The Java™ Developer's Toolkit

The Java™ Developer's Toolkit

Joshua Marketos

WILEY COMPUTER PUBLISHING

John Wiley & Sons, Inc.

New York • Chichester • Brisbane • Toronto • Singapore • Weinheim

This text is printed on acid-free paper.

Library of Congress Cataloging-in-Publication Data:

Marketos, Joshua.
    The Java Developer's Toolkit : Techniques and Technologies for Experienced Web Programmers / Joshua Marketos.
        p. 400 cm.
    Includes index.
    ISBN 0-471-16519-0 (pbk. : alk. paper)
    1. Java (Computer program language). 2. Computer software-
-Development. I. Title.
QA76.73.J38M35   1997
005.13'3--dc20   96-35812
                                                                     CIP

Printed in the United States of America
10   9   8   7   6   5   4   3   2   1

Contents

Who Should Read This Book?

This book is for people who would like to know more about the Java language. If you have an interest in networking, user interfaces, native methods, the Virtual Machine, and the like, this is the book for you.

In general, this book is intended for people with some previous computer experience. If you've ever written a macro in Microsoft Word or Lotus 1-2-3, you should be able to follow most of the material in this book. If you have any doubts, try this simple algorithm:

1. Pick a chapter in the book that sounds interesting to you.
2. Start reading.
3. If you can't understand what you're reading, pick a point halfway between where you are and the beginning of the book and go back to step 2.
4. If you end up back at this paragraph, put this book down and find another.

If you are unfamiliar with object-oriented programming (OOP) concepts, start with Chapters 2 and 3. These chapters should teach you how to set up your Java environment and the basics of OOP in short order, and then you can move on to the specifics of Java language. Then you should be prepared to tackle the rest of the book.

Some of the other chapters include the following:

Chapter 4: Simple Java Applications and the java.lang Package. This chapter focuses on the core of the Java class library. These are the classes you'll end up using on a daily basis.

Chapter 5: Applets. This chapter discusses the specifics of applet programming and introduces graphics and fonts.

Chapter 6: Inside AWT. In this chapter you'll learn about the Abstract Window Toolkit, Layout Managers (including how to write your own), Components and Containers, events, and event handling.

Chapter 7: A Tangled Web: Java Multithreading. This chapter covers threads and multithreading in Java. Special attention is paid to critical sections and thread synchronization.

Chapter 8: The Java I/O Package. This chapter covers Java I/O and the java.lang.io package, including general stream and file I/O.

Chapter 9: Java Networking. This chapter shows how to make your programs "networthy" and how to use network connections and Remote Method Invocation. As a bonus, you will learn how to steal processor cycles from everyone browsing your Web page and use them to factor large numbers.

Chapter 10: Native Methods. First you will learn how to call Native methods from Java and pass data to them. Then you'll learn how to call back from a native method into Java. Finally, we'll look at the deep voodoo of the Virtual Machine.

Chapter 11: Internet Capitalism: Shopping Carts and Databases. In this chapter we examine two commercial applications for Java: virtual shopping and database access

About the Author

Joshua Marketos is a programmer, propagandist, and singer-songwriter from Providence, Rhode Island. He is currently head of research and development for SMT. Recent projects have included the Shemp mailreader, the Shempscape WWW browser, the ShempIt and UnShempIt compression utilities and the Shempcryption encryption standard. When not playing with his avant-garde rock-n-roll band, Schwa, he can usually be found writing songs about United Nations black helicopters and attempting to rule the world from his desktop.

Acknowledgments

I'd like to take this opportunity to thank all the people who made this book possible. Brian "Colonel Panic" Jepson convinced me to write this book in the first place and so shares much of the credit and/or blame. Sean "Dr. Cretog" O'Neill, my attorney and fellow member of the band Schwa, helped to temper some of my abuses of the English language, doctored ailing code, and was of great help in the preparation of many of the tables for this book. Scott "Cool Mafia Nickname" Schoen was the impetus behind the Shempcryption project and was there with the hardware when the inevitable system failures occurred. Wayne "Sixty-Four Megabyte" Alvarez helped by lending me his experimental computer for testing (is that chip still classified?).

The other members of Schwa, namely Motom Boutique, MC Schwa, and Major Hemisphere, helped out by giving me something to keep my mind off Java for a while when my brain was in danger of overloading. The members of SMT also played a big role with their constant nagging and demands for updates on the status of the book, especially Shawn "I am the Walrus" Wallace and Bert "Artistic Expression" Crenca (who I am convinced to this day doesn't even know what Java is). Last, but by no means least, I must thank the folks at Wiley for their patience and for putting up with the corrupted and/or virus-infected files I sent them. It wasn't intentional. Honest.

Joshua Marketos

Providence, Rhode Island

About The Web Site

You can download the source code for any of the applets/applications in this book through our World Wide Web site. The URL is www.wiley.com/compbooks. The Source listings are all contained in one zipped file. This site also contains examples of some of the applets at work, plus some links to various Java resources on the Web. Enjoy!

www.wiley.com/compbooks/marketos/

Chapter 1

Politics and the Java Language

Zen and the Art of Software Maintenance

Java had its start in 1991 when James Gosling and a team of Sun engineers were developing software and operating systems for consumer electronics. They started out using C++, but found it lacking in several critical respects. The Sun team decided to take a leap of faith and create a new language from scratch to support the features they needed. At this point there was no thought of Web pages or applets or taking over the world from their desktops—just a desire to get the job at hand done in the best possible way. From this primordial, nutrient-rich ooze sprang Java, and in the few years since, Java's growth has been nothing short of phenomenal, though, ironically, the consumer electronics market is one of the few areas where Java has not yet caught on.

A recent search of the World Wide Web and Usenet using the Altavista search engine revealed 1,574,406 occurrences of the word *Java*. Still, peer pressure alone is no reason to switch from what you are using now. After all, if all your friends started using Pascal, would you do it too? When I'm asked for one good reason programmers should use Java, I respond, "For the Zen-like feeling of inner calm." Sun describes Java as a "simple, object-oriented, distributed, interpreted, robust, secure, architecture-neutral, portable, high-performance, multithreaded, and dynamic language," and I can't think of a better description of the sound of one hand clapping.

Simple

The basic philosophy the Java team used when designing the language is KISS. As you may know, KISS stands for "Knights In Satan's Service," and it indicates their commitment to the worship of Our Dark Lord and all his minions. *Just kidding!* KISS stands for "keep it simple, stupid." Some indication of this dedication to simplicity is the quote from Antoine de Saint-Exupery included in the Java White Paper: "You know you've achieved perfection in design, not when you have nothing more to add, but when you have nothing more to take away."

Because of this approach to design, Java is very easy to learn. One must realize that much of the initial difficulty in learning object-oriented languages is actually caused by the basic concepts of object-oriented programming, not the basic syntax of the language itself. Therefore C++ programmers should be able to learn the Java language in short order, and Java programmers shouldn't have too much trouble picking up C++. In fact, Java may be the ideal off ramp for those wishing to learn C++, and there isn't much excuse for not learning both. However, a sudden shift from one environment to the other should be undertaken with caution—though Java has much in common with C++, it *looks* more like C++ than it actually *is*.

Interpreted, Portable, Architecture Neutral

Three more adjectives that describe Java—interpreted, portable, and architecture neutral—boil down to the same thing. Instead of compiling to the native instruction set of any given computer, Java compiles to a set of bytecodes that are meant to be interpreted by a *virtual machine*. This method has two advantages. The more obvious advantage is the fact that your "compiled" Java programs will run on any platform which has an implementation of the Virtual Machine. The second, not-so-obvious, advantage of this scheme is that productivity is increased over that of the traditional "edit-compile-link-load-test-crash-debug" cycle. The bytecode is type-checked and everything-else-checked at compile time, something which is impossible with a true compiled language.

Object Oriented

Java is not a pure object-oriented language. The basic (known as *primitive,* which isn't exactly politically correct) data types are not objects, and that fact has kept away some of the OO purists. One of the favorite pastimes of many language proponents is playing the more-object-oriented-than-thou game. Who cares? I believe it was cybernetics pioneer F. Gump who said "Object is as Object does." or was it "Life is like a box of Objects." The most important thing is not how fully "object oriented" a language is, but how well the object-oriented features in it work to your advantage. Java seems to be a winner in this case.

Distributed

Java has the ability to treat objects located across the network as if they were local. Using a standard called RMI (remote method invocation), you can make a method call to an object in Outer Mongolia (almost) as easily as you can to one in the box sitting on your desk. Also, classes may be loaded from a remote machine as necessary.

Robust

I can tell you that Java is robust, but there is no guarantee you'll believe me. Java does extensive checking at both compile time and run time to eliminate type mismatches and other potential problems. Most of the features that could get a program into trouble (e.g., *pointers!*) have been locked away out of reach, and the global memory heap is automatically garbage collected to eliminate memory leaks.

High Performance

High performance is obviously a relative term, but for an interpreted language Java is relatively fast. For an architecture-neutral interpreted language that also keeps you from shooting yourself in the foot, it's astoundingly fast. Benchmarks time in at about 1/10 the speed of compiled C. As long as you're not using your code for Patriot missile guidance systems— oh, I forgot, *those didn't work*—and are writing the most common kinds of applications, those that are interactive or do a lot of I/O or network operations, the difference in speed is not very important. And it's faster than Perl.

Dynamic

No, we're not talking about the personality of the language, but rather about the fact that Java is dynamically linked. New classes are loaded only when needed, and that class loading can take place across the network, if necessary. Throw out your old, outdated linkers!

Secure

In these uncertain times, we all need to feel a sense of security, and a malicious attack on one's desktop can send one falling into a nihilistic downward spiral. Therefore, it's no surprise that *security* in network environments is one of Java's most seductive attributes. Much of this cyberdomestic tranquillity comes from some of the features already mentioned, such as the fact that Java has no pointers (hallelujah!), as well as the lack of structures, and in general, anything that can lay out memory in a predictable way: memory "locations" in Java bytecode are really more like "suggestions."

Many of the features left out of Java were excluded in the name of safety as well as simplicity. You might think the capability to load classes across the network should have been excluded. Fortunately, classes aren't loaded without restrictions. It is the job of Java's class loader to decide from where classes may be loaded and what kind of access they will have to your system. This can be truly annoying when a Java-enabled browser starts throwing security exceptions whenever you look at it sideways, but it's necessary for widespread acceptance.

The restrictions on class loading may seem fairly onerous, but Java enforces security with yet another check, the bytecode verification process. Every class loaded by the Virtual Machine must first undergo rigorous examination to make sure it won't do anything ghastly before it is allowed to run.

The process starts with an overall check of the class file's structure. The verifier checks to see that the proper magic number (0xCAFEBABE) is in the right place, all the segments of the class file are the right size, and no extra, possibly malicious, code has been tacked on to the end of the file.

Next, the verifier performs all the verification that can be performed without examining individual bytecode instructions. First it makes sure that classes marked as final are not subclassed and that methods declared as final are not overridden. Next it checks to see if every class (except object, the root of the class hierarchy) has a superclass and that the constant pool, the area where constants such as method names are stored, contains valid information. The verifier then checks to make sure that all field references and method references in the constant pool have legal names, legal classes, and legal signatures. This is actually a relatively shallow check: if a method call looks valid (i.e., has a valid signature), it is accepted, even though it may be a call to a method in a class which does not really exist.

The third stage of the verification process performs a complex data flow analysis which proves mathematically that no matter how a given point in the program is arrived at, the following five facts are true:

- The operand stack is always the same size and contains the same type of arguments.
- Any registers accessed can be shown to always contain the proper data type.
- Methods are called with the proper argument types.

- Fields are modified with values of the appropriate type.
- The values on the stack are appropriate for the instruction being executed.

Bytecode verification is independent of the compiler and the high-level definition of the language, so a malicious compiler (or a malicious Virtual Machine language programmer) cannot sidestep it.

Multithreaded

Multithreading is the ability to have multiple threads of execution operating concurrently. Java supports multithreading at the most basic level with primitives to keep threads from cramping each other's style. Since these thread synchronization methods are built in, they are easy to use and work the same way everywhere (even where native code is used).

Bjarne Stroustrup Marked for Death

One of the most popular misinterpretations of Java's place in the computer universe is that it is the "C++ Killer." I very much doubt this is the case. After all, old languages never die; they just cease to be supported. If better languages did actually kill off the inferior ones, COBOL would be nothing but a distant memory, but instead we get such atrocities as object-oriented COBOL. The Java language is essentially a subset of C++, with the more egregious complications removed. Don't get me wrong, C++ is a fine language, and it works well, but just about the last word anyone ever uses to describe it is "simple." The Java team thought long and hard about which features of C++ to leave in and which to leave out. Their goal was to strike a balance of ease of use, power, and flexibility. In general they took the "when in doubt, leave it out" approach. After all, no language feature is truly necessary, and many of the features that make life easier for the expert make it a living hell for the beginner and can lead to unreadable and/or unmaintainable code from the intermediate programmer. Take operator overloading, for example. The ability to change the way the basic operators work to handle new data types is one of the most attractive features of C++, and it can lead to beautiful, understandable, concise code in the right hands. But to say that operator overloading leads to good code in general would be like saying handguns are a tool for law and order just because that's how they are used by police. Unfortunately, too many programmers are the computer equivalent of a crazed subway gunman in a hostage situation. Don't think that the Java team hasn't taken slack for not including operator overloading, but they stood by their decision, and I, for one, respect them for it.

Several other features from C++ did not make it into Java, including the following:

- Functions—I can guess your reaction, "What? No functions? You're kidding!" Actually no. Before you burn this book, you should know that Java differentiates methods, which exist inside classes, and functions, which exist outside the object universe. Java has methods but not functions. In other words you won't find any functions that are not part of some class. So you don't have to give up the functionality of functions, so to speak; it just gets shifted to another place.

- The Preprocessor—This is another thing that some folks will have a hard time giving up. Some programmers spend so much time writing macros that they would probably be happy to eliminate the actual language itself as long as they have a decent preprocessor. The problem with this, and the reason that there is no Java preprocessor, is that programming with #defines and typedefs essentially results in every programmer inventing a new programming language. If you spent 10 minutes writing your #defines, chances are it will take someone else 20 to figure out what you were trying to do. Don't worry—the design of the Java language makes these features unnecessary. By the way, Java methods are self-prototyping, so there's no place you can look to get just the skinny on a method's signature. The javadoc program will extract this information along with specially formatted comments and produce decent hypertext documentation. Hypertext documentation in general takes up precious real estate on a computer screen, where there isn't any to spare, instead of on a desk, in a filing cabinet, or on the floor, where there is plenty.

- Automatic coercions—Any coercions that would result in a loss of precision require an explicit cast. By the way, Java also eliminated one form of the casting syntax. The "function call" style cast is not supported. Grumble all you want.

- Structures and unions—You won't need them, because classes can achieve the same effect. (When in doubt, . . .)

- Multiple inheritance—Multiple inheritance can be useful. Useful, but not necessary, so out it goes, into the dustbin of pre-Java history. Java does not leave us fans of object miscegenation out in the cold, because it supports the concept of interfaces. An interface is simply a description of the methods a class must support. Although an object may only inherit from (extend, in Java parlance) a single class, it may implement as many interfaces as necessary. For example, we could declare a class named Moe which implements the ShempWorthy interface and the Stooge interface. Moe acts for all intents and purposes as if he were inheriting from two parents. Moe could be cast as a ShempWorthy in some situations and a Stooge in others. The difference is that no code is actually inherited, but a written pact is made that Moe will implement methods of both interfaces.

- Pointers—Again, I can imagine the reaction of most C/C++ programmers out there. Pointers are powerful. Pointers are elegant. Pointers will overrun and crash your system in a methamphetamine millisecond. Java has features that make pointers unnecessary, so out they go. If you are a C/C++ programmer, you can expect to pass through five stages:

  1. Denial—"It's a vicious lie! Every Real Language has pointers!"
  2. Anger—"^^$#@ Java!"
  3. Bargaining—"I've got it! I'll use pointer arithmetic on an array variable!"
  4. Depression—"Why me?"
  5. Acceptance—"What's a pointer?"

This list is only partially facetious. I remember going through stages analogous to these when I was porting a C++ program to Java. Of course, with the hubris which seems to be my hallmark, I was attempting this without ever having read the Java Language Specification. I assumed that since it looked so much like C, it was close enough for government work. I distinctly remember exclaiming, "It *must* have pointers!" and then attempting various strategies to "forge" a pointer. What I didn't understand at the time is that you don't need pointers in Java for three reasons:

- Just about everything in Java already is a pointer. All nonprimitive types are passed by reference, that is, by pointer. The pointers are there; you just aren't allowed to perform Unnatural Acts with them.
- Java gives you real bounds-checked arrays that can hold any data type. You can put an object in an array (or even array of arrays), access elements in that array with an index, and access member functions and variables with dot notation.
- The goto statement—Probably not too many people are complaining about this one. Most people know better, but if you're a fan of goto, you're out of luck. Java provides multilevel break and continue statements that make goto entirely superfluous. Toss it out!

Objectivity

Now that you know the things which were eliminated, let's adopt the "vat is half-full" mindset and look at the features which were added. First of all, we get a completely object-oriented language. Java programs have no separate "main" method which exists outside the objects in order to manipulate them. I don't know how much this distinction really matters for real-world programming, but it does make the language cleaner.

Strings

It's sad to see languages that do not support strings as a basic data type. You could rationalize this as a decision to not foist another data type on the programmers when they would be happier building their own custom string handling routines. Right. Strings are about as basic a data type as you will find these days, and Java supports them fully. Strings are actually objects in Java, but they are a special breed of object that the language knows how to handle.

Fanatical Type Checking

Java is, if I may wax Freudian for a moment, extremely anal-retentive when it comes to data types. Some programmers who make a habit of playing fast and loose with data conversion will hate this, because it forces you to litter your code with explicit casts, but it prevents more problems than it causes.

Arrays

Arrays are quasi-objects in Java. They are bounds checked at run time, so going past the end of an array will result in an exception being thrown, giving not completely unpredictable results at some unpredictable time in the future. Surprisingly, the speed penalty for this is not that great.

Garbage Collection

Java uses the concept of heap memory as does C++. Java even has a new keyword (though it isn't exactly the same as new in C++). One thing you won't find is delete, because Java's heap is garbage collected, making it unnecessary to delete unused memory. The garbage collector determines when no more references to an object on the heap exist and deletes objects in the background, eliminating one of the main uses for C++ destructors. Java has a destructor equivalent (finalize methods), but you won't see them used nearly as often. The only time finalizers are necessary is when the object is holding some sort of resource not stored on the heap.

This arrangement leads to some pretty strange-looking code from a C++ viewpoint. Programmers new to Java may see new objects allocated over and over inside a loop and scream, "Memory leak!" Java programmers, just let go, get behind it, and groove with it.

Java comes with a truly standard class library, which means that you get not only simple features like string manipulation and stream I/O, but more sophisticated traits like networking support and hashtables for free. Of course, you may not like the particular implementation of some of these classes, but you can always write your own from scratch or subclass the existing ones.

True and False

It's always seemed strange to me that many computer languages that depend so much on binary logic for their very existence do not include true Boolean constants as part of the language. In Java true is true and false is false. These are keywords in the language and not simple constants defined in a header file somewhere. Java won't let you treat other data types as Booleans, which is as it should be.

Language, Thought, and Reality

Linguist Benjamin Lee Whorf (who I believe was also chief security officer of the Starship Enterprise) popularized the idea that language may shape the way you think or that, at the least, the outward form of a language may be an indication of unique modalities of thought that its (native) speakers share. Can the same be true of computer languages?

To me at least, Java just feels different from other computer languages. The attention paid to simplicity and safety seems to lead to a feeling of calm detachment from the act of programming. One can be *in* the program without being *of* the program.

There is no doubt that some computer languages are better at certain tasks than others, so a programmer will utilize one language more readily for those objectives more easily expressed in that language. Take graphical user interfaces (GUIs), for example. Using something like Visual C++ to get a simple window on the screen with AppWizard is a qualitatively different experience than accomplishing the same task with two lines of Java code. Although creating the machine-generated code may be just a matter of a few mouse clicks, you end up with several files with contents you don't even want to know about. You place your program's fate in the hands of whoever wrote the code that in turn writes your code. You end up with some code labeled "DO NOT EDIT THIS CODE" and a few tiny segments labeled "YOUR CODE HERE." The result may be feelings of suspicion, unease, alienation, and loss of control. In addition to suspicion of the generated code, you may also wonder if all the pointers in your program are actually under control at all times under all circumstances.

With Java, on the other hand, the code to put the window on the screen is three lines. Adding a menu may take another 10. And event handling may take another 20 lines, but at least you wrote the code! It isn't too hard to follow the classes involved back to their parents and see how everything works. The result is a feeling of confidence.

You can accomplish the same thing and get identical results in both languages, but with Java you'll likely end up tackling more ambitious projects because Java limits the number of things that can go wrong, making those projects less intimidating.

Visual Basic programmers may protest at this point. Visual Basic does make windows, forms, and event handling very simple, but large projects can soon become almost unmaintainable. In addition, the code isn't portable. You may be willing to settle only for the Wintel market, but think about it. What if you could put in the same amount of effort and also target the Macintosh platform. And UNIX. Java already makes hacking together user interfaces fairly easy, and the GUI builder applications are on their way. Besides, BASIC is a second-class language, no matter how much you enhance it.

What You Should Tell Your Boss

In general, programmers are the easiest to convince, but now you have to convince your boss to throw away countless staff hours invested in code in another language and switch to Java. What do you say?

First, tell the boss Java is not an all-or-nothing proposition. You could start by coding the front end to your program in Java and move over other parts at your leisure. In many cases this would allow a client to do things like use a WWW browser to hook up to the database using a Linux box in Hong Kong or a PC in Tanu Touva and check the accounts receivable. You can also make use of native code libraries you've already written by simply providing a Java wrapper around them. Then you can go about the work of porting the native code to Java or wait for someone else to release a Java library that does the same thing. In either case, the end result is an architecture-neutral application with a far larger potential consumer base than you had previously.

Second, Java leads to greater productivity. By eliminating the most common causes of program failure before they can occur, Java increases the number of bug-free lines written in a given time. Another way Java increases productivity is by allowing one programmer to do the work of four. You do not need to have a Mac programmer, a Windows programmer, and a Solaris programmer. With Java, these are all the same person.

Finally, you can try to frighten the boss into using Java by pointing out the security flaws and lack of robustness in other languages. Terrorist tactics often work, so if all else fails, demonstrate how you could plant a virus on the boss's hard drive or in the latest product the company is shipping.

Of course, you may feel that Java is a fatally flawed language with no hope for success. If so, you have plenty of company on Usenet. I have only one comment: there are none so blind as those who will not see.

Chapter 2

Getting Ready to Brew

Setting Up Your System

In this chapter we look at how to get the Java Developer's Kit (JDK), how to install and configure it, and how to use the various tools the JDK provides. The kit contains the interpreter, compiler, appletviewer, utilities to disassemble classes and generate headers for native methods, and other tools. You will find pointers to places where you can download the JDK on the Web page for this book. As of this writing, Sun provides versions of the JDK for the following operating systems:

- SPARC Solaris
- x86 Solaris
- Windows NT
- Windows 95
- MacOS

On the Wintel platform JDK is served up as a self-extracting archive file, so the initial extraction is as easy as putting the executable file wherever you want to install the JDK and running it. This will produce a directory named "java" with a few directories underneath it. The most important of these is "bin" where the java compiler, interpreter, and other associated binaries live. You'll probably want to put this directory in your PATH environment variable. Fire up an editor and add it to your autoexec.bat now. You'll also need to add a CLASSPATH environment variable. If you extracted the JDK into the root directory on drive C, this should look something like the following:

```
SET CLASSPATH=.; C:\java\lib\
```

We can't emphasize enough the importance of setting CLASSPATH. It seems that about 60% of the questions on the comp.lang.java news group boil down to problems with this environment variable. As you can see above, the minimum you should have in this environment variable is the java\lib\ directory and the dot to represent the current directory.

Testing It Out

Now you'll want to know if you did everything correctly. If you're using Windows, you'll have to reboot for the changes in the autoexec.bat to take effect. After rebooting, start your favorite editor again and enter the following program:

```
public class Clem{

  public static void main(String args[]){

    System.out.println("Hello, uh Clem");

  }
}
```

Save the file as "Clem.java" in the directory of your choice. Now go to a DOS prompt, change to that directory, and enter the following command to compile your program:

```
javac Clem.java
```

You may get the following message:

```
Clem.java:1:Warning: Public class Clem must be declared in a file called "Clem.java"
```

If so, you probably forgot to capitalize the word "Clem" in either the file name or the class definition in the file. Java is case sensitive. Now let's run the program! At the DOS prompt, issue the following command:

```
java Clem
```

You'll know right away if everything is installed properly. The output should be as follows:

```
Hello, uh Clem
```

You may get the following error message:

```
Can't find class Clem
```

If so, there is a problem with your CLASSPATH variable. It sounds simple, but you would be surprised at the number of people who have problems setting a simple environment variable. Do it now!

Chances are you don't want to use a text editor and the command line to compile and edit your programs. Let's take a look at some of the other tools you might want to check out. Much excitement has been generated by integrated development environments (IDEs) for Java. The big three of the compiler world—Borland, Microsoft, and Symantec—all have their own competing IDEs. These are called Latte, Visual J++, and Cafe, respectively. In general, you should expect the following minimum set of features from an IDE:

- A really good editor with auto-indent, brace matching, etc.
- Some sort of project management capability
- Some sort of resource editing or GUI-building capability
- Class hierarchy browsing
- Integrated context-sensitive help

The three products above add their own whistles and bells. Remember that bells and whistles don't come free, so you might end up paying for features you never use or use very infrequently. About 90% of your time is spent editing your files, compiling them into class files, and running the results. If you are very new to Java, you might also spend a lot of time perusing the documentation to find the methods you need. However, there is a *free* solution that will do all these things. Don't buy a commercial product until you have explored other options. Of course, if your company is footing the bill, you might want to consider a commercial IDE for the (perhaps slight) productivity advantage it may provide.

Free: The Programmer's File Editor

Although it may not be a Java-specific tool, one program we recommend highly is the Programmer's File Editor (PFE) by Alan Philips. PFE is a fast, small, sophisticated, yet simple file editor with the following features (and more):

- The size of file it can handle is limited only by the total amount of virtual memory available.

- It can edit multiple files, the number being limited only by the available system resources.
- It has a multilevel undo facility.
- It can read and write files in UNIX format using LF as line terminator, with automatic format detection.
- DOS commands, such as compilers, can be run with the output captured in an edit window.
- Commonly used text can be inserted in a simple operation from template libraries.
- Keystrokes and menu commands can be recorded in a replayable keyboard macro.
- Commonly used program development tools can be configured into a list and started simply from a dialog.
- Automatic line indenting and removal of trailing spaces

The ability to tailor editing modes for different file types allows you to use the same editor for Java, C/C++, Pascal, and others. It even loads faster than the (very lame) Window's Notepad. Best of all, Programmer's File Editor is absolutely 100% free! Not shareware. Not nagware. Free. It has no GUI builder or resource editor, but what do you expect for free? Those capabilities will soon be available in free Java programs anyway.

Dippy Bird's Java Documentation

If you decide to go the no-budget route using PFE, you might also want to look into Dippy Bird's Java Documentation. Bill Bercik has taken the following Java HTML files and converted them in to one whopping Windows Help file:

- The Java API
- The Java Language Environment: A White Paper
- The Java Virtual Machine Specification
- The Java Tools Reference Pages
- Java Frequently Asked Questions
- Java Tips and Tricks
- Guide to Java Resources
- Java JDBC Database API
- Java Object Serialization Spec
- Java Remote Methods Invocation Spec
- Java RMI and IDL Spec
- Java Electronic Commerce Spec

What's even better is that PFE allows you to define up to five help files and associate each with a menu item that is appended to the end of its Help menu, so all this is just a click away.

TABLE 2.1 usage: javac [options] file

Option	Meaning
-classpath <path>	Where to look for classes. By default javac uses the CLASSPATH environment variable.
-d <directory>	Output directory for class files. By default javac writes class files in the same directory as the source.
-g	Generate debugging info for use by jdb.
-nowarn	Turn off warning messages.
-O	Optimize the compiled code.
-verbose	Turn on verbose mode, which gives a detailed description of everything javac is doing.

You can even define a help file for use as "context-sensitive" help. Or you can just use the Dippy Bird Help to avoid having to launch a browser just to read the documentation.

Java Tools

Tables 2.1–2.7 list the various options and commands for the Java tools javac, java, javadoc, javap, appletviewer and jdb.

The Java Compiler The Java compiler takes plain text files with the .java extension and generates compiled classes as shown in Table 2.1.

The Java Interpreter The Java interpreter, java, takes compiled class files and runs them on a copy of the virtual machine.

```
usage: java [-options] class
```

Note that "class" is just the name of the class, *without* the .class extension. java treats dots in the class argument as file separators, so if you have a class file named Shemp.class in the current directory and you try to run it using the first line below, java looks for a file in the class-path named Shemp/class.class and gives the error in the second line:

```
java Shemp.class
Can't find class Shemp/class
```

The options are shown in Table 2.2.

TABLE 2.2 Java Options

Option	Meaning
-help	Print out a help message.
-version	Print out the build version.
-v -verbose	Turn on verbose mode, which will cause java to print a message whenever it loads a class.
-debug	Enable remote Java debugging.
-noasyncgc	Don't allow asynchronous garbage collection: java will garbage collect only when gc() is called or when it runs out of memory. The default is to have the garbage collector running as its own thread.
-verbosegc	Print a message when garbage collection occurs.
-cs or -checksource	Check to see if the modification time of the source file is more recent than that of the class file.
-ss<number>	Set the C stack size of a process.
-oss<number>	Set the stack size of each Java thread. The default is 400K.
-ms<number>	Set the amount of memory in bytes to initially allocate for the Java heap. The default is 1MB.
-mx<number>	Set the maximum heap size, in bytes, allocatable by java. The default is 16K.
-classpath <directories separated by colons>	Directory to look for classes in. By default java uses the value of the CLASSPATH environment variable.
-prof	Output profiling data to ./java.prof.

Continued

Option	Meaning
-verify	Verify all classes with the bytecode verifier when they are read in.
-verifyremote	Verify classes read in over the network. This is the default.
-noverify	Do not verify any classes.

The Java Documentation Generator The javadoc program generates HTML documentation for Java class files or packages. Information for the documentation is taken from the class definitions and special "doc comments" included in the source. (A doc comment is a comment that begins with /** and ends with */.) (See Table 2.3.)

The Java Header Generator The javah program automatically generates header files and C "stub" files for native methods from compiled class files. The options are shown in Table 2.4.

TABLE 2.3 usage:javadoc [flags] [class | package]

Option	Meaning
-version	Include the version field.
-author	Include the author field.
-sourcepath <directories separated by colons>	Directories to find class source.
-classpath <directories separated by colons>	Synonym for -sourcepath. If not used, javadoc uses the value of the CLASSPATH environment variable.
-doctype <type>	Documentation type to generate either HTML or MIF. The default is HTML.
-noindex	Do not generate an index of all methods and fields.
-notree	Do not generate a class hierarchy.

TABLE 2.4 usage: javah [options] classname

Option	Meaning
-o outputfile	Put all output in outputfile.
-d directory	Save files in directory. By default javah saves the files it generates in the current directory.
-td directory	Set the directory where javah saves temporary files. The default temp directory is /tmp.
-stubs	Generate stub files and do not generate .h header files. By default header files are generated.
-verbose	Verbose output.
-classpath path	The path where class files may be found. By default javah uses the value of the environment variable CLASSPATH.

The Java Disassembler The javap program disassembles Java class files to human readable form. See Table 2.5.

TABLE 2.5 usage: javap [options] class

Option	Meaning
-l	Prints out line and local variable tables. Local variable information is available only if the class was compiled using javac -g, and classes compiled with the -O option have no line number information.
-p	Prints private and protected methods. By default javap prints only methods that are public or have the default visibility.
-c	Prints out disassembled code; i.e., the virtual machine instructions for all other methods in the specified classes.
-classpath	The path where javap looks for classes. By default the value of the environment variable CLASSPATH is used.
-verify	Verifies the class.
-v	Prints verbosely.

Continued

Option	Meaning
-h	Creates information that can be put into C header files.
-version	Prints the javap version string.

The Appletviewer The appletviewer allows you to view applets embedded in an HTML page without having to use a browser.

```
usage: appletviewer [-debug] html_file
```

-debug starts the appletviewer in the debugger jdb.

The Java Debugger The jdb program is a rudimentary command-line debugger for java programs, similar to the UNIX dbx or gdb debuggers. It runs in its own copy of the Virtual Machine. See Table 2.6 for options.

There are two ways to use jdb. The first is simply to pass it a class name on the command line as if it were the normal Java interpreter. In this case it takes the same options as java. The jdb program will fire up a copy of java to run the specified file, which halts before the first instruction. The second way to use jdb is to attach it to a currently running java program. To do this, start the program with the -debug option. Java will print out a password for use with jdb. Next, start jdb using the -host and -password options. Table 2.7 lists the commands.

TABLE 2.6 jdb [java options] class or jdb [options]

Option	Meaning
-host <hostname>	The host where the program is running
-password <password>	Password for this session

TABLE 2.7 JDB Commands

Command	Action
threads [threadgroup]	List all threads in the specified threadgroup (by default use the current threadgroup).
thread <thread id>	Set default thread. Thread may be specified either by name or by number.

Continued

TABLE 2.7 Continued

Command	Action
suspend [thread id(s)]	Suspend the specified threads. By default suspend all running threads.
resume [thread id(s)]	Resume the specified threads. By default resume all suspended threads.
where [thread id] | all	Dump a stack trace of the specified thread.
threadgroups	List all threadgroups.
threadgroup <name>	Set current threadgroup to the specified threadgroup.
print <id> [id(s)]	Print the value of the specified object, field, local variable, or class.
dump <id> [id(s)]	Print all the fields of the specified object(s).
locals	Print all local variables in current stack frame. The class must have been compiled with the -g option to javac for this to work.
classes	List all currently known classes.
methods <class id>	List a class's methods.
stop in <class id>.<method>	Set a breakpoint in a method. If used with no arguments, list all current breakpoints.
stop at <class id>:<line>	Set a breakpoint at a line. If used with no arguments, list all current breakpoints.
up [n frames]	Move n frames up the current thread's stack. Default n=1.
down [n frames]	Move n frames down the current thread's stack.
clear <class id>:<line>	Clear a breakpoint.
step	Execute current line and stop.
cont	Continue execution from breakpoint.
catch <class id>	Break for the specified exception.

Continued

Command	Action
ignore <class id>	Ignore the specified exception.
list [line number|method]	Print source code.
use [source file path]	Set the path to look for source files or display the current path if no path is given.
memory	Report memory usage.
gc	Free unused objects.
load classname	Load Java class to be debugged.
run <class> [args]	Start execution of a loaded Java class with the given arguments.
!!	Repeat the last command
help (or ?)	List commands.
exit (or quit)	Exit debugger.

When compiling for debugging, use the -g option to tell javac to include line number and local variable information in the compiled files.

Chapter 3

Teach Yourself Object-Oriented Programming Java in 21 Minutes

The World According to OOP

Before we get into the specifics of the Java language, we should probably review a few object-oriented programming (OOP) concepts. If this is your first brush with OOP, you may be better served by a more elementary text to introduce you to the basic concepts, but here's a quick review.

The basic vocabulary necessary to learn or discuss OOP has probably scared away more potential programmers than anything else. The problem is that many of these terms are normal English words with non-OOP meanings that have been forced to mean so many different things by so many people that they have become almost totally devoid of meaning. The fact that computer folks would give this situation a silly name like *vocabulary overloading* or *homonymy* certainly doesn't help. Take this sentence, for example: "I just can't bear to watch that pathetic dancing bear any longer." Can you resolve the meaning of the repeated word? Congratulations—you have mastered homonymy!

Objects and Classes

If some OOP terms seem intentionally obscure and specialized, others seem all too common and nonspecific. The most basic term involved here is perhaps the most unspecialized word in the English language: *object*. Why *object* and not something equally vague like *thing*? What exactly is an object? Ask 10 programmers and you'll get 10 (or more) different answers. The following definition is used in this book:

> *An object is a software entity that may combine both data structures and algorithms in one self-contained unit.*

In other words, objects combine variables (state) and functions (behavior) into one chunk. In Java the functions are called methods, and the variables, which can be objects themselves, are called, in an amazing coincidence, variables.

A class is the blueprint from which objects are built. It describes the methods and variables in objects of that class. The process of actually using this blueprint to make an object is known as instantiation. Objects are instances of their class.

Why bother with these pesky objects? One reason is that if you design your programs so that there is a direct mapping between your objects and the objects they represent in the real world, they become more logical and easier to understand. For example, if you were modeling a simulation of a car, it would make sense to combine variables like speed, temperature, and windshield_washer_fluid_level with methods such as accelerate, turn, brake, and collide_with_innocent_pedestrian to make a Car object.

Data Hiding

Consistently bundling your methods with your data like this also allows you to take advantage of a feature known as *data hiding* or *encapsulation*. Data hiding means that you can make your data visible to only the parts of your program that need access to it, and invisible to those parts of your program that have no need to access or modify that data. This makes it easier to keep from stepping on your own foot and accidentally changing critical data. In fact, it is common, and considered good form, to restrict access to an object's data to the methods inside the object itself. This is especially handy to protect your data from other programmers, malicious or benign. The theory behind this is that if you give people the ability to make a mistake using your data, they probably will. Java and other OOP languages avoid this problem by allowing you to strictly control access to critical parts of your objects.

The extra stability data hiding gives you allows you to treat your objects as "black boxes" that take input and produce output without the programmer necessarily knowing all the details of how the black box operates. Once the black box is tested and working properly, it will continue to work properly forever, because other parts of your program aren't allowed to mess around with the black box internals and dilute its precious bodily fluids.

Many OOP programmers prefer to think of method calls as sending the black box a message telling it to execute a method rather than calling the method directly. This is a bit more in keeping with the OOP philosophy, but it's mostly a conceptual difference. The extra level of abstraction makes things a bit more confusing, so we simply speak of making a method or function call to an object. You can think of the process as sending a message if you wish.

Inheritance

Another feature OOP provides is inheritance, the ability to derive new classes of objects from your old ones. Let's say you have already defined the generic Car class above, and you now want to create a Drag_Racer class. Since a drag racer is a type of car, it makes sense to inherit the things they have in common and add the extra functionality you need rather than starting from scratch. In this case Car is known as the parent class, superclass, or base class, and Drag_Racer is the child or derived class, which is said to extend or subclass its parent class. You can continue the process and derive new types of drag racers from this definition. The group of classes consisting of a derived class and all its superclasses is called a class family.

In a derived class you can implement methods that have the same names as methods in the parent class. This process goes by the name of method overriding. The methods in the derived class are said to override (replace) the parent's methods (which remain accessible).

Multiple inheritance is the ability to derive from more than one base class. For example, you could derive from both the Car and the Fiery_Deathtrap classes to create a new Ford_Pinto class. Although this can be useful in the right situation, it's far from necessary. It's harder to implement multiple inheritance than single inheritance, and it may make your programs harder to understand. Many OOP languages such as Smalltalk and Java do not support multiple inheritance, and Java offers the concept of interfaces as a kind of inferior substitute, but we'll discuss that later.

Polymorphism

Another confusing OOP term you'll see is *polymorphism*. This is another example of something much easier to *do* than to *define*. Put most simply, polymorphism is the ability of different objects to respond to the same message in different ways. For example, a Drag_Racer object would respond to a "Brake" message by deploying its parachute, while a Ford_Pinto object might respond by locking its brakes and skidding into a bridge abutment. In fact there are cases in which the compiler may not be able to determine the actual method to be called. This occurs if you have a pointer that may point to either a Ford_Pinto or a Drag_Racer and attempt to access the object by means of the pointer. There is no way for the compiler to resolve which of the two types of objects the pointer will actually be pointing to when the method call takes place. The solution to this problem is known as late binding. With late binding, the process of determining which function will be called is deferred until run time. You can accomplish this in C++ by specifying this function as virtual in the base class. This step is unnecessary in Java. The compiler automatically decides which of your functions are virtual, so the whole operation is transparent to the programmer. In general, the terms *virtual function* call and *polymorphism* are most useful for putting a name to something you'll be doing all the time without even thinking about it. The less frequently you utter these magic phrases, the better.

There you have it: objects, encapsulation, inheritance, and polymorphism, the major components of object-oriented programming. In general, you will find it easier to write programs taking advantage of these concepts than to talk about them with other programmers. It is impossible not to use these features in Java, whether you know what they are called or not. I'll point out any clear examples of these concepts as they come along, but it would almost be possible to finish the book without using the word *polymorphism* ever again, and I'll give it my best shot.

Java: The Non-OOP Parts

Now that you know what all those OOP terms mean, let's forget about them for a while and deal with the basic non-OOP parts of the language. We'll cover all the basic statements you need to write fully functional programs the way programmers did in the Dark Ages (1960s and 1970s). If you know C, most of this material will look familiar, but you may want to look over such things as the size of the primitive data types. If you are unfamiliar with C, don't fear! I'll give you all the basic information you need to get started, and you can always pick up a copy of the timeless classic *The C Programming Language* by Brian Kernighan and Dennis Ritchie to give you all the gory details. If you already know C++, may God have mercy on your soul.

Comments

Comments are the most important statements in any language. After all, it takes only a few seconds to comment a block of code, but it could take 10 minutes to figure out that uncommented code that seemed so logical when you wrote it at 2:30 in the morning. A comment may begin with "/*", in which case it is terminated by "*/". Java also recognizes comments that begin with "//" and end at a carriage return, a linefeed, or a carriage return/linefeed combination. A comment can also start with "/**", in which case it is a special *doc comment* that can be used by the javadoc program to automatically generate HTML documentation for your programs. Note that "/*...*/" type comments can span more than one line but cannot successfully be nested inside each other. Some legal comments:

```
// This is a 'C++-style' comment that ends at the end of the line.
/* This is a 'C-style' comment */.
/* This is a long 'C-style' comment that can safely contain carriage
returns and span more than one line. */
/** This is a 'doc comment' */.
```

Variable Declaration

Variables can hold either a reference to an object or array or one of the eight primitive data types. The basic format of a variable declaration is as follows:

```
Variable_Type Variable_Name;
```

Variable_Type is either the name of one of the eight primitive data types or the name of an object type, and Variable_Name is any valid variable name. A variable name may not begin with a number and may not contain a reserved symbol. Variable names are case sensitive. Some valid names are as follows:

- Myclass
- _hello_kitty
- DextroMethorphan
- CallMeIshmael

Java variable declarations can reside just about anywhere in a Java program, not just at the beginning of a function definition as in C, as long as they are declared before use. Some examples are the following:

```
boolean moe;     /* moe is a boolean variable */
char larry;      /* larry is a  char variable */
int shemp;       /* shemp is an int variable */
Curly curly_joe; /* curly_joe is a reference to a Curly object */
String S;        /* S is a reference to a String object */
```

Unlike C/C++, variables are automatically initialized to a default value, which is zero for numeric values and null (a special value indicating reference to nothing) for object data types. We'll look into the specifics of Java data storage for primitive data types later in this chapter, but for this section we use only variables of type *int*, 32-bit signed integers, for demonstration purposes.

Array Declarations

Java allows you to define arrays in two ways:

- Array_Type [] Array_Name;
- Array_Type Array_Name[];

In both cases the variable Array_Name is declared to hold a reference to an array of Array_Type. Multidimensional arrays are declared and accessed as arrays of arrays, as they are in C:

- Array_Type[][] Array_Name;
- Array_Type Array_Name[][];

Some array examples:

```
int b[]; /* b is a reference to an array of ints */
int b[][]; /* b is a reference to an array of arrays */
```

Arrays are actually quasi-objects in Java, so we'll discuss them more later.

Assignment

Assignment statements have exactly the same syntax as they do in C/C++, with a variable name on the left side, the assignment operator (=) in the middle, and an expression on the right:

```
I=6;  // set I to six
I=(35*2)-69; //set I equal to result of calculation (one)
I=you; // set I equal to you
I=A[3]; // set I equal to element 3 of array A
```

Of course you can combine the declaration and assignment as in C/C++:

```
int I=3; // declare and assign
int j=0;
```

A Slew of Operators

Table 3.1 summarizes the various operators and their functions in compact form.

TABLE 3.1 Java Operators

Operator	Function
+	Addition
−	Subtraction
*	Multiplication
/	Division
%	Modulus
++	Increment
--	Decrement
&	Boolean and arithmetic AND
|	Boolean and arithmetic OR
^	Boolean and arithmetic XOR
&&	Conditional AND
||	Conditional OR
>>	Right shift with sign extension
>>>	Right shift with zero extension
<<	Left shift
<	Less than
>	Greater than
==	Equal
!=	Not equal
=	Assignment
+	String concatenation (special case)
?:	Ternary conditional
instanceof	Type comparison

The operator meanings and precedence are mostly the same as in C, but there are a few differences and additions.

All integers in Java are signed, and >> performs a right shift with sign extension. Therefore the operator >>> is necessary if you want to do a right shift with zero extension.

The bitwise AND and OR operators & and |, when applied to objects of type Boolean, perform *logical* operations, much like their compatriots && and | |. However, they are guaranteed to always evaluate both of their arguments, so if

```
int i = 1;
int a = 1;
```

then

```
(i == 1) || (++a == 2)
```

evaluates to true, and a is unchanged, whereas

```
(i == 1) | (++a == 666)
```

is also true, but a becomes 2.

The instanceof operator returns true if its left-hand operand (which must be an object) is an instance of the type named by the right-hand operand, and false if it is not:

```
curly_joe instanceof Curly      // true!
moe instanceof Curly            // false!
```

instanceof also returns false if the left-hand operator is null.

Shorthand combinations of the assignment operators with the arithmetic operators are supported as follows:

```
i+=3; // same as i=i+3
i-=7; // same as i=i-7
i/=2; // same as i=i/2
```

If Statements

The if/else statement selectively executes a block of code depending on a condition that evaluates to a Boolean true or false:

```
if (Condition){
//the code in this block executes only if the condition is true
}else{
```

```
//this block executes if the condition is false
}
```

Note the block of code could be either a single statement terminated by a semicolon or a group of statements grouped by the curly braces and that the else portion is optional. This allows the following short statement:

```
if (a==3) a=4; // if a is 3, make it 4
```

While Loops

The while statement executes a block of code as long as the given condition evaluates to true. Since this test takes place before the block executes, the block will never execute if the condition is not true:

```
while (true){
//this block will execute over and over and over...
}
while (false){
// the fact that this statement never executes
// causes a compile-time error
}
```

The second while statement above demonstrates that the test occurs before the block is executed. In the process, it also shows an interesting Java quirk. *The Java Language Specification* defines it as an error for a statement to be unreachable. A smart enough compiler will complain because false will never be true and the block of code will never be reached. This feature helps you weed out bits of old code you forgot were still living in your programs.

Do Loops

The do/while statement makes its test at the end of the loop, as the syntax implies:

```
do {
// this block would execute forever
}while (true)
do {
// this block would execute once
}while (false)
```

Since the code block in the second example executes before the test, no compiler error results.

For Loops

The for loop has the same syntax as it does in C/C++, with an initialization statement, a test statement, and an increment statement separated by semicolons and enclosed by parentheses:

```
for (i=0;i<10;i++){
// this block executes ten times
}
```

The initialization statement executes once when the loop is first encountered and sets the variable i to zero. Next, the test is evaluated and the code block and the increment statement are executed only if it is true. When the end of the block is reached, the process starts over again with the testing of the condition. Note that you can omit the test, in which case the loop goes on forever:

```
for (i=0;;i++){
//this block executes forever.
}
```

The increment portion of the for loop is also optional; you can omit it entirely or replace it with another statement that does something other than increment your loop variable. Java also allows the use of the comma to separate multiple initialization or increment statements:

```
for (i=0,j=5;i<j;j=j+i,i=i+j){...}
```

This is similar to using the comma operator in C to join multiple statements but is actually a special case of the for loop syntax; it won't work outside a for loop definition!

Breaking Out of Loops

What do you do when you're in the middle of a loop and you decide you want out? You can use the break statement, which breaks out of the loop, or the continue statement, which will simply skip over the rest of the statements in the loop:

```
for (i=0;i<100;i++){
// some stuff here would be executed once
// because the next statement breaks us right out of the loop.
break;
    //
}
```

```
// execution would continue here
for (i=0;i<100;i++){
// statements here execute 100 times
continue;
// these statements are skipped and loop starts over
}
```

This behavior is the same as in C/C++. Java does add some new functionality in the form of labeled break and continue statements. By putting a label (an arbitrary name followed by a colon) in front of a loop definition, you can break or continue out of it at any time, even if you are inside another (nested) loop:

```
outer: (i=0;i<100;i++){
for (j=0;j<100;j++){
break outer;// this will break us out of both loops!
    }
}// execution would continue here.
```

Goto Considered Harmful

Although goto is a reserved word in the Java language, it's not implemented! Including the most feared programming construct in the universe as a reserved word and then refusing to implement it appears to be an admirable piece of code-based performance art on the part of the Java team. Unfortunately, it also means you have to work a bit harder to write confusing spaghetti code.

Almost All You Need

Those are the basics, and we didn't mention classes once! These statements will probably make up about 90% of the volume of code you write. You could even get away with just one type of loop if you were willing to do a little extra typing. Now you can see why Java is so easy to learn: if you know C/C++, you already know the basics of the language. Now we can get to some of the differences.

Primitive Data Types

One of the major differences between Java and C/C++ (and quite a few other languages) is that the sizes of the primitive data types are defined by the *Java Language Specification* instead of being left to the whims of compiler designers (see Table 3.2).

TABLE 3.2 Primitive Data Types

Name	Size	Minimum	Maximum
Boolean	1-bit logical value	true	false
byte	8 -bit integer	–128	+127
short	16-bit integer	–32768	+32767
int	32-bit integer	–2147483648	+2147483647
long	64-bit integer	–9223372036854775808	+9223372036854775807
float	32-bit floating point	NEGATIVE_INFINITY	POSITIVE_INFINITY
double	64-bit floating point	NEGATIVE_INFINITY	POSITIVE_INFINITY
char	16-bit unicode character	\u0000	\uffff

Booleans The Boolean type can hold a single logical value of true or false and must not be confused with numeric one and zero. Treating a Boolean as a numeric type or a numeric type as a Boolean (a common practice in C/C++) will generate a compile-time error. For example, the following will generate an "Incompatible type for while. Can't convert int to boolean" error message:

```
int i=1;
while (i){/* do something */ } /* ERROR:i is not a boolean */
```

The following will give an "Incompatible type for +. Can't convert boolean to int." message:

```
int i=0;
i=i+(i<0); /* ERROR: (i<0) is a boolean, not an int.*/
```

Integer Data Types Note that bytes, ints, shorts, and longs are all assigned integer values and are stored in two's complement format, which uses the uppermost bit to represent the sign of the number. This means that in case of an overflow or underflow, you may wind up changing the sign accidentally. Consider the following example:

```
byte b=0;
while (true){
System.out.println(b++); // print b then increment it
}
```

It would count upward until it reached 127, roll over to –128, and continue counting back toward zero again! This is the nature of the two's complement system. When b has the value 127, the binary representation would be 01111111. Adding one to this number gives 10000000, which also happens to be the binary two's complement representation of –128. This kind of overflow can be hard to track down, because Java gives no warnings or errors at compile time or run time. If you were to add two bytes and check to see if the total is greater than 100, yo could very well end up with a (negative) number less than 100, and the comparison would be invalid. The lesson here is to use the larger data sizes if there is a chance of overflow.

Floating Point Types You may wonder how floating point variables can handle infinitely large and infinitely small numbers. They don't, really. The actual maximum is around 3.40282e+038 (signed) for floats and 1.79769e+308 for doubles. Floats and doubles can, however, also take on three special values: POSITIVE_INFINITY and NEGATIVE_INFINITY for overflowed numbers, and NaN (short for Not a Number) for the result of undefined operations like division by zero. The value of any comparison between NaN and any other value is always false, so even a comparison of NaN==NaN will return false!

Characters The char data type represents a 16-bit unicode character. The unicode standard, so far, supports 24 alphabets; the normal ASCII character set is mapped to the range 32 to 127. Even though the internal representation is guaranteed to be 16 bits long, some input and output functions may strip off the upper byte.

A Brief Digression: Literals Java uses some special codes to indicate different types of literal values in Java source code. A base 10 integer literal is represented by its normal decimal value. A base 16 (hexadecimal) integer literal is indicated by "0x" or "0X" followed by the hex digits of the number, and a base 8 (octal) literal is represented by "0" followed by the octal digits of the number. Numeric literal values are assumed to be of type int unless they are suffixed with "L" or "l," in which case they are type long.

```
int i=123;    /* decimal literal  (base 10 value=123) */
int i=0x123;  /* hex literal  (base 10 value=291) */
int i=0123;   /* octal literal  (base 10 value=83) */
long i=1L     /* long decimal literal */
int i=1L      /* ERROR: can't assign a long value to an int without cast! */
```

Floating Point Literals Floating point numbers can be represented in a variety of ways. The basic components of a floating point literal are as follows:

- A whole number part
- A decimal point
- A fractional part
- An exponent consisting of "e" or "E" followed by a (optionally signed) integer
- An optional type suffix consisting of either "f" or "F" (for float), "d" or "D" (for double)

A floating point literal must have at least one digit in either the whole or fractional part and either an exponent or a decimal point:

```
/* some  floating point literals */
float f=1.1F; /* "F" is optional */
float f=1.1; /* same as previous */
float f=1.1 e 1;
float f=.1;
double d=2.2D;
double d=1D;
float d=1.1D; /* ERROR: can't assign double to float! */
```

If no type suffix is provided, the compiler assumes type float.

Unicode Character Literals A unicode character literal consists of either a single character or an escape sequence enclosed in single quotes. The escape sequences make it possible to represent nonprinting characters like carriage returns, as well as the full 16-bit unicode character set. The basic unicode escape sequence is "\u" followed by the hexadecimal value of the character (without the 0x prefix) . The following two statements are equivalent:

```
char c='A';
char c='\u0041'; /* unicode 41(hex) is "A"
```

Several additional escape sequences are also defined as shown in Table 3.3.

TABLE 3.3 Escape Sequences

Escape	Value
\b	backspace (\u0008)
\t	tab (\u0009)

Continued

Escape	Value
\n	linefeed (\0000A)
\r	carriage return (\u000D)
\"	double quote (\u0022)
\'	single quote (\u00027)
\\	backslash (\u005C)

These special escapes are necessary because of the way Java treats normal unicode escapes during compilation. The "\u000A" escape sequence, in the following

```
char c='\u000A';
```

is turned into an actual linefeed character very early in the compilation process, resulting in

```
char c='
';
```

When the compiler comes back to this statement later in the compilation, it sees a single quote followed by a linefeed followed by another single quote and interprets this as an empty set of single quotes. The compiler then complains that this is an "Invalid character constant." Using "\n" causes no such problems.

String Literals A string literal is represented by one or more characters and escapes enclosed in double quotes.

```
String s="What is the frequency, Kenneth?";
String s="\t";
String s="1234";
```

A string literal may not span more than one line. To represent a very long string, use the string concatenation operator (+):

```
String s="Hello, " + "World! I am a very long string which" +
" would normally be longer than one line so " +
"I get broken into pieces and put back together using the" +
" string concatenation operator!";
```

The compiler actually does a little voodoo behind the scenes using the StringBuffer class to add the strings together. In other words, this is *not* an example of operator overloading, but we'll get into that later.

Source File Format The Java compiler (javac) accepts plain text files with the ".java" extension and compiles them into class files that have the ".class" extension. More than one class may be defined in a source file, and this will result in separate class files being produced. Here is an example of a simple Java source file:

```
package java.simple;
import java.shemp;
public class Simple{
// an empty class
}
```

Packages The *package* statement on the first line identifies the package to which the classes defined in this file belong—in this case it's "java.simple." Every class is part of a package of classes. If you do not specify a package name at the beginning of your source file, your classes get automatic membership in a default, unnamed package. Packages are used to group cooperating classes and to control access to those classes.

By convention a package name consists of one or more names separated by periods, and you declare to what package (if any) the classes defined in a source file belong by using the package statement at the beginning of your source file. Note that the package statement must be the first statement (noncomment) in the source file. The following are all valid package statements:

```
package java.lang;
package java.shemp;
package COM.nixon.plumber.watergate;
```

Note that a package statement must end with a semicolon. When the interpreter goes to find a package, it replaces the periods in the package name with directory separators (i.e., "/" or "\" depending on the platform) to make a path. Then it attempts to access the classes using that path, starting with the directories listed in the CLASSPATH environment variable. For example, if the package name is "java.util," this is converted to the path "java\util\" on the PC. If the CLASSPATH variable contains the entry "C:\java\lib," the Virtual Machine will attempt to load the classes from "C:\java\lib\java\util," which is where they happen to be. If it has no luck with the first entry in CLASSPATH, it tries the remaining ones in turn. If none of the paths contain the desired subdirectories, a run-time error results.

The package name "COM.NIXON.watergate.plumber.watergate" demonstrates Sun's suggested convention for globally unique package names. To generate a globally unique package name, you start by reversing your domain name and append as many dot-separated names as necessary.

The combination of a class's package name with the name of the class is known as the *fully qualified name*, because it exactly specifies where a class resides. For example, if the fully qualified name of a class is

```
java.stooge.Shemp
```

the compiler knows that the name of the class is "Shemp" and that the class resides in the directory "Java/stooge/."

Import Statements After the package statement comes an *import* statement. This doesn't really import anything the way an analogous "#include" preprocessor directive would in C/C++. What the import statement actually does is allow you refer to classes in the packages without having to give their fully qualified names. If the fully qualified name is

```
java.stooge.Shemp
```

the import statement

```
import java.stooge.Shemp;
```

would allow you to refer to the class as simply "Shemp" instead of "java.lang.Shemp." There is another "wildcard" form of import that will import every class in a package. The statement "import java.stooge.*" would import all the classes in the "java.stooge" package. This allows you to refer to the class "java.stooge.Curly" as simply "Curly."

All Java programs get access to the "java.lang" package automatically, so the statement "import java.lang.*" would be redundant but would not generate an error. Remember that import statements don't really import anything, and they will not affect the size, speed, or religious affiliation of the compiled programs. The only side effect import statements could have, theoretically, would be slightly slower compilation; this doesn't seem to be the case in practice, so import away!

Classes

The next part of the source file is a simple class definition. Every Java statement or variable that is not a comment, package statement, or import statement must reside inside a class. This is a departure from C++ in which it was possible to write programs that didn't have any classes at all. Classes can be defined using the class keyword:

```
class Class_Name{/* class body here */}
```

As you can see, a class definition consists of the word "class" followed by the class name, followed by the actual class body enclosed in curly braces. By convention class names are capitalized, but this convention is not enforced by the compiler. This defines a class named Class_Name which by default extends, or inherits from Object, the root of the Java class library, so this statement is equivalent to the following:

```
class Class_Name extends Object{/* class body here */}
```

Of course an empty class like this doesn't have much use, but it's perfectly valid and will compile anyway.

The complete format for the class definition is as follows:

```
Class_Modifiers class Class_Name extends Parent_Class implements Interface_Name {/*
class body */}
```

Class_Modifier can be *public*, *final*, or *abstract*. Public classes can be accessed by classes from other packages. If public is omitted, access is restricted to other classes in the package.

```
public class class1{/* this class is visible to other packages */}
class class2{/* but this class is visible only in the current package */}
```

Classes marked *final* may not be subclassed (extended). Marking classes final may allow some compilers to perform some optimizations that would otherwise be impossible. Attempting to extend a final class results in a "Can't subclass final classes" error:

```
final class Class1{/*class body */}
class Class2 extends Class1{/*ERROR: can't extend a final class */}
```

If a class is defined with the *abstract* modifier, it can never be instantiated. Again, this rule is enforced by the compiler. Abstract classes exist only to serve as parents for derived classes.

Now that you have the basic shell of a class, what do you put inside? The simple answer is the following:

- Variable declarations
- Methods
- Constructors/finalizers
- Static initializers

Variable Declarations We have already looked at variable declarations. There is a slightly more verbose format for declaring class member variables, which declares who can access the variable (or even know of its existence):

```
Access_Specifier Variable_Type Variable_Name;
```

Access_Specifier can be *public, private, protected,* or *private protected* to reflect the desired level of visibility. If none of these is specified, the *default* (but actually nameless) access level is assumed.

Variables with *default* visibility are visible in the current class, in the current package, and also in any subclasses in the current package. They are not accessible to any subclasses that do not reside in the current package, and they will not be inherited by a subclass from a different package.

Public variables are visible everywhere and are always inherited. One should use these sparingly if one values one's object-oriented credentials.

Variables declared *private* are visible in the current class and invisible in any subclasses. Private variables are never inherited by subclasses.

Variables declared *protected* have the same visibility as the default; that is, they are visible in the current class and in subclasses in the current package, but not visible to subclasses residing in another package, which means that those subclasses cannot access protected variables in its superclass. However, protected variables are *inherited* by subclasses no matter what package they are in.

So as you can see, Java has *four* visibility types to deal with, instead of C++'s already confusing three.

Variables may also be declared *static* or *final*. Static variables are also known as *class variables* because they belong to a class rather than an instance of a class. If a variable is declared static, it is allocated and initialized exactly once, when the class is loaded. Don't let the word *static* fool you into thinking static variables are unchanging; they're just as variable as any other variable. For instance:

```
public class Item{
public static int numitems;
}
```

No matter how many Item objects exist in your program, they all share the numitems variable. If each Item object increments the numitems variable when it is instantiated (we'll see how to do this in a bit), we would have a handy running count of the number of Items in existence.

Variables marked *final*, however, cannot be changed once they are initialized. Final variables can also be thought of as constant variables, a phrase that has a nice contradictory ring to it.

Casting As you probably know, Java is a very strongly typed language. This means you cannot do something like assign a floating point value to a variable of type int. In general, if an assignment would require a run-time validity check or may possibly result in loss of information (as a float-to-int conversion would), an explicit *cast* is necessary. By using a cast, you can convert any numeric type to any other numeric type, regardless of any information loss that may be possible. The basic format of the cast is to place the required type name in parentheses in front of the value to be converted, like so:

```
float f=3.141;
int i=(int)f;
```

The compiler would not allow these statements to compile without the explicit cast. Object data types (references) can also be cast, but only to a superclass. Thus, a reference to any object can be cast to the Object class, because Object is the root of the Java class hierarchy. One thing C++ programmers should note is that Java does not support the function call syntax for casts. The following is not legal:

```
float f=3.141;
int i=float(f);//Nope!
```

Accessing Variables If the variable is part of the current class, you're in luck. You can refer to the variable by name. If the variable resides in another class, you must use *dot notation*. To use dot notation, you simply prefix the name of the class in which the variable resides and a dot (.) to the variable. An example follows:

```
a=Shemp.numitems; // Set a equal to the variable numitems in the Shemp class.
```

Of course this access is subject to the restrictions outlined above. An attempt to access a private variable, for example, will produce a compile-time error.

Methods Classes may contain *methods*, which are also called *member functions*. The basic method declaration format is as follows:

```
Access_Modifier Return_Type Method_Name(Argument_list){/* method body
*/}
```

Access_Modifier functions exactly as it does for variable declarations and is optional. The Return_Type, as the name implies, specifies what type of value the method returns. This may be a primitive type, an object reference, or void to indicate that no value is returned. The parenthesized list of arguments, which may be empty, specifies the name and type of the variables passed to the function. If we wanted to declare a method named "sum," which takes no arguments and returns no value, we could do it like so:

```
public void sum(){/* add something */}
```

The void keyword specifies *"nada"* as the return type, and the lack of declared arguments in parentheses indicates that this method expects to receive no parameters. Attempting to call this method with arguments would result in a compile-time error. A method, accessible only to other parts of this class, which takes two integers and returns the sum as an integer, would look something like this:

```
private int sum(int a, int b){
int c;
c=a+b;
return c;
}
```

Because these two functions have the same name, you might think it would be an error to define them both in the same class. Far from considering it an error, Java encourages this type of behavior. This is a perfect example of overloading in action. Method overloading allows you to have as many methods with the same name as you want, as long as they differ in either the *number*, *type*, or *order* of their arguments. The combination of a method's name and its argument list is sometimes called the *method signature*, because it uniquely defines each method. In this case one sum method takes no arguments and the other takes two integers. Which method is actually called can be determined at run time by the arguments (or lack of them) passed to the function. So, calling sum() with no arguments would call the first method, and calling sum(5,5) would invoke the latter. This is one example of polymorphism. It's not quite as exciting as the fancy Greek name would imply.

Note that it is not enough for the overloaded methods to have different return types. They must have different method signatures, or the compiler will complain. It *is* possible for the methods to differ only in the order of the arguments they take. The following is perfectly acceptable, if somewhat confusing, method overloading:

```
public sum(int a, float b){/* do something */}
public sum(float b, int a){/* do something */}
```

The Main Method One very special method for stand-alone Java applications is the *main* method. The main method must have the following form:

```
public static void main (String Args[]){/* main code here */}
```

This is the method called automatically when you feed a class file to the Java interpreter. As you can see, this is a static (class) method that takes an array of String objects as its sole argument and returns no value. The String array contains the command-line arguments (if any) passed to the program.

Method Overriding When you extend a base class, you inherit all the methods and variables of the parent class that are not marked as being private. What if you want to have a method with the same name as one of these methods? This is where *method overriding* comes in. If you define a method with the same signature as one of the inherited methods, the second method is said to override the original, and it will be called instead. The superclass method remains accessible through use of the super keyword, as will be explained later.

Calling Methods Method access is similar to variable access. The following will call the sum() method in the current class:

```
sum();
```

Through dot notation the following will call the sum() method in the Shemp class if it has previously been imported:

```
Shemp.sum();
```

If it hasn't been imported, the following will do the trick nicely for the sum() method of a Shemp object in the java.stooge package:

```
java.stooge.Shemp.sum();
```

When we make the following call, we are making a call to the println() function of the "out" object, a printstream that belongs to the System class:

```
System.out.println("Hello World");
```

Instantiation The process of creating a new instance of an object is known as instantiation and is accomplished with the new operator. The basic syntax is as follows:

```
new Class_Type();
```

In this syntax Class_Name is the name of the class of which you want to make an instance. The new statement reserves space for the new object on the free memory heap, makes an instance of the class, and returns a reference to that instance. So, to set the variables to a reference to a new Shemp object, we could use the following:

```
Shemp s;              // declare s is a reference to a Shemp object
s=new Shemp();        // set s equal to a new instance of the Shemp class
Shemp s=new Shemp(); // this will do the same thing in one line
```

When s is declared to be a reference to a Shemp object, it is initialized to null by default. Any attempt to reference s before the new statement will result in a run-time error.

Constructors You may wonder why you need the parentheses after the class name. This looks like a method call, doesn't it? It turns out the new operator does make a call to a special method known as a *constructor*. Constructors are methods that are called automatically whenever you create an instance of a class and perform any necessary initialization. Constructors must have the same name as the class to which they belong, must be declared public, and must not have a return type (not even void). We could define a class as follows:

```
class ConstructorTest{
public ConstructorTest(){
System.out.println("ConstructorTest Constructor called with no arguments!");
    }
public ConstructorTest(int a){
System.out.println("ConstructorTest Constructor called with an int argument!");
    }
}
```

Then the following lines would instantiate two ConstructorTest objects:

```
ConstructorTest T1=new ConstructorTest();
ConstructorTest T2=new ConstructorTest(3);
```

As a result, two different constructors would be called:

```
ConstructorTest Constructor called with no arguments!
ConstructorTest Constructor called with an int argument!
```

As you can see, we are overloading the constructor, and the run-time decides which to call based on the type and number of arguments. If you do not specify a constructor for your classes, the default constructor (which takes no arguments) is called. When you define a constructor that takes no arguments, you are, in fact, overriding this default constructor. Constructors are not inherited per se, but each constructor starts off with an invisible call to the default constructor of the parent class. We could extend the ConstructorTest as follows:

```
class SonOfConstructorTest extends ConstructorTest{
public SonOfConstructorTest(){
System.out.println("SonOfConstructorTest Constructor called with no arguments!");
    }
}
```

When we instantiate a new SonOfConstructorTest object, as in the first line below, we get the messages shown below that:

```
SonOfConstructorTest= new SonOfConstructorTest();
    :

ConstructorTest Constructor called with no arguments!
SonOfConstructorTest Constructor called with no arguments!
```

What we don't see here is that the original ConstructorTest constructor also calls the default constructor of this parent class, in this case Object, before it executes. This whole process is called *constructor chaining*, and it ensures that the parent class constructors always execute before the constructors in the derived classes. You can explicitly call the default superclass constructor using the super keyword:

```
super(); // this would call the default constructor of the superclass
```

The call to the superclass constructor, whether you make the call with super( ) or let it occur automatically, performs one other invisible action; it causes the instance variable initializers to be called. For example, your class could contain the following code:

```
class A{
int t=6; // instance variable initialization on these two lines
int s=8; // occurs transparently when superclass constructor is called
public A(){
super(); // redundant, this call occurs implicitly
// variables are initialized at this point
System.out.println("t="+t+" s="+s);
    }
}
```

In this case, the two variable assignments take place when the super() constructor is called and the print statement gives the expected output:

```
t=6 s=8
```

There are some cases in which you want to use some constructor in the superclass other than the default constructor. Then you would include a call to whichever specific superclass constructor you wish as the first statement of the derived class constructor, like so:

```
class SonOfConstructorTest extends ConstructorTest{
public SonOfConstructorTest(){
super (3); /* Call the parent constructor which takes an int. */
System.out.println("SonOfConstructorTest Constructor called with no arguments!");
    }
}
```

When we create a new SonOfConstructorTest object using new(), we get the following output:

```
ConstructorTest Constructor called with an int argument!
SonOfConstructorTest Constructor called with no arguments!
```

Destructors In C++, the opposite of the constructor is the *destructor*. Destructors are called when an object goes out of scope, and they can perform any cleanup actions you may feel are necessary. The Java equivalent of the destructor is the finalize() method or *finalizer*. The difference is that Java makes no guarantee that the finalizer of an object will be called as soon as the object goes out of scope, although it does guarantee that the finalize() method will be called before the object is garbage collected. This gives you a chance to free up any system resources the object may be using. The finalize method must be declared with the following format:

```
protected void finalize() throws Throwable{/* Cleanup code here */}
```

We'll get to the exact meaning of the Throwable part of this declaration later. Sometimes a finalizer will *never* be called because an object may be garbage collected before a program exits.

Take the following code:

```
public class CT{
public static void main(String args[]){
FinalizerTest T1=new FinalizerTest();
```

```
int N=15000;
for (int f=0;f<N;f++){T1=new FinalizerTest();}
    }
}
class FinalizerTest{
int a=1;
protected void finalize() throws Throwable{
System.out.println("Finalizer called!");
    }
}
```

This produces no output for values of N less than 14574 on my system. Values of N greater that 14574 cause the finalizers of about 30 of the FinalizerTest objects to be called at a time, at fairly random intervals. Since the *Java Language Specification* does not specify what garbage collection policy should be used, your finalize methods may never be called at all. There is a java.lang.System.gc( ) method that is supposed to initiate garbage collection, but this method actually acts more like a *request* that garbage collection take place. Note that it is probably a good idea to call the finalizer of any superclass you extend with super.finalize( ); in case it does any extra cleanup.

Summary

At this point you know how to declare classes which are templates for objects. Objects begin their lives when they are instantiated the new keyword that causes the constructors of the class and all its superclasses to be called. Objects can contain variables and methods that can be referenced with dot notation. When objects are removed by the garbage collector, their finalize( ) method is called to give the object a chance to do any cleanup. That's the complete life cycle of an object from birth (instantiation) to death (garbage collection).

Chapter 4

Simple Java Applications and the java.lang Package

Applets and Oranges

Java programs come in two flavors: applications and applets. Java applications are stand-alone programs interpreted directly by Java.exe, while applets are designed to live on web pages and be executed by a web browser (or Sun's Appletviewer program) to provide the familiar seizure-inducing animation and scrolling Netscape status bars we all know and love. The differences do not end there, however. Because of the inherently insecure nature of today's Internet, many restrictions are placed on applets. Specifically, applets cannot

- Read files
- Write files
- Rename files
- Check a file's size
- Create directories
- Check for the existence of a file
- Check a file's size or extension
- Check the time stamp of a file

In addition to these restrictions, applets are allowed to make connections over the Internet only to the host from which they originated and have their windows branded with ugly "untrusted applet window" title bars. In addition to being crippled in these ways, bare-bones applets are slightly more complex than minimal applications. In this chapter we start with applications to give you a feel for the basic Java language and the Java class library.

A Basic Application Shell

A basic text-only application is shown in Listing 4.1 (Application.java). This program simply echoes back the command-line arguments you give it. Sounds simple, doesn't it? The first thing to notice about this program is that everything is contained inside a class that is declared public, which stands to reason if we want other classes to access it. One thing that may not be obvious from this small example is that it would be an error to define more than one public class in a single file. You may define as many classes as you want in a file, as long as only one is public. The Java compiler will also complain if the file does not have the same name as this single public class with the **.java** extension.

LISTING 4.1

```java
/*

    Application.java
    Echoes command line args.
*/

import java.lang.*; // automatic, included for clarity
public class Application{

    public static void main (String args[]){

        int length=args.length;
        System.out.println("You passed me "+length+" arguments.");
        for (int i=0;i<length;i++){
            System.out.println("Argument "+i+" was "+args[i]);

        }
    }
}
```

Note that the main method must be a static method. Java never actually instantiates an Application object; it merely loads the Application class. This means that if you want to have any nonstatic variables or methods in your program, you must instantiate an Application object in order to reference it. It is an error to make a static reference to a nonstatic variable or method. The reverse is perfectly acceptable, however.

One other fact this simple example makes clear is that command-line arguments are passed as an array of strings. Since arrays are quasi-objects in Java, we use the array.length field to find out how many elements are actually allocated in the array. The ouput of the program shows that the zeroth array element contains the first argument and not the name of the command as it would in C/C++.

```
java.exe Application foo bar
You passed me 2 arguments on the command line.
Argument 0 was foo
Argument 1 was bar
```

Now would be a good time to explain the System.out.println ("foo"). It is calling the println (String) method of a static java.io.PrintStream object, which belongs to the java.lang.System class. We get this and its opposite, InputStream, for free. PrintStream is a subclass of the FilterOutputStream class, which is in turn a subclass of the abstract OutputStream class. This explanation will have to suffice for now, but we'll come back to it later. Just note that this is the method call equivalent of using the C++ insertion operator (<<). The major differences are that you are using a method call instead of an operator, and you can't use any of the C++ stream manipulators.

A Package Tour: java.lang

What follows is a whirlwind tour of the java.lang package (Table 4.1), the core of the Java class library. Here you will meet the root of the entire class hierarchy, Object, along with its closest friends and family. The java.lang package is implicitly imported into every program and is the only package guaranteed to be available in even the most rudimentary Java implementation. Let's start at the top!

TABLE 4.1 The Java.lang Package

Boolean	An object wrapper for Boolean values.
Character	An object wrapper for char values

Continued

TABLE 4.1 Continued

Class	A class to encapsulate classes
ClassLoader	Abstract parent for classes that load classes
Compiler	A class to encapsulate a compiler
Double	An object wrapper for double values
Float	An object wrapper for float values
Integer	An object wrapper for int values
Long	An object wrapper for long values
Math	Various math constants and functions
Number	An abstract parent class for numerical objects
Object	The One True Base Class
Process	A class to encapsulate an exec()'ed process
Runtime	An object representation of the run-time environment
SecurityManager	A class to keep ClassLoaders honest
String	An immutable string
StringBuffer	A mutable string
System	A class to encapsulate system services
Thread	A class to encapsulate threads of execution
ThreadGroup	A class representing a group of threads
Throwable	The base class for exceptions

The java.lang.Object Class

Object is "the mother" of all objects. The methods of the Object class are shown in Table 4.2, and a short Java program to demonstrate some of these features is shown in Listing 4.2 (myObject.java).

TABLE 4.2 Java.lang Object

public Object()	Creates a new Object object
protected native Object clone() throws CloneNotSupportedException	Just tosses the exception
public boolean equals(Object obj)	Returns true if 'this' and 'obj' refer to the same object
protected void finalize() throws Throwable	Called before garbage collection
public final native Class getClass()	Returns the Class object for this Object's class
public native int hashCode()	Returns a unique integer hashcode
public final native void notify()	Notifies a single waiting thread
public final native void notifyAll()	Notifies all waiting threads
public String toString()	Returns string of form "objectName@hexhashcode"
public final void wait(in) throws InterruptedException	Wait forever to be notified
public final void wait(long timeout, int nanos) throws InterruptedException	Wait until notifed or (timeout milliseconds + nanos nanoseconds) have elapsed
public final native void wait (long timeout) throws InterruptedException	Wait until notified or timeout milliseconds

LISTING 4.2

```
/*
    myObject.java
    Tests some methods in the Object class.
*/

import java.lang.*;

public class myObject extends Object{
```

Continued

```
public static void main(String args[]){
    /* create a couple of new objects */
    Object o1=new Object();
    Object o2=new Object();

    /* now print out some info about our objects */
    System.out.println("Object1 belongs to "+o1.getClass());
    System.out.println("Object2 belongs to "+o2.getClass());
    System.out.println("\nObject1 hashcode:"+o1.hashCode());
    System.out.println("Object2 hashcode:"+o2.hashCode());
    System.out.println("\nObject1 String value:"+o1.toString());
    System.out.println("Object2 String value:"+o2.toString());
    System.out.println("\nObject1 equals Object1?:"+o1.equals(o1));
    System.out.println("Object1 equals Object2?:"+o1.equals(o2));
try{
    o1=o2.getClass().newInstance();

}catch (InstantiationException e){ }
 catch (IllegalAccessException e){ }
 System.out.println(o1);


}

}
```

Here is a sample output:

```
Object1 belongs to class java.lang.Object
Object2 belongs to class java.lang.Object

Object1 hashcode:20526920
Object2 hashcode:20526928

Object1 String value:java.lang.Object@1393748
Object2 String value:java.lang.Object@1393750
```

```
Object1 equals Object1?:true
Object1 equals Object2?:false
```

As you can see, we use the getClass() method to get a reference to a Class object representing the current object's class. We use this Class object's toString() method to print each object's class as a string. Next we print each object's hashcode using the hashCode() method, which returns an integer that should be different for different objects (as it is in this case). Next we use Object.toString() to print a string representation of the objects. This consists of the object's class name followed by an ampersand and the object's hashcode (converted to hexadecimal). The compiler knows how to take advantage of the fact that every object inherits this method, so the following statements are equivalent and generate the same bytecodes when compiled.

```
System.out.println(AnObject);
System.out.println(AnObject.toString());
```

The next few lines demonstrate something interesting about the basic implementation of the equals() method. The default Object.equals method simply compares the **this** pointer of an object to an object reference you pass to it. This method will return true only if both references point to the same object, even if the two objects in question may have the same value at the binary level.

```
Object a=new Object(); // identical
Object b=new Object(); // but not the same!
Object c=a;   // c is now a reference to a
a.equals(a); // true
a.equals(c); // true
a.equals(b); // false
```

If you want a more sophisticated approach, such as a member-by-member comparison, you may override this method.

There are a few more java.lang.Object methods not demonstrated in the myObject.java program for various reasons. The clone() method is supposed to return a new object that is a binary copy of the current object. As it is implemented in Object, clone() simply throws a CloneNotSupportedException, so it isn't much use. Another problem is that clone() is a protected method, so it is not accessible from a subclass from a different package. We would have had to declare our myObject class part of the java.lang package in order to access it. The different variations of wait() and notify() are used for thread synchronization and will be covered in Chapter 7.

The java.lang.Class Class

A minute ago we used the Class class to get a string representing an object's class. Table 4.3 shows the other Class methods. The run-time instantiates a Class object for every class it loads.

The Class Class Method The ForName () method takes the (fully qualified) name of a class as an argument and returns a reference to a Class object for that class. This may throw a ClassNotFoundException if the class cannot be found. Note that this is the only class (static) method in the Class class.

Instant Instantiation The newInstance() method is supposed to return a new object for the class in question. This should have the same effect as using new(), but it currently throws a NoSuchMethodError.

Getting Class Information Several other Class methods are demonstrated in Listing 4.3 (ClassDumper.java).

TABLE 4.3 java.lang.Class

public static native Class forName (String className) throws ClassNotFoundException	Gets a reference to named class. Loads it if necessary
public native ClassLoader getClassLoader ()	Returns a reference to the ClassLoader that loaded this class (null by default)
public native Class getInterfaces ()	Returns the interfaces this class implements
public native String getName ()	Returns the name of the class
public native Class getSuperclass ()	Returns a handle to the superclass
public native boolean isInterface ()	Returns true if this is an interface
public native Object newInstance () throws InstantiationException , IllegalAccessException	Instantiates a new object of this class
public String toString ()	Returns "className@hashCode"

LISTING 4.3

```
/*
    ClassDumper.java
    Prints some interesting info using java.lang.Class methods.
*/

import java.lang.*;
import java.awt.*;

public class ClassDumper extends Object{
    public static void main(String args[]){

        /* Try to load the class supplied on the command line. */
        /* Freak out if we can't!                              */
        Class c=null;
          try {
              c= Class.forName(args[0]);
          }catch (Exception e){
              System.out.println("Danger! Danger! "+e);
          }

        /* is it a class or an interface? */
        if (c.isInterface()){
            System.out.print("Interface ");
        }else{
            System.out.print("Class ");
        }

        /* the class, and its superclass*/
        System.out.println(c.getName()+"\n extends "+c.getSuperclass());

        /* List the interfaces it implements. */
        Class s[]=c.getInterfaces();
        if (s.length>0){
```

Continued

```
            for (int i=0;i<s.length;i++){
                System.out.println(" implements "+s[i].toString());
            }
        }

    }// main

}
```

The getName() method returns the name of the class as a string, while the toString() method returns a slightly more verbose description. The getSuperclass() method returns a reference to the superclass of the class. The get Interfaces() method returns an array of Class objects containing the interfaces implemented by the class, and the isInterface() method will tell you if this class is actually an interface itself. Trying this on the java.awt.FlowLayout class, for example, will give the following output:

```
java.exe myClass java.awt.FlowLayout


Class java.awt.FlowLayout
 extends class java.lang.Object
 implements interface java.awt.LayoutManager
```

The java.lang.System Class

We've been using the standard output stream in the System class (Table 4.4) for some time now. The System class also provides the standard input stream, in, and the standard error stream, err. The err stream is useful when you have redirected standard output to a file and you want to have the error messages still go to the screen. The different types of input and output streams will be covered in detail later, but we'll examine some of the other features of java.lang.System here.

TABLE 4.4 java.lang.System

public static InputStream in	Stdin
public static PrintStream out	Stdout
public static PrintStream err	Stderr

Continued

public static native void arraycopy (Object src, int src _position, Object dst, int dst _position, int length)	Copy array elements from src to dst
public static native long currentTimeMillis ()	Milliseconds elapsed since midnight 1/1/70
public static void exit (int code)	Bail out with exit code
public static void gc ()	Suggest that garbage collection take place
public static String getenv (String name)	Gets environment string
public static Properties getProperties ()	Returns a referenceto the object holding the current system properties
public static String getProperty (String key)	Gets a single property named by key
public static String getProperty (String kcy, String value)	Sets single property to value
public static SecurityManager getSecurityManager ()	Return a reference to the current SecurityManager
public static void load (String path_n_filename)	Loads a dynamic library path_n_filename
public static void loadLibrary (String libname)	Loads a dynamic library libname
public static void runFinalization () awaiting garbage collection	Runs the finalize() methods of objects
public static void setProperties (Properties props)	Sets current properties
public static void setSecurityManager (SecurityManager s)	Can be called only once without throwing an exception

Copying Arrays One very useful static method in the System class is arraycopy(). This method will save you from having to code a loop just to copy elements of one array to another. The syntax is

```
arraycopy(source,source_start,destination,destination_start,length);
```

So to copy all the elements of array A into array B, we could use

```
System.arraycopy(A,0,B,0,A.length);
```

Not only is this much cleaner than using a loop, it's also about 40 times faster. Note that this method does not follow the naming convention used in most of the class library. It's arraycopy(), not arrayCopy().

Timing The System.currentTimeMillis() method returns the number of milliseconds since midnight 1/1/70 as a long integer. According to Sun's documentation this will not overflow until the year 292280995. Very useful when performance tuning your programs.

Exit(0), Stage Left The System class also provides the exit(int code) method to bail out of the Virtual Machine immediately with an error code. Attempting to use this in an applet may be considered a security violation.

Taking Out the Trash The System class provides the gc() method to request that garbage collection take place and the runFinalization() method to run the finalize() methods of any objects awaiting garbage collection. There is no official Java garbage collection policy, so you can use these as a hint to the run-time as to when it would be most convenient for garbage collection to take place.

Properties There are several System methods that return a java.util.Properties object. The Properties class itself is used to store system properties as string values and access them by name. We'll cover these when we get to the java.util class, but for now suffice it to say that the first line below should yield something similar to the standard output under it:

```
System.getProperties().list(System.out); // dump system properties
```

```
-- listing properties --
java.home=C:\JAVA\BIN\..
awt.toolkit=sun.awt.win32.MToolkit
java.version=1.0
file.separator=\
line.separator=
```

```
java.vendor=Sun Microsystems Inc.
user.name=Lester Bangs
os.arch=x86
os.name=Windows 95
java.vendor.url=http://www.sun.com/
```

```
user.dir=C:\chp4
java.class.path=.;C:\SC\JAVA\LIB;;C:\JAVA\BIN\..\clas...
java.class.version=45.3
os.version=4.0
path.separator=;
user.home=C:\JAVA\BIN\..
```

Note that an actual carriage return/linefeed string is returned as a line separator and shows up as two blank lines above.

Is It Safe? The System setSecurityManager() and getSecurityManager() methods allow you to get or specify the SecurityManager used by the system. The SecurityManager implements a security policy and will check to see if things like file and network I/O can take place without a SecurityException being thrown. The SecurityManager can be set only once and will throw a SecurityException if it has already been set. Unless you are using things like Remote Method Invocation, you probably will never need to use this feature.

The java.lang.Runtime Class

The java.lang.Runtime class encapsulates a representation of the run-time environment. Some of the methods are similar to those in the java.lang.system class. In fact, many of the methods in the System class actually call their counterparts in the Runtime Class to do their dirty work. All the methods of java.lang.Runtime are shown Table 4.5.

TABLE 4.5 java.lang.Runtime

public static Runtime getRuntime ()	Returns a reference to the current Runtime
public Process exec (String command)throws IOException	Executes command and returns reference to the process
public Process exec (String command, String envp [])throws IOException	Executes command with evp[] as arguments and returns reference to the process
public Process exec (String cmdarray []) throws IOException	Executes command[0] with other array elements as arguments and returns reference to the process
public Process exec (String cmdarray [], String envp [])throws IOException	Executes command[0] with evp[] as arguments and returns reference to the process
public void exit (int code)	Bails out with exit code

Continued

TABLE 4.5 Continued

public native long freeMemory ()	Returns number of _estimated_ number of free bytes as a long
public native void gc ()	Request garbage collection; called by Systemgc()
public InputStream getLocalizedInputStream (InputStream in)	Gets an InputStream that converts from local format to unicode
public OutputStream getLocalizedOutputStream (OutputStream out)	Gets an OutputStream that converts from unicode to local format
public synchronized void load (String path_n_filename)	Loads a dynamic library path_n_filename
public synchronized void loadLibrary (String libname)	Loads dynamic library by name
public native long totalMemory ()	Returns total system memory as a long
public native void runFinalization ()	Causes finalize() method of objects awaiting garbage collection to be called
public native void traceInstructions (boolean on)	Enable/Disable instruction tracing
public native void traceMethodCalls (boolean on)	Enable/Disable method call tracing

You can get a reference to the current Runtime using the following:

```
Runtime R=Runtime.getRuntime(); // static method to get runtime
```

Once you have this reference, you can do some useful things including launching another process using exec(), which returns a Process object. The Process class (see Table 4.6) has methods for getting the input, output, and error streams of the child process. Listing 4.4 (Runtime.java) shows the use of the Runtime class to execute the MS-DOS editor, edit.com. First we use the System.totalMemory() and System.freeMemory to print the amount of memory available for this copy of the Virtual Machine. Then we use the version of exec() that takes an array of String objects and executes the process named in the zeroth element and passes the other elements as command-line arguments. Next we use the methods in the Process class to get the input, output, and error streams for this process.

TABLE 4.6 Java.lang.Process

abstract public void destroy ()	Destroys the process
abstract public int exitValue ()	Returns the exit code of the process
abstract public InputStream getErrorStream ()	Returns a handle to process error stream
abstract public InputStream getInputStream ()	Returns a handle to process stdout stream
abstract public OutputStream getOutputStream ()	Returns a handle to process stdin
abstract public int waitFor ()throws InterruptedException	Waits for this process to return

LISTING 4.4

```
/*
* Runtime.java
* use the runtime class to execute an external process */
import java.io.*;
public class Runtime{
    public static void main(String Args[]){
        try{

            String S[]=new String[2]; // command and args
            S[0]="/dos/edit.com";    // zero element=command t
            S[1]="test.txt";          // command line args

            Runtime R=Runtime.getRuntime(); // get a ref to runtime
            Process P=R.exec(S);
    // note path separator is forward slash! (even on MS-DOS)


            InputStream in=P. getInputStream();   // the OUPUT of the child process
            OutputStream out=P.getOutputStream(); // the INPUT of the child process
            InputStream err=P.getErrorStream();    // the error OUTPUT
```

Continued

```
        int exitcode=0;

        try{
            exitcode=P.waitFor(); // wait for process to exit
        }
        catch (InterruptedException e){
        }
        System.out.println(S[0]+" exited with code "+exitcode);

    }catch (java.io.IOException e){}


}
```

Wrap It Up—The Wrapper Classes

The java.lang package also provides the Boolean, Character, Double, Float, Integer, and Long *wrapper classes,* which are useful when you want to treat a primitive data type as an object. One case in which you may want to do this is when you are passing primitive data types in a method call. Normally, primitive values are passed by *value;* a copy of each variable is made and passed to the method as a local variable. Changing this local variable will not change the value of the original variable. This is the place where the wrappers come in. Since these are objects, you can pass them to a method by *reference,* which means any changes made in the method will change the original variable. As you can discover by perusing the representative java.lang.Integer class (Table 4.7), these classes also provide several static methods for converting strings to numbers and numbers to strings. The Integer.parseInt(String) method will return the Integer's value as an int, and the static Integer.toString(int) method will return a string representation of an int.

TABLE 4.7 java.lang.Integer

public static final int
MIN _VALUE =_x80000000

public static final int
MAX _VALUE =_x7fffffff

Continued

public Integer (String s)throws NumberFormatException	Constructs a new Integer object from a string
public Integer (int value)	Constructs a new Integer with the given value
public double doubleValue ()	Returns a double with this Integer's value
public boolean equals (Object obj)	If obj is an Integer, compares its value with this Integer; otherwise, returns false
public float floatValue ()	Returns this Integer's value as a float
public static Integer getInteger (String name, Integer val)	Uses System.getProperty(String name) to return the given property as an Integer; if the property does not exist, returns val
public static Integer getInteger (String name,int val)	Uses SystemgetProperty(String name) to return the given property as an Integer; if the property does not exist, returns val
public static Integer getInteger (String name)	Uses SystemgetProperty(String name) to return the given property as an Integer; if the property does not exist, returns zero
public int hashCode ()	Returns a unique hashcode for this Integer
public int intValue ()	Returns the value of this Integer as an int
public long longValue ()	Returns the value of this Integer as a long
public static int parseInt (String s) throws NumberFormatException	Returns the value of the given string as an int
public static int parseInt (String s, int radix)throws NumberFormatException	Returns the value of the given string (base radix) as an int
public String toString ()	Returns a string representation of this Integer
public static String toString (int i)	Returns a string representation of the given int
public static String toString (int i, int radix)	Returns a string representation of the given int, base radix
public static Integer valueOf (String s)throws NumberFormatException	Returns the Integer value of the given string

Continued

TABLE 4.7 Continued

public static Integer valueOf (String s, int radix)throws NumberFormatException	Returns the Integer value of the given string, base radix

Strings and Things

If you are coming from a C/C++ background, you're in for a pleasant surprise: real strings! The java.lang.String class is shown in Table 4.8. One thing to note about Java Strings is that they are immutable. Once it is created, you cannot alter the value of a String object. If you are looking for mutable strings, the StringBuffer (Table 4.9) class is what you want. These are fairly large classes, and they provide about every string manipulation function you could hope for. Note that both classes override the equals(Object O) method to do a character-by-character comparison. One other thing to note at this point is how the compiler uses the StringBuffer class to implement the string concatenation operator. A statement such as that in the first line below is compiled to the lines beneath it:

```
String S="James Taylor " + "marked for death!"
```

```
String S=new StringBuffer().append("James Taylor ").append("marked for
death!").toString();
```

TABLE 4.8 java.lang.String

public String()	Constructs a new empty String
public String(String S)	Constructs a new String that is a copy of String S
public String(char[] chars)	Constructs a new String from an array of characters
public String(char[] chars, ≈ int start, int end)	Constructs a new String from a subarray of characters starting with chars[start] and ending with chars[end]
public String(byte[] chars, int highbyte, int offset, int length)	Constructs a new String from a subarray of bytes starting with chars[offset] and ending with chars[offset+length]; high byte of the characters is set to highbyte

Continued

public String(byte[] chars, int highbyte)	Constructs a new String from an array of bytes; high byte of the characters is set to highbyte
public String(StringBuffer)	Constructs a new String from the given StringBuffer
public char charAt(int n)	Returns nth character of the String
public int compareTo(String S)	Scans Strings to find first unequal characters and returns difference between those characters as an int; if all characters match, returns the difference in the length of the Strings
public String concat(String S)	Adds S to the end of this String and returns the result
public static copyValueOf(char[] chars, int offset, int len)	Turns num characters in chars[] into a String, starting with chars[offset]
public static copyValueOf(char[])	Turns entire character array into a String and returns it
public boolean endsWith(String S)	Returns true if this String ends with substring S
public boolean equals(Object O)	Returns true if this String matches (String) O (character-by-character comparison)
public boolean equalsIgnoreCase(String)	Returns true if this String matches String S (character-by-character comparison ignoring case)
public void getBytes(int start, int end, byte[] bytes, int offset)	Copies characters start through end from this String into the specified byte array starting at bytes[offset]
public void getChars(int start, int end, char[] chars, int offset)	Copies characters start through end from this String into the specified char array starting at chars[offset]
public int hashCode()	Returns a hashcode derived from character values in this string
public int indexOf(int char)	Returns the index of first occurrence of char, or –1 if none
public int indexOf(int char, int startindex)	Returns the index of first occurrence of char after startindex, or –1 if none
public int indexOf(String S)	Returns the index of the first occurrence of substring S, or –1 if none
public int indexOf(String S, int startindex)	Returns the index of the first occurrence of substring S after startindex, or –1 if none

Continued

TABLE 4.8 Continued

public String intern()	Returns a copy of this String; guaranteed to be a unique entity, not just another reference to this String
public int lastIndexOf(int char)	Returns the index of the last occurrence of char, or –1 if none
public int lastIndexOf(int char, int startindex)	Returns the index of the last occurrence of char after startindex, or –1 if none
public int lastIndexOf(String S)	Returns the index of the last occurrence of substring S, or –1 if none
public int lastIndexOf(String S, int startindex)	Returns the index of the last occurrence of substring S after startindex, or –1 if none
public int length()	Returns the length of the String
public boolean regionMatches (int index1, String S, int index2, int len)	Returns true if the len characters of this String after index1 match the len characters of String S starting at index2
regionMatches(boolean B, int index1, String S, int index2, int len)	Returns true if the len characters of this String after index1 match the len characters of stringS starting at index2; ignores case if B=true
public String replace(char old, char new)	Returns a String that is a copy of this String where all occurrences of the character old are replaced by the character new
public boolean startsWith (String S, int startindex)	Returns true if this String begins with the substring of S starting with startindex and ending with Slength()
public boolean startsWith(String)	Returns true if this String begins with substring S
public String substring (int startindex)	Returns the substring of this String starting at startindex and ending at the end of the String
public String substring (int startindex, int endindex)	Returns the substring of this String starting at startindex and ending at endindex
public char[] toCharArray()	Returns an array filled with this String's characters
public String toLowerCase()	Returns a copy of this String converted to lowercase
public String toString()	Returns this String

Continued

public String toUpperCase()	Returns a copy of this String converted to uppercase
public String trim()	Returns a copy of this String with white space removed from beginning and end
public String valueOf(Object O)	Returns a String that represents the String value of the object O (same as OtoString())
public static String valueOf (char[] chars)	Returns a String constructed from the array of characters
public static String valueOf(char[] chars, int startindex, int numchars)	Returns a String constructed from numchars characters starting with char[startindex]
public static String valueOf(boolean)	Returns either "true" or "false"
public static String valueOf(char ch)	Returns a string consisting of the single character ch
public static String valueOf(int num)	Returns num converted to a String
public static String valueOf(long num)	Returns num converted to a String
public static String valueOf(float num)	Returns num converted to a String
public static String valueOf(double num)	Returns num converted to a String

TABLE 4.9 java.lang.StringBuffer

public StringBuffer()	Constructs an empty StringBuffer
public StringBuffer(int length)	Constructs an empty StringBuffer of size length
public StringBuffer(String S)	Constructs a StringBuffer that is a copy of S
public synchronized StringBuffer append(Object O)	Appends O.toString() to the buffer
public synchronized StringBuffer append(String S)	Appends S to the buffer; returns a reference to this StringBuffer

Continued

TABLE 4.9 Continued

public synchronized StringBuffer append(char[] chars)	Appends a character array and returns a reference to this StringBuffer
public synchronized StringBuffer append(char[] chars, int start, int end)	Appends characters chars[start] through chars[end]; returns a reference to this StringBuffer
public synchronized StringBuffer append(boolean B)	Appends a Boolean value; returns a reference to this StringBuffer
public synchronized StringBuffer append(char ch)	Appends a character ch; returns a reference to this StringBuffer
public synchronized StringBuffer append(int num)	Appends string value of num; returns a reference to this StringBuffer
public synchronized StringBuffer append(long num)	Appends string value of num; returns a reference to this StringBuffer
public synchronized StringBuffer append(float num)	Appends string value of num; returns a reference to this StringBuffer
public synchronized StringBuffer append(double num)	Appends string value of num; returns a reference to this StringBuffer
public int capacity()	Returns the current capacity of the StringBuffer as an int
public synchronized char charAt(int index)	Returns the nth character
public synchronized void ensureCapacity(int capacity)	Ensures that the StringBuffer can hold at least capacity characters
public synchronized void getChars(int start, int end, char[] chars, int offset)	Copies the characters start through end into chars[] starting at chars[offset]
public synchronized StringBuffer insert(int index, Object O)	Inserts OtoString at index; returns a reference to this StringBuffer
public synchronized StringBuffer insert(int index, String S)	Inserts String S at index; returns a reference to this StringBuffer

Continued

public synchronized StringBuffer insert(int index, char[])	Inserts character array char[] at index; returns a reference to this StringBuffer
public synchronized StringBuffer insert(int index, boolean B)	Inserts string value of B at index; returns a reference to this StringBuffer
public synchronized StringBuffer insert(int index, char ch)	Inserts character ch at index; returns a reference to this StringBuffer
public synchronized StringBuffer insert(int index, int num)	Inserts string value of num at index; returns a reference to this StringBuffer
public synchronized StringBuffer insert(int index, long num)	Inserts string value of num at index; returns a reference to this StringBuffer
public synchronized StringBuffer insert(int index, float num)	Inserts string value of num at index; returns a reference to this StringBuffer
public synchronized StringBuffer insert(int index, double num)	Inserts string value of num at index; returns a reference to this StringBuffer
public int length()	Returns number of characters in the StringBuffer
public synchronized void setCharAt(int index, char ch)	Changes the character at index to ch
public synchronized void setLength(int len)	Sets this StringBuffer's length to len
public String toString()	Returns a String made from the characters in this StringBuffer

Math Class 101

The java.lang.Math (Table 4.10) class defines the constants e and pi as well as all the standard trigonometric functions for both float and double data types. All trig results and arguments are in radians. The Math class also defines several functions to round numbers to the nearest integer: floor(num) rounds down, ceil(num) rounds up, and round(num) rounds numbers to the nearest integer.

TABLE 4.10 java.lang.Math

public static final double E	2.7182818284590452354
public static final double PI	3.14159265358979323846
public static double abs (double X)	Returns the absolute value of double X
public static float abs (float X)	Returns the absolute value of float X
public static long abs (long X)	Returns the absolute value of long X
public static int abs (int X)	Returns the absolute value of int X
public static native double acos (double X)	Returns the arc cosine of double X
public static native double asin (double X)	Returns the arc sine of double X
public static native double atan (double X)	Returns the arctangent of double X
public static native double atan2 (double X, double Y)	Returns the arctangent(X/Y)
public static native double ceil (double D)	Returns smallest integer larger than double D
public static native double cos (double D)	Returns the cosine of double D
public static native double exp (double Y)	Returns e (base of natural logarithms) to the power Y
public static native double IEEEremainder (double X, double Y)	Returns the remainder of (X/Y) as defined by IEE 754
public static native double floor (double X)	Returns largest integer smaller than double X
public static native double log (double X) throws ArithmeticException	Returns the logarithm of X base e
public static double max (double X, double Y)	Returns the larger of the two doubles
public static float max (float X, float Y)	Returns the larger of the two floats
public static long max (long X, long Y)	Returns the larger of the two longs
public static int max (int X, int Y)	Returns the larger of the two ints
public static double min (double X, double Y)	Returns the smaller of the two doubles
public static float min (float X, float Y)	Returns the smaller of the two floats

Continued

public static long min (long X,long Y)	Returns the smaller of the two longs
public static int min (int X, int Y)	Returns the smaller of the two ints
public static native double pow (double X, double Y)throws ArithmeticException	Returns X to the power of Y
public static synchronized doubleRandom ()	Uses javautilRandom() to get a Random number between 00 and 10
public static native doubleRint (double X)	Returns XRounded to the nearest integer
public static longRound (double X)	Returns XRounded to the nearest integer as a long
public static intRound (float X)	Returns XRounded to the nearest integer as a float
public static native double sin (double X)	Returns the sine of X
public static native double sqrt (double X) throws ArithmeticException	Returns the square root of X
public static native double tan (double X)	Returns tangent of x

Putting It All Together: Shemp for Victory!

Thus ends our whirlwind tour of the java.lang package. You can do quite a bit using only this most basic section of the class library. Take Listing 4.5 (Shempnum.java), for example. This package implements a class to encapsulate extremely large numbers of 200 digits (or larger if you change the SIZE constant). This may not seem that large, and it isn't when you are dealing with normal decimal numbers with digits ranging from 0 to 9. Shempnum digits range from 0 to 268435455, so a 200-digit Shempnum is quite large.

LISTING 4.5

```
package java.shemp;// should reside in /java/shemp/
import java.lang.*;


public class Shempnum{
    /* class to encapsulate largish numbers */
```

Continued

```java
private final static long BASE=0x10000000;
private static int numd=7; //number of bits per digit.
private final static int MASK=0xfffffff;    // annoying sign begone!
private final static int SIZE=200;// maximum size=200 digits base BASE
public final static boolean POSITIVE=false;
public final static boolean NEGATIVE=true;
private boolean sign;
private int numdigits;// Number of significant digits (always >=1)
/* Array a[] to hold values. a[1]==lowest word place */
/* Default access means this is visible to other classes in this package. */
int a[];


/** Construct a Shempnum with value=0 and numdigits=1 */
public Shempnum(){
    numdigits=1;
    a=new int[SIZE+1];// Note:we don't use a[0] to store data.
    a[numdigits]=0;
}


/** Create a Shempnum with value=v (v<BASE) and numdigits=1
 * @param v value
 */
public Shempnum(int v){
    numdigits=1;
    a=new int[SIZE+1];// Note:we don't use a[0] to store data.
    a[numdigits]=v;
}


/** Copy constructor creates a copy of Shempnum s
 *@param s the Shempnum
 */
public Shempnum(Shempnum s){
    a=new int[SIZE+1];
    System.arraycopy(s.a,1,a,1,s.numdigits);
    sign=s.sign;
```

```
            numdigits=s.numdigits;
        }


        /** Create a Shempnum from the given hex String
         * @param s a string of hex digits
         */
        public Shempnum (String string){
            a=new int[SIZE];
            String ts;
            int temp=0;
            int l=string.length();
            int count=0;
            while (l>numd){
                ts=string.substring(l-numd,l);
                a[count+1]=Integer.parseInt(ts,16);
                l=l-numd;
                count++;
            }
            String t=string.substring(0,l);
            temp=Integer.parseInt(t,16);
              a[count+1]=temp;
            numdigits=count+1;
        }


        /** Returns a string representing this Shempnum in hex.
         *
         */
        public String toString(){
            StringBuffer sb=new StringBuffer(SIZE);
            String temp=new String();
            if (sign==NEGATIVE){sb.append("-");}else sb.append("+");
            for (int i=numdigits;i>=1;i--){
                temp=Integer.toString(a[i],16);
                if ((temp.length()<numd) &
i<numdigits){temp=("0000000000".substring(0,numd-(temp.length()))+temp);}//??????
```

Continued

```java
            sb.append(temp);//base 16!
        }
        return sb.toString();
}


/** Set nth digit to x.
 *@param n digit number
 *@param value
*/
private void setDigit(int n,int x){
    if (n>=numdigits){for (int i=numdigits+1;i<n;i++)a[i]=0;numdigits=n;}
    a[n]=x;
}
/** return the nth digit.
 */
public int getDigit(int n){
    return a[n];
}
/** return the number of digits in this shempnum
 */
public int getNumDigits(){
    return numdigits;
}
/** Return this Shempnum shifted num digits (base BASE, of course) to the right.
 *@param num the number of digits to shift right.
*/
public Shempnum rshift(int num){
  if (num>numdigits) return this;
    Shempnum result=new Shempnum();
    System.arraycopy(a,1+num,result.a,1,(numdigits+num));
    result.numdigits=numdigits-num;
    return result;
}
```

```java
/** Return this Shempnum shifted num digits (base BASE, of course) to the left.
  *@param num number of digits to shift
 */
public Shempnum lshift(int num){
    Shempnum result=new Shempnum();
    for (int i=1;i<=num;i++) result.a[i]=0;
    System.arraycopy(a,numdigits,result.a,num+numdigits,(numdigits));
    result.numdigits=numdigits+num;
    return result;
}


/** Return true if this Shempnum=Shempnum b.
  * @param b the Shempnumber to compare to
**/
public boolean eq(Shempnum b){
    if (b.numdigits!=numdigits) return false;
        for (int i=0;i<=(numdigits);i++){
        if (a[i]==b.a[i]);
        else return false;
        }
        return true;
}


/** Return true if this Shempnum==int b. b<BASE
  * @param the integer to compare to
  */
public boolean eq(int b){
    if ((numdigits==1) & (a[1]==b))return true;
    else return false;
}


/** Return true if this Shempnum >=Shempnum b.
  *@param b the Shempnum to compare to
  */
public boolean geq(Shempnum b){
```

Continued

```
        if (numdigits>b.numdigits) return true;
        if (numdigits<b.numdigits) return false;
        int i=numdigits;
        while(i>=1){
            if (a[i]!=b.a[i]) break;
            i--;
        }
        if (a[i]>=b.a[i]) return true;
        else return false;
    }


    /** Return true if this Shempnum is even. **/
    public boolean even(){
        if ((a[1]&1)==0) return true;
        else return false;
    }



    /** Add a Shempnum to the  current Shempnum and return result
     * @param b Shempnum to add
     */
    public Shempnum addAbs(Shempnum b){
        int i; //loop counter
        int na=numdigits;
        int nb=b.numdigits;
        int nd=(na<nb) ? nb : na;
        int carry=0;
        int temp=0;
        long r=0;
        Shempnum result=new Shempnum();
        for(i=1;i<=nd;i++){
            if (i<=na){
                r=(long)(a[i]+carry);
            }else {
                r=carry;
```

```
        }
        if (i<=nb){r=r+b.a[i];}
        if (r>=BASE){
                carry=1;
                r=(long)(r-BASE);
        }
        else carry=0;
    result.numdigits=i;
    result.a[i]=(int)(r);


    }
if (carry>0){
    result.a[i]=carry;
    result.numdigits=i;
}
result.sign=sign|b.sign;


return result;
}


public void zero(){
    a[1]=0;numdigits=1;
}


/** Subtract a Shempnum from this Shempnum and return result.
  * @param b the Shempnum to subtract
 **/
public Shempnum sub(Shempnum b){
    Shempnum result=new Shempnum();
    Shempnum tem;
    Shempnum a=new Shempnum(this);
    if (sign!=b.sign){
        result=addAbs(b);
    }else{
    if (b.geq(a)){
```

Continued

```
            tem=b;
            b=a;
            a=tem;
            result.sign=!sign;
            }else result.sign=sign;
            long borrow=0;
            int na=a.numdigits;
            int nb=b.numdigits;
            long temp=0;
            for(int i=1;i<=na;i++){
                temp=a.a[i]-borrow;
                if (i<=nb)
                    temp-=(long)b.a[i];
                if (temp<0) {
                    borrow=1;
                    temp+=BASE;
                }
                else borrow=0;
            result.a[i]=(int)temp;
            if ((int)temp>0){result.numdigits=i;}
            }
        }
    return result;
}


/** Divide by two and return the result **/
public void div2(){
    int carry=0;
    int temp=0;
    for (int i=numdigits;i>=1;i--){
        temp=a[i];
        temp=((temp|carry)>>>1);
        if ((a[i]&1)==1){
            carry=(int)BASE;
        }else{
```

```
                carry=0;
            }
            a[i]=(int)temp;
        }
    if ((a[numdigits]==0)&(numdigits>1))
    numdigits--;
}


/** Decrement and return true if zero. **/
public boolean dec(){

        Shempnum result=new Shempnum();
        long borrow=0;
        int na=numdigits;
        int nb=1;
        long temp=0;
        for(int i=1;i<=na;i++){
            temp=a[i]-borrow;
            if (i==1) temp-=1;
            if (temp<0) {
                borrow=1;
                temp+=BASE;
            }else borrow=0;
        a[i]=(int)temp;
        if ((int)temp>0){result.numdigits=i;}
    }
    if (numdigits>1)
    return false;
    else{if (a[1]==0) return true;
    else return false;
    }
}


/** Multiply this Shempnum by another and return result.
```

Continued

```
    * @param b the shempnum to multiply by
**/
public Shempnum mult(Shempnum b){
    Shempnum result=new Shempnum();
    long carry=0;
    int nb=b.numdigits;// find number of digits in b
    int na=numdigits;// find number of digits in this
    long temp=0;
    int i;
    for (int j=0;j<nb;j++){
        carry=0l;
        for (i=0;i<na;i++){
            temp=(long)a[i+1]*(long)b.a[j+1]+(long)result.a[i+j+1]+carry;
            carry=((long)temp/BASE);
            result.a[i+j+1]=(int)(((long)temp%BASE)&(BASE-1));
        }

        if (carry>0){
            result.a[i+j+1]=(int)carry;
            result.numdigits=(i+j+1);
        }else result.numdigits=(i+j);
    }
    result.sign=(sign^b.sign);
    return result;
}
/** Return this Shempnum mod another shempnum.
  * @param b the shempnum modulus
 **/
public Shempnum mod(Shempnum b){
    if (b.geq(this))return new Shempnum(this);
    int j;
    long guess,n,d,f,s,th,ff,a1,a2,b1,b2;
    Shempnum a=new Shempnum(this);
    Shempnum t=new Shempnum(a);
```

```
long base=(long)BASE;
int nb=0;
int na= numdigits;
Shempnum mp=new Shempnum();
nb=b.numdigits;
    na=a.numdigits;
boolean hh=true;
a=t;
int y=a.numdigits;
while (!b.geq(a)){
    nb=b.numdigits;
    na=a.numdigits;
    j=na-nb+2;
    a1=(a.a[na]);//MSD of a
    a2=(a.a[na-1]);//SMSD of a
    b1=(b.a[nb]);//MSD of b
    b2=(b.a[nb-1]);//SMSD of b
    guess=(long)(((a1*BASE)+a2)/((b1*BASE)+b2));
    if ( (guess==0)){
        j--;
        guess=((a1*BASE)/(b1));
    }
    mp.setDigit(j-1,(int)guess);
    mp=mp.mult(b);
    mp.sign=a.sign;
    a=a.sub(mp);
    mp.zero();
    if(b.geq(a) |(j==0)) {
        if (a.sign==POSITIVE) {
            return a;
        }
        else {
            a.sign=POSITIVE;
            return b.sub(a);
        }
```

Continued

```
            }
        }
        if (a.sign=POSITIVE) return a;
    else {
        a.sign=POSITIVE;
        return b.sub(a);
    }
    }


    /** Return this shempnum to the power of e mod m
     * @param e the exponent
     * @param m the modulus
     **/
    public Shempnum modexp(Shempnum e,Shempnum m){
        Shempnum k=new Shempnum(e);
        Shempnum t=new Shempnum();
        if (k.eq(0)) return new Shempnum(1);// return one
        if (k.even()){
            k.div2();
            t= modexp(k,m);
            t=t.mult(t).mod(m);
            return t;
        }else{
            k.dec();
            t=mult(modexp(k,m)).mod(m);
            return t;
        }
    }

}
```

The first thing you'll notice about Shempnum.java is that we declare it to be part of the java.shemp package. This means it must reside in a directory called shemp directly under the java directory (which should already be in your CLASSPATH environment variable). If you're just playing around with Shempnums, you can remove this statement and put the class just about anywhere.

Basic Data Structures

Since Java ints are signed, the decision was made to simply ignore the sign bit and not use it for storage. We use an array of integers to store the digits of our number base 0x10000000 and a mask of 0xFFFFFFF to strip off the sign bit when necessary. The program logic is somewhat cleaner when you don't have to constantly keep testing and changing the sign just to squeeze another bit out of each int. We also throw away a couple more bits on each digit to facilitate conversion to and from hexadecimal. Because this decision adds only a few bytes of storage to even the largest Shempnums, it seemed a logical choice. In addition to an array of digits, each Shempnum has Boolean sign value for the number as a whole and a numdigits variable to keep track of the number of digits in the Shempnum.

The Algorithms

Addition, subtraction, and multiplication are all accomplished basically the way you would do them using a pencil and paper, the only difference being that the calculations are all done base 0x10000000 instead of base 10. The mod function uses a "guess and test" algorithm that guesses an answer based on the most significant digits and corrects it if it is too large or too small. Division can be accomplished with basically the same algorithm and is left as an exercise for the reader.

Things get more interesting when we get to exponentiation. The most obvious, and least efficient, algorithm to calculate A to the power of X would require X multiplications. Instead, our modExp(Shempnum A, Shempnum X) modular exponentiation function uses a clever trick to really speed things up. It's a basic fact that

```
 x    y    x+y
A *  A  = A
```

From this, it follows that

```
 X     X/2  X/2
A  = A    * A
```

and

```
 X     X-1  1
A  = A    * A
```

We can use these properties to construct a helpful recursive algorithm to calculate A to the power of X. We define the Modexp(A,X) function as follows:

```
if X is 0, return 1 else
if X is odd, return Modexp(A,X-1) times A else
If X is even, return Modexp(A,X/2) times Modexp(A,X/2)
```

Shemp will need to perform the modulus and exponentiation only approximately log X times and will finish fairly quickly compared with the straightforward algorithm, which returns an answer in geologic time.

Using Shempnums

The most important Shempnum constructor takes a string of hex digits and turns it into a Shempnum. This is implemented quite efficiently using the java.lang.Integer.parseInt(String S, int radix) function to process each seven-digit chunk of the hex string and place it in the appropriate place in our array of integers.

Notice how we override the toString() method. This allows us to print a hex representation of the Shempnum, by saying simply:

```
System.out.println(S);
```

Again, the Integer class came to the rescue, and we can easily use the static toString(int num, int base) with a base of 16 to turn our number to a string in seven-digit chunks.

The basic arithmetic functions are all implemented as methods that return a reference to a new Shempnum containing the result. In C++ we could overload the arithmetic operators and get away with the simple and familiar:

```
a=b*c+b/c;
```

Unfortunately, Java does not, and probably never will, support operator overloading. We must use the somewhat more confusing method call notation:

```
b.mult(c).add(b.div(c));
```

Uses for Large Numbers

Chances are you're not planning on calculating the orbit of Jupiter in millimeters, so you may not think such extremely large numbers are very useful. One application, which is the reason the Shempnum package was written, is cryptography. The security of an encryption key is proportional to its size. In fact, the United States of America has attempted to limit the key size used in cryptographic software exported outside the country. This decision has caused a lot of controversy, but it's essentially meaningless given the anarchic nature of the Internet. Later, we'll show how to use the Shempnum package to securely transfer data over the Internet using a public key system and possibly violate export regulations in the process. Just don't tell anyone you learned it here.

Chapter 5

Applets

Tag, You're It!

Applets are included on a page through the use of the <APPLET> HTML tag, which has three required parameters: the name of the applet class, the width of the applet, and the height of the applet (please note that the Macintosh JDK expects all lowercase, but uppercase is used here for clarity).

```
<APPLET CODE= "MyApplet.class" WIDTH=100 HEIGHT=100>
</APPLET>
```

As you can see, the mandatory CODE attribute specifies the name of the classfile to be loaded. Normally the class is loaded from the same directory as the HTML page on which it resides, but you can specify another location using the optional CODEBASE parameter. Several other optional parameters are listed below:

ALT	Description to be used by browsers that don't support java
NAME	This applet's name
ALIGN	Alignment (ABSBOTTOM, ABSMIDDLE, BASELINE, BOTTOM, LEFT, MIDDLE, RIGHT, TEXTTOP, TOP), which works as it does for images
VSPACE and HSPACE	The amount of space to place around the image (in pixels)

A slightly more complicated example of the APPLET tag would be as follows:

```
<APPLET CODE="myclass.class" WIDTH=20 HEIGHT=20 VSPACE=10 HSPACE=10 ALIGN=MIDDLE
NAME="App1" ALT="Sorry, no Java!"></APPLET>
```

Applet tags can also contain string parameters to be passed to the applet. The basic format for these is the following;

```
<PARAM NAME="param_name" VALUE="param_value">
```

The Life Cycle of an Applet

When the browser encounters an applet tag on an HTML page, it first loads the proper class (if it has not already been loaded). Next, the browser instantiates an object of that class and calls its init() method. The init() method is called only once, when the applet is first created. The init() method is typically used for things like setting the applet's foreground and background colors. After init(), start() is called. The start() method is called every time the user visits the page on which the applet resides, so it may be called more than once. The start() method is often used to launch a separate thread of execution. Finally, the stop() method is called by the browser whenever the user leaves a page, so it also may be called more than once.

A Simple Applet

The way these methods are used in practice is demonstrated by StatusMessage.java in Listing 5.1. This applet takes a series of strings separated by backslashes and displays them in the browser's status bar.

LISTING 5.1

```
import java.awt.*;
public class StatusMessage extends java.applet.Applet implements Runnable {

    String messageString;
    int length=0; // string length
    int pause;
    boolean isDead=false;

    /* called first. initialize here. */
    public void init(){
```

```
    }

    /* called after init() we call run() as a separate thread */
    public void start(){
        isDead=false;
        new Thread(this).start();
    }

    /* called when applet is stopped */
    public void stop(){


            isDead=true;


    }

    /* called after stop() */
    public void destroy(){
    }

public void run(){

    String subString;
    int end;
    int begin;
    retrieveParams();
    length=messageString.length();

    while (isDead==false){
        begin=0;
        end=messageString.indexOf(".",begin);
        do{
            end=messageString.indexOf("/",begin);
            subString=messageString.substring(begin,end);
            showStatus(subString);
            begin=end+1;
```

Continued

```
        try{
            Thread.sleep(pause);
        }catch (InterruptedException e){}


    }while(begin<length && isDead==false);
    }
}


public String getAppletInfo() {
    return "Status Bar Message Applet";
}


public void retrieveParams(){
    messageString=getParameter("message");
    if (messageString==null){
        messageString="Default message:/ LEMON CURRY!/";
    }
    try{
        pause=Integer.parseInt(getParameter("pause"));
    }catch (Exception e){pause=2000;}
}


}
```

You can include this applet in a Web page using the following tag:

```
<APPLET CODE="StatusMessage.class" WIDTH=0 HEIGHT=0 ALT="Sorry, no Java!">
<PARAM name="name" value="Andrew Carver">
<PARAM name="address" value="Stardust Hotel"
</applet>
```

Note that we set the size of the applet to be zero; this ensures it will not appear on screen. The init() method in this case is quite small. We simply set the applet's color to green (enabling us to make unforgivable puns about little green applets). Since this particular applet is designed to be invisibly small, this doesn't matter in this case, but it would if the size were set to be anything other than zero. After init() exits (which it should do rather quickly), the start method is called. Our start() method is also quite tiny:

```
public void start(){
    isDead=false;
    new Thread(this).start();
}
```

In this case, we use the start() method to launch a thread to display our message. A thread is simply an independent path of execution, and the Thread class is covered in detail in Chapter 7. For now suffice it to say that the following magical incantation causes our applet's run() method to be called and execute in its own thread automatically:

```
new Thread(this).start();
```

Just before we launch the thread, we set our Boolean state variable, isDead, to false. Later, when the stop method is called (when the browser leaves the page), we set this variable to true, telling our run() method to exit.

The first thing we do in the run() method, is call our retrieveParams() helper function to get our message string and pause values that are embedded in our applet tag using <PARAM>. To do this, we use the getParameter(String) method which gets a parameter by name and returns it as a string. If you have a parameter named message, for example, you can retrieve it with the following:

```
String message=getParameter("message"); // get parameter named 'message'
```

So to retrieve our message (a String object) and our pause value (an int), we can use the following:

```
public void retrieveParams(){
    messageString=getParameter("message");
    if (messageString==null){
        messageString="Default message:/ LEMON CURRY!/";
    }
    try{
        pause=Integer.parseInt(getParameter("pause"));
    }catch (Exception e){pause=3000;}
}
```

The getParameter(String) method returns null if the parameter cannot be found, so we take advantage of this fact to provide a default message. Next, we use the Integer.parseInt(String) method to get the pause value for our applet. The parseInt(String) will throw an exception if the String we pass it is null or does not contain a valid number, so we catch this exception and provide a default pause of three seconds. After calling retrieveParams(), the run method uses the standard string functions to break our string into substrings and display them in the browser's status bar using the showStatus(String) method. This is all enclosed in a while loop, which checks our isDead variable and exits if it is true:

```
while (isDead==false){
    begin=0;
    end=messageString.indexOf(".",begin);
    do{
        end=messageString.indexOf("/",begin);
        subString=messageString.substring(begin,end);
        showStatus(subString);
        begin=end+1;
        try{
            Thread.sleep(pause);
        }catch(InterruptedException e){}

    }while(begin<length && isDead==false);
}
}
```

The stop() method is called when the user leaves the page, and we take this opportunity to set our state variable to true, causing our thread to exit and die:

```
/* called when applet is stopped */
public void stop(){

 isDead=true;
 }
```

One interesting point to note is that our thread will keep running unless killed explicitly (see Figure 5.1).

FIGURE 5.1 Status Message Applet.

Simple Graphics

Chances are you won't be satisfied with the status bar as the display area. To display any graphics in the applet's main display area, you need to get a reference to a Graphics object. A Graphics object is basically a graphics context for a GUI component (the applet itself, in this case). Graphics is an abstract class, so you can't instantiate a graphics context. The getGraphics() method (actually defined in Applet's distant superclass, Component) will return a reference to the graphics context for your applet. The Graphics class is shown in Table 5.1. One important thing to note is that getGraphics will return null if the component in question has not yet been shown on the screen, but this is not an issue in this case. (This all has to do with late peer creation, which is covered in Chapter 6 "Inside AWT.")

TABLE 5.1 java.awt.Graphics

public abstract void clearRect (int x, int y, int width, int height)	Fills a rectangle with the current background color.
public abstract void clipRect (int x, int y, int width, int height)	Narrows the clipping rectangle.
public abstract void copyArea (int x, int y, int width, int height, int dx, int dy)	Copy a rectangular section of the screen from one location to another.
public Graphics create (int x, int y, int width, int height)	Returns a new graphics context that is a copy of this, with the specified clipping rectangle.
public abstract Graphics create ()	Returns a new Graphics Object that is a copy of this graphics context.
public abstract void dispose ()	Frees any resources this context may be using.
public void draw3DRect (int x, int y, int width, int height, Boolean raised)	Draws a raised or lowered 3D rectangle.

Continued

TABLE 5.1 Continued

public abstract void drawArc (int x, int y, int width, int height, int startAngle, int arcAngle)	Draws an arc of a circle centered on (x,y) (all angles in radians, 3 o'clock is zero).
public void drawBytes (byte data [], int offset, int length, int x, int y)	Draws an array of bytes to the screen using the current font and color (y coordinate specifies baseline).
public void drawChars (char data [], int offset, int length, int x, int y)	Draws an array of characters to the screen using the current font and color (y coordinate specifies baseline).
public abstract Boolean drawImage (Image img, int x, int y, int width, int height, Color bgcolor, ImageObserver observer)	Draws an image at (x,y) with specified background color. Scales image if necessary.
public abstract Boolean drawImage (Image img, int x, int y, Color bgcolor, ImageObserver observer)	Draws an image at (x,y) with specified background color. Scales image if necessary.
public abstract Boolean drawImage (Image img, int x, int y, int width, int height, ImageObserver observer)	Draws an image at (x,y). Scales image if necessary.
public abstract Boolean drawImage (Image img, int x, int y, ImageObserver observer)	Draws an image at (x,y) (actual size).
public abstract void drawLine (int x1, int y1, int x2, int y2)	Draw a line from (x1,y1) to (x2,y2).
public abstract void drawOval (int x, int y, int width, int height)	Draws an oval of the specified width and height centered at (x,y).
public void drawPolygon (Polygon p)	Draws a given polygon object using the current color.
public abstract void drawPolygon (int xPoints [],int yPoints [],int numPoints)	Draws a polygon whose coordinates are contained in two arrays of type int.
public void drawRect (int x, int y, int width, int height)	Draws an unfilled rectangle with its upper left-hand corner at (x,y).

Continued

public abstract void drawRoundRect (int x, int y, int width, int height, int arcWidth, int arcHeight)	Draws a rounded rectangle whose corners have the specified arc width and height.
public abstract void drawString (String str, int x, int y)	Draws a string at x,y using the current font (y coordinate specifies baseline).
public void fill3DRect (int x, int y, int width, int height, Boolean raised)	Draws a raised or lowered filled 3D rectangle.
public abstract void fillArc (int x, int y, int width, int height, int startAngle, int arcAngle)	Draws a filled arc of a circle centered on (x,y) (all angles in radians, 3 o'clock is zero).
public abstract void fillOval (int x, int y, int width, int height)	Draws an oval of the specified size at (x,y).
public void fillPolygon (Polygon p)	Draws a filled polygon object using the current color.
public abstract void fillPolygon (int xPoints [],int yPoints [],int nPoints)	Draws a filled polygon whose coordinates are contained in two arrays of type int.
public abstract void fillRect (int x, int y, int width, int height)	Draws a filled rectangle at (x,y).
public abstract void fillRoundRect (int x, int y, int width, int height, int arcWidth, int arcHeight)	Draws a filled rounded rectangle whose corners have the specified arc width and height.
public void finalize ()	Disposes of a graphics context (calls dispose())
public abstract Rectangle getClipRect()	Returns a Rectangle object that contains the current clipping region.
public abstract Color getColor()	Returns the current foreground color.
public abstract Font getFont()	Returns the current font.
public abstract FontMetrics getFontMetrics (Font f)	Gets a FontMetrics object describing the given font's appearance as drawn in this graphics context.

Continued

TABLE 5.1 Continued

public FontMetrics getFontMetrics()	Gets a FontMetrics object describing the current font's appearance as drawn in this graphics context.
public abstract void setColor (Color c)	Sets the foreground color.
public abstract void setFont (Font font)	Sets the current font.
public abstract void setPaintMode()	Returns drawing to normal after a call to setXORMode(Color).
public abstract void setXORMode (Color c1)	Sets drawing to exclusive OR mode.
public String toString()	Returns a string representation of this Graphics object.
public abstract void translate(int x, int y)	Causes future operations to be relative to (x,y) instead of (0,0).

When you have a reference to the current graphics context, drawing circles, ellipses, rectangles, polygons, and lines is straightforward. As far as color goes, the setColor(Color) method will set the current drawing color and, the getColor(Color) method will return it to you. The Color class (Table 5.2) has several static colors defined for you, so you can either use one of them or construct a new color object using the red, blue, and green color values or an integer with the RGB values packed together.

```
Graphics g=getGraphics();
g.setColor(Color.black);    // these three lines
g.setColor(new Color(0,0,0));    // all have the same
g.setColor(0x000000);        // effect.
```

You may have noticed that there is no setpixel(x,y) method in the Graphics class to draw a single point. The easiest way to work around this is to draw a filled rectangle one pixel on a side using fillRect(x,y,1,1).

TABLE 5.2 java.awt.Color

public Color (float r, float g, float b)	Creates a new color with the specified red, green, and blue values in the range 0.0–1.0.

Continued

public Color (int r, int g, int b)	Creates a new color with the specified red, green, and blue values in the range 0-255.
public Color (int rgb)	Creates a new color with the specified red, green, and blue values (in the range 0-255) packed into an int.
public final static Color white	Color constant (255, 255, 255).
public final static Color lightGray	Color constant (192, 192, 192).
public final static Color gray	Color constant (128, 128, 128).
public final static Color darkGray	Color constant (64, 64, 64).
public final static Color black	Color constant (0, 0, 0).
public final static Color red	Color constant (255, 0, 0).
public final static Color pink	Color (255, 175, 175).
public final static Color orange	Color constant (255, 200, 0).
public final static Color yellow	Color constant (255, 255, 0).
public final static Color green	Color constant (0, 255, 0).
public final static Color magenta	Color constant (255, 0, 255).
public final static Color cyan	Color constant (0, 255, 255).
public final static Color blue	Color constant (0, 0, 255).
public static int HSBtoRGB (float hue, float saturation, float brightness)	Returns the packed RGB values for the given HSB color.
public static float[] RGBtoHSB (int r, int g, int b, float []hsbvals)	Returns the HSV values for the given RGB values in the given array of floats.
public Color brighter()	Returns a color brighter than this color.
public Color darker()	Returns a color darker than this color.
public Boolean equals (Object obj)	Compares this with another color (value comparison). Returns false if the object is not a Color.
public int getBlue()	Gets the blue component (0–255).

Continued

TABLE 5.2 Continued

public static Color getColor (String nm, int default)	Returns a color constructed from the packed RGB values in default if that property can't be found.
public static Color getColor (String nm, Color default)	Gets a color property by name using System.getProperty(String). Returns default if that property can't be found.
public static Color getColor (String nm)	Gets a color property by name using System.getPropery(String).
public int getGreen()	Gets the green component (0–255).
public static Color getHSBColor (float h, float s, float b)	Returns a Color with the given hue, saturation, and brightness.
public int getRGB()	Gets red, green, and blue values (0–255) packed into an int.
public int getRed()	Gets the red component (0–255).
public int hashCode()	Returns a hashcode for this Color.
public String toString()	Returns getClass().getName() + "[r=" + getRed() + ",g=" + getGreen() + ",b=" + getBlue() + "]".

Listing 5.2 (Cool.java) demonstrates using graphics in an applet. Both the Graphics and Color classes are contained in the java.awt package, so we explicitly import that package at the start of the file. Our start() method gets the graphics for the applet and hands it off to a separate thread that does the actual drawing. In the run() method of our thread, we draw random patterns using blocks of random colors. One may question the wisdom of using a statement like the following in a loop as this applet does:

```
g.setColor(new Color((int)(0xffffff*Math.random())));
```

After all, aren't all those new Color objects being thrown away? Yes, they are, but it's not as big a waste as you might think. Automatic garbage collection will delete these for us. It's like a license to litter! (See Figure 5.2.)

Applet started.

FIGURE 5.2 The Cool Applet.

LISTING 5.2

```java
import java.awt.*;

public class Cool extends java.applet.Applet{
    Thread T;
    Graphics G;

    /* called first. initialization here*/
    public void init(){
        setBackground(Color.black);
        show();
    }

    public void start(){
        G=this.getGraphics();
        T=new CoolThread(G,this.size());
        T.start();

    }

    /* called when applet is stopped */
```

Continued

```
    public void stop(){
        T.stop();
    }


}
class CoolThread extends Thread{
    Graphics G;
    int size;
    public CoolThread(Graphics g,Dimension D){
        G=g;
        this.size=D.width>=D.height?D.width:D.height;
    }

    public void run(){
        int x=0;
        int y=0;
        int r=5;
        int nx=0;
        int ny=0;
        r=2;
        G.setColor(Color.black);
        G.fillRect(0,0,size,size);
        while (true){

            x=(int)(Math.random()*size);
            y=(int)(Math.random()*size);
            nx=size-x;
            ny=size-y;

            G.setColor(new Color((int)(0xffffff*Math.random())));
            G.fillRect(x,y,r,r);
            G.fillRect(x,ny,r,r);
            G.fillRect(nx,y,r,r);
            G.fillRect(nx,ny,r,r);
            G.fillRect(y,x,r,r);
```

```
            G.fillRect(y,nx,r,r);
            G.fillRect(ny,x,r,r);
            G.fillRect(ny,nx,r,r);
        }


    }
}
```

Paint, Repaint, and Update

In many applets you will see various combinations of paint (Graphics), Update(Graphics) and repaint() used to refresh the screen. There is much confusion over what each of these does, and when they are called. The bottom line is as follows:

- repaint(): A request that update(Graphics) be called. If too many requests arrive in too short a time, they may be collapsed into a single call to update(Graphics).
- update(Graphics): Usually erases the screen, then calls paint(Graphics).
- paint(Graphics): Called by the system whenever the component needs painting.

Both paint(Graphics) and update(Graphics) may receive a graphics object that has had its clipping rectangle set to include only the part of the display that needs to be painted. This would occur when only part of a window was obscured and then displayed again. You can set a clipping rectangle yourself using the clipRect(int x, int y, int w, int h) method. Once you narrow the clipping region of a Graphics object, you can't make it larger again; you must call getGraphics() to get a fresh graphics context.

Java Animation

Java animation at its simplest consists of drawing a series of images to the screen at regular intervals to give the appearance of motion. Although this sounds simple in theory, it requires a few tricks to avoid flicker and achieve a constant frame rate. The first thing you will want to do is override the update(Graphics) method with a version that doesn't erase the background and simply calls paint(Graphics). This significantly reduces flicker. The second thing you should do is forget about repaint(), because its habit of quietly collapsing multiple requests into a single call to update (Graphics g) will wreak havoc with your frame rate.

If you want to eliminate flicker completely, you must resort to a technique known as *double buffering*. With double buffering, all drawing is done to an offscreen buffer image and then transferred (blitted) to the screen in one fell swoop. An applet showing how to do this is shown in Listing 5.3. This applet smoothly scrolls a message across the screen, as shown in Figure 5.3.

FIGURE 5.3 The Scroller Applet.

LISTING 5.3

```
/*
PARAMETERS:
"text"=text of scroller
"pause"=pause in millseconds
"foreground"=foreground color in hex (RRGGBB format)
"background"=background color in hex (RRGGBB format)
"fontname"=name of the font
"fontsize"=font size in points

*/

import java.awt.*;
public class scroller extends java.applet.Applet implements Runnable{
    Thread me=null;
    String text;
    Font font;
    int ypos=0; // where to draw
    Image offImage; // offscreen buffer image
    Graphics offGraphics,onGraphics;
    Color foreground,background;
    int width=0; // our applet's size
    int height=0;
    int pause=0; //sleep between frames , millis
    int textwidth=0; // width of text in pixels

    public void init(){
```

```
// get applet parameters
try{
    text=getParameter("text");
    pause=Integer.parseInt(getParameter("pause"));
    int temp=Integer.parseInt(getParameter("foreground"),16);
    foreground=new Color(temp);

    temp=Integer.parseInt(getParameter("background"),16);
    background=new Color(temp);

    String fontname=getParameter("fontname");
    int fontsize;fontsize=Integer.parseInt(getParameter("fontsize"));
    font=new Font(fontname,Font.BOLD,fontsize);// a new font

}catch (Exception e){
    throw new RuntimeException("Problem with applet parameters: "+e.toString());
}

show();        // necessary for getGraphics to return non-null
onGraphics=getGraphics(); // onscreen graphics
setBackground(background);
update(onGraphics);
// calculate font height and where to draw it
FontMetrics fm=onGraphics.getFontMetrics(font);// get the metrics
height=fm.getHeight()+2; // font height plus slop
ypos=(height)-(fm.getMaxDescent())-1; // our baseline

// find string width in pixels
textwidth=fm.stringWidth(text);

// resize ourselves to new height
Dimension d=this.size();// get our size
width=d.width;     // our old width
```

Continued

```
        resize(width,height);    // resize ourselves

        // make an offscreen image for buffering
        offImage=this.createImage(width,height);// offscreen image
        offGraphics=offImage.getGraphics();    // offscreen graphics
        offGraphics.setFont(font);//use our font offscreen



    }

    public void start()
    {
        if (me==null){
            me=new Thread(this);
            me.start();
        }


    }

    public void run(){
        Thread.currentThread().setPriority(10);

        while (true){
            for (int f=0;f>(-textwidth);f-=2){
                    offGraphics.setColor(background);
                    offGraphics.fillRect(0,0,width,height+2);
                    offGraphics.setColor(foreground);
                    offGraphics.drawString(text,f,ypos);
                    paint (onGraphics);
                    try{Thread.sleep(pause);} catch(Exception e){}


            }
        }
```

```
    }
    public void update(Graphics g){paint(g);}
    public void paint(Graphics g){
        if (offImage!=null){
            g.drawImage(offImage,0,0,width,height,null);
        }
    }
}
```

The first step in double buffering is to use the Component.createImage(int w, int h) to create an Image object (see Table 5.3) to act as an offscreen buffer:

```
Image offImage=this.createImage(width,height);// offscreen image
```

TABLE 5.3 java.awt.Image

public static final Object UndefinedProperty	Returns in response to queries for nonexistent property.
public abstract void flush()	Flushes any resources this image is using but does not destroy the image itself.
public abstract Graphics getGraphics()	Gets a graphics context to draw on this image.
public abstract int getHeight (ImageObserver observer)	Returns image height. If the height is unknown, -1 is returned and the ImageObserver is notified later.
public abstract Object getProperty (String name ,ImageObserver observer)	Gets a property by name. Returns UndefinedProperty if it can't be found.
public abstract ImageProducer getSource()	Returns the ImageProducer for this image.
public abstract int getWidth (ImageObserver observer)	Returns image width. If the width is unknown, -1 is returned and the ImageObserver is notified later.

Next get a graphics context for the offscreen image and one for the applet:

```
Graphics onGraphics=this.getGraphics();      // onscreen graphics
Graphics offGraphics=offImage.getGraphics();    // offscreen graphics
```

From then on, do all your drawing to offGraphics, and blit everything to the screen whenever a complete frame is ready for display:

```
onGraphics.drawImage(offImage,0,0,width,height,null);
```

The scroller applet also demonstrates how to work with the java.awt.Font class (Table 5.4) and the associated FontMetrics class (Table 5.5). You create a new Font object by supplying the font name, the style, and the point size.

TABLE 5.4 java.awt.Font

public static final int PLAIN	Constant for plain fonts (0).
public static final int BOLD	Constant for bold fonts (1).
public static final int ITALIC	Constant for italic fonts (1).
public Font (String name ,int style ,int size)	Returns a reference to the specified font.
public Boolean equals (Object obj)	Compares this font to another; returns false if they are not equal, or the second object is not a font.
public String getFamily()	Returns the platform-specific name for this font.
public static Font getFont (String nm , Font default_font)	Retrieves a font by name from the system properties list. Returns default_font if it can't be found.
public static Font getFont (String nm)	Retrieves a font by name from the system properties list. Returns null if it can't be found.
public String getName()	Returns the logical (platform-independent) name of the font.
public int getSize()	Returns the point size of this font.
public int getStyle()	Returns either PLAIN, BOLD, or ITALIC.

Continued

public int hashCode()	Returns a hashcode for this Font.
public Boolean isBold ()	Returns true if this font is bold.
public Boolean isItalic()	Returns true if this font is italic.
public Boolean isPlain()	Returns true if this font is plain.
public String toString()	Returns getClass().getName() + "[family=" + family + ",name=" + name + ",style=" + Style + ",size=" + size + "]".

TABLE 5.5 java.awt.FontMetrics

public int bytesWidth (byte data [], int off, int len)	Returns the width of the array of bytes (off through off+len) in this font.
public int charWidth (char ch)	Returns the width of character ch in pixels.
public int charWidth (int ch)	Returns the width of character ch (stored in an int) in pixels.
public int charsWidth (char data [], int off, int len)	Returns the width of the array of characters in pixels.
public int getAscent()	Returns the distance from the baseline to the top of the characters.
public int getDescent()	Returns the distance from the baseline to the bottom of the characters.
public Font getFont()	Returns a handle to the font itself.
public int getHeight()	Returns leading + ascent + descent in pixels.
public int getLeading()	Returns spacing between lines of text in pixels.
public int getMaxAdvance()	Returns the maximum advance width in pixels, or –1 if unknown.
public int getMaxAscent()	Returns the maximum ascent of this font in pixels.
public int getMaxDecent()	Returns the maximum descent of this font in pixels. (Misspelling carried over for compatibilty.)
public int getMaxDescent()	Returns the maximum descent of this font in pixels.

Continued

TABLE 5.5 Continued

public int[] getWidths()	Returns the width of the first 256 characters of this font in the int array.
public int stringWidth (String str)	Returns the width of the string in pixels.
public String toString()	Returns a string representation of this font metric.

```
Font font=Font("Courier", Font.BOLD ,12) ; // 12 point Courier Bold
```

We use the setFont(Font) method of a Graphics object to specify a font, and its getFont() method will tell us the current font. The FontMetrics class is used to get the specific metrics of a font as displayed on a given graphics (or other) context. We can use the Graphics object's getFontMetrics() method to get a FontMetrics object for the current font. Using the FontMetrics object, we can find all the gory details of a font's size and shape. We use this technique in the applet to adjust its size automatically to accommodate different fonts.

The rest of the applet's run method is straightforward. We draw a frame offscreen, call paint(onGraphics) to blit it onscreen. Note that the coordinates used in the drawString(String, int x, int y) don't specify the upper left corner or even the lower right corner. The x coordinate specifies the left-hand edge, and the y coordinate specifies the base line (below which the descenders of some characters may extend).

The getDocumentBase() method returns the base URL of the page on which the applet resides, and the GetCodeBase() method returns the URL of the applet itself. If the images are in the same directory as the HTML document, loading an image is as easy as the following:

```
Image i=getImage(getDocumentBase(),imageName);
```

One thing to keep in mind is that every image request is processed as a separate HTTP request, and each one of these takes time. Fifteen images would require 15 separate connections to the server. Another point to note is that the image loading is asynchronous. The getImage(URL) method will return immediately, and the image will actually be loaded in a separate thread. This means that any methods that inquire about the image's size will return a nonsense value (–1) until the entire image is loaded. You can force your program to wait until an image has been loaded using the MediaTracker class. You can use the add(Image I, int ID) to add an image and an arbitrary ID number to a list of images being tracked and the waitFor(int ID) to wait for that image to load:

```
Image image=getImage(getDocumentBase(),imageName);
// Use a MediaTracker object to force image load
MediaTracker mt=new MediaTracker(this);
mt.addImage(image,0);
  try {
    mt.waitForID(0);// wait for image #0
}catch (InterruptedException e);
```

If you want to wait for all images being tracked to load, use MediaTracker's waitForAll() method instead. If you want to do something constructive in the meantime, you can simply use the checkId(int ID) method to see if an individual image has loaded or checkAll() to see if all images are ready.

An Animator

One approach to maximizing the speed on image loading is to combine smaller images into one large image and then break them up again when you have received them off the net. This technique is used in Schwa.java (Listing 5.4).

LISTING 5.4

```
/*
PARAMETERS:
"imageName"=name of imagestrip (images.gif)
"numImages"=# of images in imagestrip (1)
"pause"=pause between frames in milliseconds
"xor"=use XORMode (false)
"random"=randomize frame order? (false)
*/

import java.awt.*;
public class schwa extends java.applet.Applet implements Runnable{
    boolean xor,random;
    Font font;
    String imageName;
    Image image;      // image to animate
    Image offImage; // offscreen buffer image
    Graphics offGraphics;
```

Continued

```java
Graphics onGraphics;
int xSize=0; // our crapplets size
int ySize=0;
int numImages=0;
int pause=100; //sleep between frames , millis
int frameWidth=0;

public void init()
{

    show();         // necessary for getgraphics to return non-null
    onGraphics=getGraphics();
    Dimension d=this.size();
    ySize=d.height;
    xSize=d.width;
    offImage=this.createImage(xSize,ySize);// offscreen image
    offGraphics=offImage.getGraphics();    // offscreen graphics
    retrieveParams();

}

public void start()
{

    new Thread(this).start();

}

public void run(){
    setLayout(new BorderLayout());
    show();


    Image image=getImage(getDocumentBase(),imageName);
    // Use a MediaTracker object to force image load
```

```
    MediaTracker mt=new MediaTracker(this);
    mt.addImage(image,0);
        try {mt.waitForID(0);}catch (InterruptedException e);

            frameWidth=image.getWidth(this)/numImages;
    int frameHeight=image.getHeight(this);

    //resize(xSize,ySize+scrollerHeight+30);
     System.out.println(xor);
     if (xor){
         onGraphics.setXORMode(Color.black);
     }
    int x=0;
        int f=0;
    while (true){
        f=(f++)%numImages;
        if (random){f=(int)(Math.random()*numImages);}
        x=(-1*f*xSize)
        offGraphics.setColor(new Color((int)(Math.random()*0xffffff)));
        offGraphics.fillRect(0,0,xSize,ySize);
        offGraphics.drawImage(image,x,0,xSize*numImages,ySize,this);
        paint (onGraphics);

        try{
            Thread.sleep(pause);
            }catch(InterruptedException e){}

    }

}
public void paint(Graphics g){

    if (offImage!=null){
        g.drawImage(offImage,0,0,xSize,ySize,this);
    }
```

Continued

```
    }

    public void stop()
    {
        super.stop();

    }
    public boolean handleEvent(Event evt)
    {
        switch(evt.id)
        {
            default:
            return false;
        }
    }
    public void retrieveParams(){
        // get applet parameters
        try{
            imageName=getParameter("imageName");
            if (imageName==null){imageName="images.gif";}
            numImages=Integer.parseInt(getParameter("numimages"));
        }catch (Exception e){numImages=1;}

        try{
            pause=Integer.parseInt(getParameter("pause"));

        }catch (Exception e){pause=2000;}

        try{
            if (getParameter("xor").equals("true")){xor=true;}

        }catch (Exception e){xor=false;}

        try{
            if (getParameter("random").equals("true")){random=true;}
```

```
        }catch (Exception e){random=false;}



    }
}
```

In this case, we assume that the images are all the same size and are laid out in a strip. We get the number of images in the file from the applet parameters. To do the animation, we simply draw the image using the appropriate (usually negative) x offset and allow the graphics context to clip it appropriately.

```
while (true){
        f=(f++)%numImages;
        if (random){f=(int)(Math.random()*numImages);}
        offGraphics.setColor(new Color((int)(Math.random()*0xffffff)));
        offGraphics.fillRect(0,0,xSize,ySize);
        x=(-1*f*xSize)
        offGraphics.drawImage(image,x,0,xSize*numImages,ySize,this);
        paint (onGraphics);

        try{
                Thread.sleep(pause);
        }catch(InterruptedException e){}


}
```

This applet also has two applet parameters to specify special effects. If the "xor" parameter is true, we use the setXORMode(Color c) method to "psychedelicize" things. If the "random" parameter is true, we override the normal frame order and shuffle the frames randomly. (See Figure 5.4.)

Applet Audio

Silent animation isn't much fun. Fortunately, it's easy to add sound to your animation. To retrieve an AudioClip object, simply use the following:

```
AudioClip clip;
clip=getAudioClip(getDocumentBase(), "sound.au")
```

FIGURE 5.4 The Animator Applet.

Then use one of the following three methods to play or stop the clip:

```
clip.loop(); // Starts playing the clip in a loop.
clip.play(); // Starts playing the clip.
clip.stop(); // Stops playing the clip.
```

Stupid Applet Tricks: Communication and Navigation

Often you will want to be able to have applets on the same page communicate with each other. One simple way to do this, if the applets are all of the same type, is to use a static variable to act as a "mailbox" to hold your data. Another way to have applets (no matter what their type) communicate is to use the applet's AppletContext object. An AppletContext is basically a wrapper around the browser itself. You can use the applet's getAppletContext() to get a handle to the applet's AppletContext. Once you have that, you can use its methods to get a list of the other applets on the page and even take limited control of the browser itself. If you know the name of the applet in question (the name specified by NAME in the APPLET tag, not the class name), you can get a reference to it using AppletContext's getApplet(String) method. This technique is demonstrated by the applets in Listing 5.5 In this case, we use the second applet to change the color of the first applet. The method is simple, but it proves the concept is feasible.

If you want to know all the names of the other applets, you can use the getApplets() method. This method returns an object that implements the java.util.enumeration interface that contains all the applets on the page. The enumeration interface has two methods — hasMoreElements() and nextElement() — so to loop through the enumeration and print the elements (which include the applet itself), use something akin to the following:

```
AppletContext AC=getAppletContext();
Enumeration E=AC.getApplets();
 while(E.hasMoreElements()) {
        System.out.println(E.nextElement());
    }
```

There are occasions, with applet image maps, for example, when you may want to send the browser to another page, as if the user had clicked on a hyperlink. To do this, simply use the AppletContext's showDocument(URL) method:

```
try{
URL link=new URL("http::/www.shemp.com/doc.html");
AppletContext AC=getAppletContext();
AC.showDocument(link);
}catch (MalformedURLException e){
System.err.println("D'ohh");
}
```

See the chapter on networking to find other ways to construct a java.net.URL object. Note that showDocument(URL) may be ignored by some AppletContexts (as it is by the AppletViewer's AppletContext).

A Generic Applet Template

Listing 5.6 shows a generic applet template. All the methods you might wish to override are included, and the start() method is already set to run the run method in a single thread. You can use this in any editor that supports code skeletons or simply use cut and paste. One other resource you might consider looking up is Nelson Yu's AppletGen utility, which can automatically generate a skeleton applet and its associated HTML page.

LISTING 5.5

```
import java.applet.*;
import java.awt.*;
```

Continued

```java
public class App1 extends java.applet.Applet{


  /* called after init() we call run() as a separate thread */
    public void start(){


    }


}
class App2 extends java.applet.Applet{


  /* called after init() we call run() as a separate thread */
    public void start(){
        AppletContext AC=getAppletContext();
        Applet otherApplet=AC.getApplet("App1");

        for (int f=0 ;f<0xFFFFFF;f++){
                otherApplet.setBackground(new Color(f));
                otherApplet.repaint();
        }


    }


}


public class App2 extends java.applet.Applet{


  /* called after init() we call run() as a separate thread */
```

```
public void start(){
  AppletContext AC=getAppletContext();
  Applet otherApplet=AC.getApplet("App1");



  for (int f=0 ;f<0xFFFFFF;f++){
        otherApplet.setBackground(new Color(f));
        otherApplet.repaint();
  }


}
```

}

LISTING 5.6

```
public class AppletShell extends java.applet.Applet implements Runnable{

Thread T;// this applet's single thread

  /* do any initialization here*/
  public void init(){


  }

  /* called after init() we call run() as a separate thread */
  public void start(){

      // next lines call run() method as a separate thread
      T=new Thread(this);
      T.start();


  }

  /* main run method, launched as a thread by start() */
```

Continued

```java
public void run(){

}

 /* called when applet is stopped */
public void stop(){

 }

 /* called after stop() */
public void destroy(){

 }

 /* called when applet needs painting */
    public void paint(Graphics g){

}

    /* normally erases background before    */
    /* call paint(g) to avoid this behavior, */
    /* or super.update(g) to retain it.      */
  public void update(Graphics g){

 }

}
```

Chapter 6

Inside AWT

In Through the AWT Door

Contrary to popular belief, the AWT is not a mythical beast with the head of a Motif widget, the body of a Macintosh dialog, and the tail of a Windows menu. AWT stands for Abstract Window Toolkit and is, in fact, a generic windowing system that sits on top of native graphical user interfaces (GUIs) to provide a cross-platform GUI capability. For each component in a Java GUI, there are actually three different entities involved. First there is the native component, let's say a button. Next there is a so-called *peer* object (java.awt.ButtonPeer in this case), which acts as a sort of wrapper around the native button. Finally there is the java.awt.Button object, with which programmers actually deal. In general, it is safe to ignore peer objects entirely because their operations all take place behind the scenes. There are some cases in which this three-tier structure has some side effects, but we'll discuss that later.

Components

At the top of the AWT component hierarchy is the generic Component class (all the AWT components are shown in alphabetical order at the end of this chapter). As you can see, this is a fairly complicated class. The Button, Canvas, Choice, Container, Label, List, Scrollbar, and TextComponent classes all inherit Component's basic functionality. Note that Container is a special case, as it is a component that may contain other components. The Window, Panel, Applet, Frame, and Dialog classes are all descended from Container. Since we usually need a place to put our components in order to make use of them, let's start our investigation of the AWT with the Container class.

Container

The Container class serves as the abstract parent of all components that are capable of holding other components. Since Container is itself a component, it may hold other containers as well. For an example, let's look at a Frame. Frame is a simple window with an optional title and menu bar. A simple program that pops up an empty frame on the screen should look something like this:

```java
import java.awt.*;


public class MyFrame {

    static final int XSIZE = 400;
    static final int YSIZE = 400;

    public static void main(String args[]){

        Frame frame=new Frame("Howdy!");

        frame.resize(XSIZE,YSIZE);
        frame.show();


    }


}
```

One thing to note is that we must explicitly call the frame's show( ) method, because Frames are initially invisible. It is also necessary to use the resize( ) method; otherwise, all we would see is the frame's title bar. One side effect of using so little code to put a frame on the screen is that it will refuse to disappear when you try to close it. This is because we are not yet handling the WINDOW_CLOSE event. For now you can just shut down the Java interpreter to close the window.

Now we need to add components to our frame. Before we start, a brief digression concerning layout managers is in order. Normally, an object that implements the LayoutManager interface is responsible for positioning and resizing components within a container. To do this, the layout manager usually queries the components using their minimumSize( ) and preferredSize( ) methods and then lays them out according to some strategy using their reshape(int x, int y, int w, int h) methods. The theory is that this type of arrangement is more likely to look presentable on many different platforms than if one were to use absolute coordinates to position the components. Using a layout manager also allows your containers to redistribute space among components when the window is resized. In practice, some layout managers reach a new level of compatibility by producing layouts that look equally ugly on all platforms and just get worse when the component is resized. Using a layout manager is a better strategy than none at all, but most of the layout managers that come with the JDK are fairly brain damaged.

The reason this is important at this point is that there are three different ways to add a component to a container, and only one of them also tells the layout manager about the component. The most basic, add(Component), does not. This means the component will have to be moved to the correct position and resized to a nonzero width and height in order to become visible. Consider the following:

```
Button button=new Button("A Button");
frame.add(button);
button.show();
button.move(20,20);
button.resize(50,50);
```

In this case, the button doesn't actually show up on the screen until the last statement is executed. The second add method, add(Component c, int position), has this same problem. Note that the position referred to in this method call is the position in the container's internal list of components, and this has no relation to the physical position of the component in the container. Of course, you *could* manually position all your components this way, if you had the patience, but the first time someone resizes the frame, your application will look cretinous.

The third method, and the only one that involves the container's layout manager, is add(String name, Component comp). You may be wondering what kind of layout manager we're adding the component to. Every subclass of Container has a default layout manager. The default layout manager for the Frame class is BorderLayout. BorderLayout positions components at the four sides of the container or in the center, depending on their names. The valid names are "North," "South," "East," "West," and "Center," and they are case sensitive. The West and East components stretch to fill the container vertically and are resized to their preferred horizontal sizes, and the North and South components stretch to fill the container horizontally and are resized to their preferred vertical size. The Center component is stretched in both directions to take up any space left over. Here is a simple demonstration of the BorderLayout:

```java
import java.awt.*;

public class MyFrame {

    static final int XSIZE = 400;
    static final int YSIZE = 200;

    public static void main(String args[]){

        Frame frame=new Frame("The Celestine Prophecy");

        frame.resize(XSIZE,YSIZE);
    // try moving frame.show() here!

        Button Nbutton=new Button("N Button");
        Button Sbutton=new Button("S Button");
        Button Ebutton=new Button("E Button");
        Button Wbutton=new Button("W Button");
        Button Cbutton=new Button("C Button");
        Button Xbutton=new Button("X Button");
```

```
frame.add("Center",Cbutton);
frame.add("West",   Wbutton);
frame.add("East",   Ebutton);
frame.add("South",  Sbutton);
frame.add("North",  Nbutton);
frame.show();


    }
}
```

This should produce something that looks something like Figure 6.1.

One interesting thing to note is when the laying out of a container actually takes place. As an experiment, comment out the frame.show() call from the end of the example to the line indicated. You will end up with an empty frame. If you resize the frame, the buttons will magically appear. When a component is added to a container, it is marked invalid, meaning that it needs to be laid out. This does not force the layout to occur. As we have seen, resizing the container or calling its show() method will do the trick. You can also use the validate() method to force the layout manager to lay out the container.

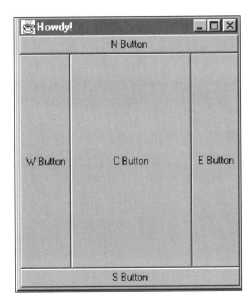

FIGURE 6.1 BorderLayout.

The Department of Redundancy Department

Now you know how the default layout manager for frames works, and chances are you loathe it. Luckily, Java does come with several other layout managers. To set the layout manager, we can use the setLayout(LayoutManager) method. Currently, the JDK gives you several to choose from: BorderLayout(the default for Dialogs, Frames, and windows), FlowLayout (the default for Panels), GridLayout, CardLayout, and GridBagLayout.

FlowLayout

The FlowLayout manager lays the components out in a row, from left to right. If no more components fit in a row, a new row is started. By default, the components are centered within the rows. To construct a new FlowLayout with a different alignment, use one of the following constructors:

```
FlowLayout(int alignment);
FlowLayout(int alignment, int vgap, int hgap);
```

vgap and hgap indicate the vertical and horizontal space to put between components (default is 5 pixels), and alignment is either FlowLayout.LEFT, FlowLayout.RIGHT, or FlowLayout.CENTER to indicate how to align the components in a row. You will often see this manager used when buttons are being laid out on a subpanel. This next snippet shows how to create a panel and set its layout to a centered FlowLayout with a vertical and horizontal gap of 10 pixels. When this is added as the southern component in a BorderLayout, it should look something like Figure 6.2. Note that we use the same string names we did earlier to add the components, but FlowLayout ignores them.

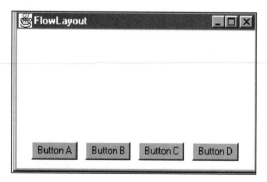

FIGURE 6.2 FlowLayout.

```
Frame frame=new Frame("FlowLayout");
frame.resize(XSIZE,YSIZE);

Panel panel=new Panel();
panel.setLayout(new FlowLayout(FlowLayout.CENTER,10,10));

Button A=new Button("Button A");
Button B=new Button("Button B");
Button C=new Button("Button C");
Button D=new Button("Button D");

panel.add("Center",A);
panel.add("West",  B);
panel.add("East",  C);
panel.add("South", D);

frame.add("South",panel);
frame.show();
```

GridLayout

The GridLayout layout manager lays out components in a grid of cells (see Figure 6.3).
Components are resized to fill the entire cell in which they reside. This layout manager has
two constructors:

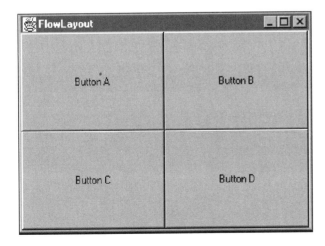

FIGURE 6.3 GridLayout.

```
new GridLayout(int rows, int columns)
new GridLayout(int rows, int columns,int hgap, int vgap)
```

If the entry for either rows or columns is zero, GridLayout takes that to mean "any number," and the grid will expand if necessary. At least one of the two must be nonzero. The hgap and vgap act as they do in FlowLayout, except the default gap is zero. Here's a snippet showing how this works:

```
frame.setLayout(new GridLayout(0,2,0,0));

Button A=new Button("Button A");
Button B=new Button("Button B");
Button C=new Button("Button C");
Button D=new Button("Button D");

frame.add("Center",A);
frame.add("West",  B);
frame.add("East",  C);
frame.add("South", D);

frame.show();
```

CardLayout

The CardLayout layout manager treats its components as if they were a deck of cards. Only the top card is showing at any time, and the component is resized to fill its parent's area. This works especially well when each component is a panel with its own layout, in which case you can get a sort of "tabbed dialog" effect by providing buttons to flip to different cards. CardLayout has two constructors. One takes no arguments, and the other takes two ints specifying the horizontal and vertical gaps to place around the card. Here's an example of how to set up a CardLayout with three buttons:

```
CardLayout CL=newCardLayout()
frame.setLayout(CL);

Button A=new Button("Button A");
Button B=new Button("Button B");
Button C=new Button("Button C");
```

```
frame.add("A",A);
frame.add("B",B);
frame.add("C",C);

frame.show();
```

When first displayed, the A button will be the only thing visible, but we can flip through the cards using the following methods:

```
CL.next(frame);// flip to next card
CL.previous(frame);// flip to previous card
CL.first(frame);// flip to first card
CL.last(frame);// flip to last card
CL.show(frame, "A");// flip to card named "A"
CL.show(frame, "C");// flip to card named "C"
```

The deck "wraps around" so that if you call previous when the first card is being displayed, the last card will be displayed (and vice versa). Also note that in this case the names that you give the components are important. If more than one component has the same name and you call show for that name, the *last* component matching that name is displayed.

GridBagLayout

GridBagLayout has been described as "ten pounds of grids in a five-pound bag." It is complicated, it has a stupid name, and few people agree that it is worth the effort it takes to master. I have mixed feelings. On the one hand, I agree that it may be too complicated, and I don't agree with some of the choices made in implementing it. On the other hand, it is the most flexible of all the layout managers shipped with Java, and it is possible to produce some very nice layouts using it.

The basic idea behind GridBagLayout is the positioning components in a grid of cells like GridLayout. Unlike GridLayout, the components can span more than one cell, and the cells need not be the same size.

The first complication is that GridBagLayout doesn't get its information on how to position components from the add() method and the components themselves, the way the other layout managers do. A GridBagConstraints object is used to provide information to the GridBagLayout about the object's position, size, and behavior when it is resized. You create a GridBagConstraints object, set its fields to the desired values, and then use the

GridBagLayout's setConstraints(Component, GridBagConstraints) method to tell the Grid-BagLayout to use those values for the specified component.

```
Frame frame=new Frame("GridBagNightmare!");

GridBagLayout GBL=new GridBagLayout();
GridBagConstraints GBC=new GridBagConstraints();
frame.setLayout(GBL);
Button button=new Button("I am the unpleasant GridBagButton!");
frame.add("hello",button);


GBL.setConstraints(button,GBC);
```

A copy of the GridBagConstraints is made when you call setConstraints, so you can reuse the same GridBagConstraints object for different components.

In the following discussion we refer to constants in the GridBagConstraints class by their field name alone (e.g., RELATIVE, not GridBagConstraints.RELATIVE), because GridBagConstraints is a cumbersome class name.

The most important fields to set are gridx and gridy. These specify the row and column where the component will reside. If you specify RELATIVE for gridx, the component will be placed just to the left of the last component added. Similarly, specifying RELATIVE for the gridy field causes the component to be placed just below the last component added. The default value for both gridx and gridy is 0.

You may also specify how many cells you wish the component to span using gridwidth and gridheight. The default for both is 1. You may also use REMAINDER to specify that the component be the last in its row or column.

If a component is larger than the cell area you have specified, you can set the fill field to VERTICAL, HORIZONTAL, or BOTH. The default is NONE.

The ipadx and ipady fields specify how much internal padding to add to the minimum width and height of the component. An ipadx value of 10, for example, will increase the width of the component by 20 pixels (because the padding is added to both sides of the component). The default for both is 0.

The insets field accepts a java.awt.insets object (see Table 6.1) specifying the amount of external padding to add to the component. This is the minimum amount of space between the component and the edges of its display area.

TABLE 6.1 java.awt.Insets

public int top	The top inset in pixels.
public int left	The left inset in pixels.
public int bottom	The bottom inset in pixels.
public int right	The right inset in pixels.
public Insets (int top, int left, int bottom, int right)	Create a new Insets object with the given top, left, right, and bottom insets.
public Object clone ()	Returns a duplicate of this Insets object.
public String toString ()	Returns a string representation of this object.

The anchor field specifies where to place the component inside its display area. The possible values are CENTER EAST, NORTH, NORTHEAST, NORTHWEST, SOUTH, SOUTH-EAST, SOUTHWEST, and WEST. The default is CENTER.

Finally, the weightx and weighty fields (both of type double) specify how to distribute any extra space to the components in a row or column. GridBagLayout adds up all the weights in a row or column and then distributes the extra space proportionately. This requires some explanation. If the weights of the three components in a row are 1, 2, and 3, respectively, the first component will receive 1/6; the second, 2/6; and the last, 1/2 (3/6) of the space. The default is 0.

There you have it. You can probably imagine why most people avoid GridBagLayout like the plague.

The Goldilocks Syndrome

Now that you've seen the layout managers that are included with Java, odds are you are suffering from the Goldilocks Syndrome. You probably think some of them are too simple, some are too complicated, but none of them are "just right." There's a simple solution to this problem. Write your own.

Rolling Your Own: FloatLayout

Although the FloatLayout class is a good example of how to write a layout manager, it was never intended to be used by humans. It came about as part of a simple GUI builder I was writing, where the computer would generate all the necessary information to position the components. A funny thing happened when I was hand coding some examples to test it: I liked it better than any of the existing layout managers. So if this approach seems odd, keep this in mind.

The FloatLayout (shown in Listing 6.1) layout manager uses floating point values stored in a FloatLayoutConstraints (see Listing 6.2) object to specify the position and size of the component as a fraction of the container's width and height. For a component that is centered in the container and takes up one-quarter of the vertical area and half the horizontal area, we could use the following:

```
FloatLayout lm = new FloatLayout();
Button button =new Button("FloatLayout");
this.add(button);
flc=lm.getConstraints(button);
flc.ypos=(float).5; // halfway across
flc.xpos=(float).5; // halfway down
flc.xsize=(float).5; // width 1/2 of container's width
flc.ysize=(float).25; // height 1/4 of container's height
flc.resizable=true; // resizable
```

A component is automatically assigned a FloatLayoutConstraints with its preferred size when it is added to the container. To get the associated FloatLayoutConstraints for a component, we can use the getConstraints(Component) method. Unlike GridBagLayout, we can change the constraints of a component after we have added it to a container without removing it and adding it again. If the size calculations using the FloatLayoutConstraints would cause the component to be smaller than its minimum size, the minimum size is used. A good example of the FloatLayout in action is the chat applet in Chapter 9.

LISTING 6.1

```
import java.util.*;
import java.awt.*;
public class FloatLayout implements LayoutManager{
    /* hashtable for components */
    Hashtable components=new Hashtable(100);

    public void addLayoutComponent(String name, Component comp){
```

```
    // Container we are laying out.
    Container parent=comp.getParent();
    parent.show();

    Insets insets = parent.insets();
        int pw = parent.size().width - (insets.left + insets.right);
    int ph = parent.size().height - (insets.top + insets.bottom);
    comp.show();
    FloatLayoutConstraints FLC=new FloatLayoutConstraints();
    Dimension d=comp.preferredSize();
    Point p=comp.location();
    // convert absolute coords to floatlayoutconstraints
    FLC.xsize=(float)((float)d.width/(float)pw);
    FLC.ysize=(float)d.height/(float)ph;



    FLC.xpos=(float)p.x/(float)pw+FLC.xsize/2;
    FLC.ypos=(float)p.y/(float)ph+FLC.ysize/2;


    components.put((Object)comp,(Object) FLC);



}


public void removeLayoutComponent(Component comp){
    components.remove(comp);
}

public Dimension preferredLayoutSize(Container parent){

    return parent.size();
}

public Dimension minimumLayoutSize(Container parent){return parent.size();}
```

Continued

```
        public FloatLayoutConstraints getConstraints(Component c){
            if (!components.containsKey(c))layoutContainer(c.getParent());
            return (FloatLayoutConstraints)components.get(c);
        }
        public void layoutContainer(Container parent){
            int cxsize=0;// component width (pixels)
            int cysize=0;// component height (pixels)
            int cxpos=0;// component position (pixel)
            int cypos=0;// component position (pixel)
            int numcomps = parent.countComponents();


        FloatLayoutConstraints flc=null;


        // find inner size of parent (w and h)
            Insets insets = parent.insets();
            int w = parent.size().width - (insets.left + insets.right);
            int h = parent.size().height - (insets.top + insets.bottom);

            //now loop through all the components
            //contained in the parent
            Component c;
            for (int i=0;i<numcomps;i++){
                c=parent.getComponent(i);

                //if this componenmt has not been added yet, do it!
                if (!components.containsKey(c)) {
{this.addLayoutComponent("auto",c);
            }

                // get the constraints for component c
                flc=(FloatLayoutConstraints)components.get(c);
                Dimension d=c.minimumSize();
                if (flc.resizable==true){
```

```
                    cxsize=(int)((float)flc.xsize*(float)w);
                    cysize=(int)((float)flc.ysize*(float)h);


                    if (cxsize<d.width)cxsize=d.width;// use min size
                    if (cysize<d.height)cysize=d.height;


                }

            cxpos=(int)((float)flc.xpos*(float)w)-cxsize/2;
            cypos=(int)((float)flc.ypos*(float)h)-cysize/2;
            c.reshape(cxpos+insets.left,cypos+insets.top,cxsize,cysize);


        }
    }
}
```

LISTING 6.2

```
public class FloatLayoutConstraints{
    public float xpos;
    public float ypos;
    public float xsize=0;
    public float ysize=0;
    public boolean resizable=false;

    public String toString(){
        StringBuffer sb=new StringBuffer().append("FLoatLayoutConstraints:\n");
        sb.append("\nxpos : ").append(xpos);
        sb.append("\nypos : ").append(ypos);
        sb.append("\nxsize: ").append(xsize);
        sb.append("\nysize: ").append(ysize);
        return sb.toString();

    }
}
```

TABLE 6.2 java.awt.Event Objects

Name	Description	Type
target	The object in which this event originated.	Object
when	The time stamp of the event	long
id	The event type.	int
x	The x coordinate of the event	int
y	The y coordinate of the event.	int
key	The key pressed or released.	int
modifiers	What modifier keys were pressed (i.e., shift, alt, etc.).	int
clickCount	The number of times the mouse was clicked.	int
arg	An arbitrary argument.	Object
evt	A reference to the next event. Used when events are put into a linked list.	Event

Happenings

One good thing about the AWT is that you don't have to go out and check for user input. Your objects can sit back, relax, and let the GUI events be delivered to them in neat little packages. The packages in this case are java.awt.Event objects (see Table 6.2). This class is mostly constants, but it does have 10 public fields.

The most important fields for most purposes are id and target. Note that not all fields in the event class have meaningful values for all types of events. The key field, for example, doesn't make much sense if the event is a mouse move event. The various events generated by different components are listed later, but you may be wondering where these events come from and where they are headed. See Table 6.3.

TABLE 6.3 java.awt.Event

public static final int SHIFT _MASK	Key modifier constant.
public static final int CTRL _MASK	Key modifier constant.

Continued

public static final int META _MASK	Key modifier constant.
public static final int ALT _MASK	Key modifier constant.
public static final int HOME	Key constant.
public static final int END	Key constant.
public static final int PGUP	Key constant.
public static final int PGDN	Key constant.
public static final int UP	Key constant.
public static final int DOWN	Key constant.
public static final int LEFT	Key constant.
public static final int RIGHT	Key constant.
public static final int F1	Key constant.
public static final int F2	Key constant.
public static final int F3	Key constant.
public static final int F4	Key constant.
public static final int F5	Key constant.
public static final int F6	Key constant.
public static final int F7	Key constant.
public static final int F8	Key constant.
public static final int F9	Key constant.
public static final int F10	Key constant.
public static final int F11	Key constant.
public static final int F12	Key constant.
private static final int WINDOW _EVENT	Event ID constant.
public static final int WINDOW _DESTROY	Event ID constant.
public static final int WINDOW _EXPOSE	Event ID constant.

Continued

TABLE 6.3 Continued

public static final int WINDOW _ICONIFY	Event ID constant.
public static final int WINDOW _DEICONIFY	Event ID constant.
public static final int WINDOW _MOVED	Event ID constant.
private static final int KEY _EVENT	Event ID constant.
public static final int KEY _PRESS	Event ID constant.
public static final int KEY _RELEASE	Event ID constant.
public static final int KEY _ACTION	Event ID constant.
public static final int KEY _ACTION _RELEASE	Event ID constant.
private static final int MOUSE _EVENT	Event ID constant.
public static final int MOUSE _DOWN	Event ID constant.
public static final int MOUSE _UP	Event ID constant.
public static final int MOUSE _MOVE	Event ID constant.
public static final int MOUSE _ENTER	Event ID constant.
public static final int MOUSE _EXIT	Event ID constant.
public static final int MOUSE _DRAG	Event ID constant.
private static final int SCROLL _EVENT	Event ID constant.
public static final int SCROLL _LINE _UP	Event ID constant.
public static final int SCROLL _LINE _DOWN	Event ID constant.
public static final int SCROLL _PAGE _UP	Event ID constant.
public static final int SCROLL _PAGE _DOWN	Event ID constant.
public static final int SCROLL _ABSOLUTE	Event ID constant.
private static final int LIST _EVENT	Event ID constant.
public static final int LIST _SELECT	Event ID constant.
public static final int LIST _DESELECT	Event ID constant.

Continued

private static final int MISC _EVENT	Event ID constant.
public static final int ACTION _EVENT	Event ID constant.
public static final int LOAD _FILE	Event ID constant.
public static final int SAVE _FILE	Event ID constant.
public static final int GOT _FOCUS	Event ID constant.
public static final int LOST _FOCUS	Event ID constant.
public Object target	The object this event originated in.
public long when	The time stamp of the event.
public int id	The ID code of the event.
public int x	The x coordinate of the event.
public int y	The y coordinate of the event.
public int key	The value of the key pressed.
public int modifiers	What modifier keys were pressed (ORed together).
public int clickCount	The number of times the mouse was clicked.
public Object arg	An arbitrary argument; significance varies.
public Event evt	A reference to the next event. Used when events are put into a linked list.
public Event (Object target, int id, Object arg)	Create a new event with the given values.
public Event (Object target, long when, id, int x, int y, int key, int modifiers)	Create a new event with the given int values.
public Event (Object target, long when, int id, x, int y, int key, int modifiers, Object arg)	Create a new event with the given int values.
public boolean controlDown ( )	Returns true if the control key was held down during a keypress.

Continued

TABLE 6.3 Continued

public boolean metaDown ( )	Returns true if the meta (alt) key was held down during a keypress.
protected String paramString ( )	Returns a string containing this event's state.
public boolean shiftDown ( )	Returns true if the shift key was held down during a keypress.
public String toString ( )	Returns a string representation of this event.
public void translate (int x, int y)	Translates the coordinates of the event to be relative to x,y.

A Long, Strange Trip

A Java event starts when something happens in the native GUI. For simplicity's sake, let's say the user presses a key in a TextField. The first thing that happens is that some sort of native event is generated. The details of this native event do not concern us. The TextField's peer object grabs this event and uses whatever information it contains to generate a java.awt.Event object encapsulating the different parameters of the event. The peer then sends this event on its journey by calling the TextField object's postEvent(Event) method, which simply calls the handleEvent(Event) method. The code is something like the following:

```
public boolean postEvent(Event e){
    if (handleEvent(Event){
    return true;
    }
. . . .
```

For now we will ignore the details of how the handleEvent(Event) method works, but we will assume that it returns true if it has handled the event and no further action needs to be taken, and false if the event has not been handled by the TextField and it needs further processing. If TextField returns true, the event simply disappears and the postEvent(Event) method returns to the peer that called it.

In this case the TextField does want the event to continue on its journey because sooner or later it wants the character of the key that was pressed to show up in the native text field, so the TextField.HandleEvent(Event) method returns false. This causes the execution of TextField's postEvent(Event e) method to continue with the following lines:

```
Component parent = this.parent;
if (parent != null) {
    e.translate(x, y);
    if (parent.postEvent(e)) {
        return true;
    }
}
```

If this component has a container above it, the event is passed along to that component's postEvent(Event), and the process continues until some component returns true or a top-level component (one with no parent) is reached. In that case, the following code executes:

```
if (peer != null) {
    return peer.handleEvent(e);
    }
return false;
}
```

Now what happens is that the event gets passed back down through the component hierarchy, but this time through peer objects. Eventually the event reaches the original peer object that generated the AWT event in the first place. The peer then does two things. First, it finally displays the proper character in the TextField! Next, the peer returns true. This causes execution to pop back through all the method calls and eventually return to the peer. To summarize, if the TextField is contained in a Frame, the Event's path should look like this:

```
 TextFieldPeer ‡TextField ‡Frame ‡ FramePeer ‡TextFieldPeer
```

Why This Trip Matters

If any of the objects in this chain return true before the event reaches the TextField's peer, the keypress will never appear on the screen! The native text field will never know anything happened. The lesson to learn here is to return true from a handleEvent(Event) method if you wish to short-circuit this whole process. One by-product of this system is that you can filter, destroy, or modify events at any level. One example is shown in the following listing.

```
import java.awt.*;

public class EventFilter extends Frame{

    public EventFilter(){
        super("EventFilter");
    }
    public static void main(String args[]){

        EventFilter frame=new EventFilter ();
        frame.setLayout(new FlowLayout());
        frame.add("text",new TextField(10));
        frame.show();


    }
    public boolean handleEvent(Event evt){
        if (evt.id==Event.KEY_PRESS){
            evt.key=evt.key-23;
        }

        return super.handleEvent(evt);
    }
}
```

This program creates a wacky TextArea that displays a totally wrong character whenever the user presses a key. To do this, we subtract 23 from the value of every keypress.

Helper Methods

Luckily we don't have to check for every event type, because the default code in Component's handleEvent(Event) routine will sort out events for you and automatically call some helper methods for you. The Component.handleEvent(Event) method contains some code similar to the following:

```
switch (evt.id) {

    case Event.MOUSE_ENTER:
```

```
        return mouseEnter(evt, evt.x, evt.y);

    case Event.MOUSE_EXIT:
        return mouseExit(evt, evt.x, evt.y);

    case Event.MOUSE_MOVE:
        return mouseMove(evt, evt.x, evt.y);

    case Event.MOUSE_DOWN:
        return mouseDown(evt, evt.x, evt.y);

    case Event.MOUSE_DRAG:
        return mouseDrag(evt, evt.x, evt.y);

    case Event.MOUSE_UP:
        return mouseUp(evt, evt.x, evt.y);

    case Event.KEY_PRESS:
    case Event.KEY_ACTION:
        return keyDown(evt, evt.key);

    case Event.KEY_RELEASE:
    case Event.KEY_ACTION_RELEASE:
        return keyUp(evt, evt.key);

    case Event.ACTION_EVENT:
        return action(evt, evt.arg);
    case Event.GOT_FOCUS:
        return gotFocus(evt, evt.arg);
    case Event.LOST_FOCUS:
        return lostFocus(evt, evt.arg);
}
```

If you are interested in keypresses, for example, you can simply define a keyDown(Event e,int I), and it will be called automatically. Remember that you should, as a rule, return false from all of these routines.

Where to Handle Events

There are two approaches to handling events. One school of thought holds that events should be handled at the highest level, in the parent container. This makes a lot of sense, because the events happen inside the container, so it is logical for the container to take care of them. The good thing about this is that the event handling all occurs in one place; if you make any modifications to the event handling, it will affect the entire container. The bad thing is also that the event handling all occurs in one place: you may end up with one huge event handling routine that is more confusing than a bunch of smaller ones.

The second school of thought holds that events are best handled in the component in which they originate, if possible. We can call this the "Visual Basic" approach. Although this approach makes sense in some cases, it's easy to end up with a lot of isolated code snippets that are as easy to maintain as a 600-pound gorilla. However, this approach may be very sensible from an object-oriented viewpoint because once you make one component with some event handling (changing all keypresses to uppercase, for example), you can reuse it in many different containers and inherit its functionality in subclasses.

A Mystery Solved

By now, you've probably figured out why the Frame in the earlier examples refused to close. We never handled the WINDOW_DESTROY method, but this is simple to do. All we have to do is override the Frame's handleEvent(Event) method:

```
public boolean handleEvent(Event evt){
    If (evt.id==Event.WINDOW_DESTROY){
        System.exit(0);
    }
    return false;
}
```

All the Components

What follows are brief descriptions of all the Awt components and the events they generate. See the tables at the end of this chapter for a listing and description of all the methods of each class.

Button

The Button class represents a simple push-button. It has two constructors: one that takes no arguments and creates a blank button and one that takes a string to be used as a label. When a user clicks on a button, an ACTION_EVENT is generated with the button as the target and the button text as the argument.

Canvas

Canvas is by far the simplest subclass of Component. It represents a simple rectangular drawing area. There isn't much to say about this one; it exists only to be drawn on.

Checkbox and CheckboxGroup

A Checkbox represents a simple "radio button" style checkbox with an optional label. If a checkbox is a member of a CheckboxGroup, only one of the buttons in the group may be checked at a time. You get the checkbox's state using the getState() method, which returns a Boolean, and set it with setState(Boolean state). If a checkbox is part of a group, you can use its getCurrent() and setCurrent(CheckBox) methods to get and set the currently checked box. When clicked, checkboxes generate an ACTION_EVENT with the checkbox as the target and the new state of the button as the argument.

CheckboxMenuItem

A CheckboxMenuItem is a menu item (see below) that may be checked. You can get and set its state as you would a normal checkbox. Except for having a state, it behaves like a MenuItem (see below).

Choice

The Choice component is drop-down menu of items. You can add items to a Choice with addItem(String), but there is no method to remove an item. When an item is selected, an ACTION_EVENT is generated with the Choice component as the target and the text of the item selected as the argument. You can find the index of the currently selected item with getSelectedIndex() and the item at that index with getItem(int index).

Dialog

Dialog (a subclass of Window) is a simple dialog box. It has two constructors:

- Dialog (Frame parent, String title, Boolean modal)
- Dialog (Frame parent, Boolean modal)

If the modal flag is set to true, the dialog's show() method is supposed to block until the dialog has been dismissed. This may or may not actually work as advertised, depending on the platform. Note that the parent frame need not be visible on the screen, so if you just want to pop up a dialog from a text-only application, you can use the following:

```
Dialog (new Frame(),  "I have no real parent!")
```

File Dialogs

File dialogs are file selectors that operate in a fairly straightforward way. One thing to note is that the setFilenameFilter (FilenameFilter filter) takes an instance of a class that implements the FilenameFilter interface, which has one method:

```
boolean accept (File dir, String name)
```

This allows your filter to decide whether the given file in the given directory passes through the filter. What's nice about this is that your filename filters can be as intelligent as you want to make them and not just simple wildcard-style filters. You could, for example, make a filename filter that rejects file names beginning with any other letter of the alphabet, if you wanted to be perverse.

Frames

Frames are top-level windows that may have a Menubar. You use the setMenuBar(Menubar) method to bind a menu bar to a Frame (see below). This is demonstrated in the following snippet, and the result is seen in Figure 6.4.

```java
import java.awt.*;

public class MenuTest {

    public static void main(String args[]){

        Frame frame=new Frame ("Menu Sample");
        String string;

        Menu menu=new Menu("Numbers", true);
        MenuBar menubar=new MenuBar();

        for (int i=1;i<10;i++){
```

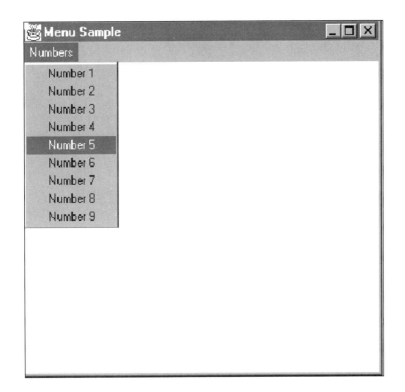

FIGURE 6.4 A Java Menu.

```
        string ="Number "+Integer.toString(i);
        MenuItem M=new MenuItem(string);
        menu.add(M);
    }
    menubar.add(menu);
    frame.setMenuBar(menubar);

    frame.show();

    }
```

Label

Labels are one-line text labels, plain and simple. They can be set to automatically align their text using Label.LEFT, Label.RIGHT, or Label.CENTER.

List

A List component is a listbox of string items that may be selected by the user. You can control whether multiple items may be selected through the setMultipleSelections (Boolean multi) method. If the listbox contains more items than can be displayed at the current size, a scrollbar will be added automatically. A List component will generate a LIST_SELECT event when a user selects an item and a LIST_DESELECT event when an item is deselected. Double-clicking on an item on the list generates an ACTION_EVENT with the text of the item clicked on as the argument and the List as the target.

Menu, MenuBar, and MenuItem

Menus are simple drop-down menus that contain MenuItems and are themselves contained in a MenuBar, which is in turn bound to a Frame. Since MenuItems themselves implement the MenuContainer Interface, they can contain other "fly out" menus. Note that the Menu class hints at having "tear off" menu functionality, but this is not currently supported.

The MenuBar class has only one constructor that takes no arguments. You can add menu items to a menu bar with the add (Menu) method and remove them with remove (Menu-Component). It is also possible to add and retrieve menus from the menu bar based on their position on the menu bar using the getMenu (int) and remove(int) methods. Menu bars are bound to a frame using its setMenuBar(MenuBar) method. This arrangement allows you to easily change menu bars displayed in different contexts. The "help" menu is a special case. You can retrieve a reference to it using getHelpMenu () and set it with setHelpMenu(Menu). The help menu need not be titled "help" and need not even exist at all.

As far as menu items go, there isn't much you can do to them. You can enable and disable them using enable() and disable (), and you can set their text using setLabel (String), but that's about it. Clicking on a menu item generates an ACTION_EVENT with the list as the target and the text of the list item on which the user double-clicked as the argument.

Scrollbar

The Scrollbar component provides a control for scrolling through a range of values. Usually they are used to scroll a viewport over a larger area, but scrollbars are very flexible. The Scrollbar class has two constructors:

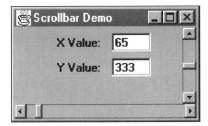

FIGURE 6.5 Scrollbar Demo.

- public Scrollbar(int orientation)
- public Scrollbar(int orientation,int value, int visib,int minimum,int maximum)

Orientation is either Scrollbar.HORIZONTAL or Scrollbar.VERTICAL, value is the position in the current window, visible is the amount of the total range visible per page, minimum is the minimum value of the scrollbar, and maximum is the maximum value. You can also set the page increment (the amount to move when the user clicks somewhere in the range) using setPageIncrement(int) and the line increment (which is the amount to move when the user clicks on one of the scrollbar arrows) with setLineIncrement(int i).

To set the value of a scrollbar, use setValue(int). To get the current value, use getValue(). When clicked on, a scrollbar generates the following events: SCROLL_LINE_UP, SCROLL_LINE_DOWN, SCROLL_PAGE_UP, SCROLL_PAGE_DOWN, and SCROLL_ABSOLUTE.

Listing 6.3 shows a simple example of how to use a Scrollbar to set the values in a couple of TextFields (see Figure 6.5).

LISTING 6.3

```
import java.awt.*;

public class ScrollDemo extends Frame{
        static Scrollbar Hscroll,Vscroll;
     static TextField Xtext, Ytext;

    public static void main(String args[]){

        /* make a new ScrollDemo
        ** and set attributes
```

Continued

```
        */

        ScrollDemo frame=new ScrollDemo ();
        frame.setTitle("Scrollbar Demo");
        frame.setBackground(Color.lightGray);


        /* add a couple of scrollbars
        ** to the BorderLayout
        */

        Vscroll=new Scrollbar(Scrollbar.VERTICAL,6,10,0,666);
        frame.add("East",Vscroll);

        Hscroll=new Scrollbar(Scrollbar.HORIZONTAL,25,10,0,1000);
        frame.add("South",Hscroll);


        Panel panel=new Panel();
        panel.add(new Label("X Value: "));
        Xtext=new TextField(3);
        panel.add(Xtext);
        panel.add(new Label("Y Value: "));
        Ytext=new TextField(3);
        panel.add(Ytext);


        frame.add("Center",panel);

        frame.show();
        frame.pack();

    }
    public boolean handleEvent(Event evt){
```

```
    if (evt.target==Hscroll){
        Xtext.setText(Integer.toString(Hscroll.getValue()));

    }else{
        Ytext.setText(Integer.toString(Vscroll.getValue()));
    }
    return true;
  }
}
```

TextComponent, TextArea, and TextField

The TextComponent class serves as the parent for the components for text input and output. Note that TextComponent has no public constructor, so you can't instantiate a TextComponent. It is included here because its methods are inherited by its children, TextField and TextArea. To get all the text of the component, use the getText() method; to set the text, use the setText(String) method. You can select a range of text with select (int start, end) and get only the selected text using getSelectedText().

A TextField is a text component that has only a single line of optionally editable text. One interesting thing to note is the setEchoChar(char) method, which sets the character used to echo keyboard input. This is useful when you are entering passwords where you don't want the keystrokes to appear on the screen as-is. The TextArea class is similar to the TextField class, but it can contain multiple lines. If the text is too large for the size of the TextArea, scrollbars will magically appear.

Window

A Window is a component with a title but no MenuBar. Like its subclass, Dialog, the constructor for Window requires a Frame parent, but this need not be a visible frame.

Peers

Earlier we said it was safe to ignore peers, which is generally true. One thing you should know is that the peer objects are created lazily, just before the object is shown on the screen for the first time. This means that calls to a component's size(), preferredSize(), and minimumSize() methods will return a width and height of 0 until the peer actually comes into existence. You may wonder where peers come from in the first place. The abstract

Toolkit class is the superclass of classes that are responsible for generating peers. You can get a reference to the default toolkit for your system using the static Toolkit.getToolkit() method. The toolkit has a few other interesting methods not involved with peer creation. Here's an interesting snippet showing how to learn about the video capabilities of the computer on which it's running:

```
Dimension D;
Toolkit TK=Toolkit.getDefaultToolkit();
D=TK.getScreenSize();
System.out.println("Screen size:"+D.width+" by "+D.height);
System.out.println("Resolution:"+TK.getScreenResolution()+" DPI");
```

java.awt.image

The ImageProducer interface is implemented by classes that wish to deliver data to classes that implement the ImageConsumer interface. This is a very simple interface. The addConsumer(ImageConsumer) registers an image consumer with the producer, and the startProduction() starts delivering image data. It actually delivers the data by making one or more calls to the setPixels() method. Image observers are, as the name implies, classes interested in details of an image's status. Many calls querying image data (for instance, the Image.getHeight(ImageObserver) method) require an ImageObserver. If the image is local, and you know it will be fully prepared, you can probably get away with using null for this argument, but this is not a good habit to get into.

TABLE 6.4 ImageProducer

public void addConsumer (ImageConsumer ic)	Adds a consumer to the list of those interested in data from this producer.
public boolean isConsumer (ImageConsumer ic)	Returns true if the given consumer is already registered with this producer.
public void removeConsumer (ImageConsumer ic)	Removes the given consumer.
public void requestTopDownLeftRightResend (ImageConsumer ic)	Requests the producer start sending data in top-down, left-right order.
public void startProduction (ImageConsumer ic)	Starts delivering data to the consumers.

TABLE 6.5 ImageConsumer

int RANDOMPIXELORDER	Constant for setHints(int). The pixels will be delivered in random order.
int TOPDOWNLEFTRIGHT	Constant for setHints(int). The pixels will be delivered in top-down, left-right order.
int COMPLETESCANLINES	Constant for setHints(int). The pixels will be delivered in complete scan lines.
int SINGLEPASS	Constant for setHints(int). The pixels will be delivered in a single pass.
int SINGLEFRAME	Constant for setHints(int). This image consists of a single frame.
int IMAGEERROR	Constant for imageComplete(int). A single frame of a multiframe animation is complete.
int SINGLEFRAMEDONE	Constant for imageComplete(int). A single frame of a multiframe animation is complete.
int STATICIMAGEDONE	Constant for imageComplete(int). A single frame static image is complete.
int IMAGEABORTED	Constant for imageComplete(int). The production of data was aborted.
void imageComplete (int status)	Called to report image status.
void setColorModel (ColorModel model)	Sets the color model.
void setDimensions (int width, int height)	Reports the size of the image.
void setHints (int hintflags)	Sets the hints. Several hints may be ORed together.
void setPixels (int x, int y, int w, int h, ColorModel model, int pixels [], int off, int scansize)	Delivers a chunk of pixels as ints. Pixel (m,n) is pixels [n * scansize + m + off].
void setPixels (int x, int y, int w, int h, ColorModel model, byte pixels [], int off, int scansize)	Sends a chunk of pixels as bytes. Pixel (m,n) is pixels [n * scansize + m + off].
void setProperties (Hashtable props)	Sets the properties hashtable for this image.

Continued

TABLE 6.6 ImageObserver

public static final int WIDTH	Constant for infoflags.
public static final int HEIGHT	Constant for infoflags.
public static final int PROPERTIES	Constant for infoflags.
public static final int SOMEBITS	Constant for infoflags.
public static final int FRAMEBITS	Constant for infoflags.
public static final int ALLBITS	Constant for infoflags.
public static final int ERROR	Constant for infoflags.
public static final int ABORT	Constant for infoflags.
public boolean imageUpdate (Image img, int infoflags, int x, int y, int width, int height)	Called to notify the observer of image status.

Some Examples

MemoryImageSource Class   One useful class that implements the ImageProducer interface is MemoryImageSource. This class will take an array containing pixel data for an object and turn it into an image. To make a new image from an array named pixels, one must use createImage( ):

```
Image I = createImage(new MemoryImageSource(wdth, height, pix, 0, width));
```

PixelGrabber Class   PixelGrabber is a class that implements the ImageConsumer interface to get data from an ImageProducer. This class takes the pixel data for an image and puts it in an array. Here is a short example:

```
public Vector makecv(Image i, int color){

    Vector v=new Vector(); // collision detection vector

    int x=0;
    int y=0;
    int width=-1;
    int height=-1;
    while(width!=-1&&height!=-1){
```

```
        width=i.getWidth(null);
        height=i.getHeight(null);
     }
    int[] pixels = new int[width * height];
    //now we'll fill our pixel array using pixelGrabber()
    PixelGrabber pg = new PixelGrabber(i.getSource(),x,   y,width,height,pixels,0,
width );
        i.getSource().addConsumer(pg);  // shouldn't be necessary, but it is
        try {
      pg.grabPixels(15000L);
        }catch (InterruptedException e){}
     // now scan through the array and put some pixels in cv
       for (x=0;x<width;x++){
           for (y=0;y<height;y++){
               if (pixels[x+y*width]==color) {
               v.addElement(new Point(x,y));
               }
           }
       }
}
```

In this case, we put all pixels with the given color in the vector. We have used this type of code to make collision detection vectors for sprite animation. To do this, change the last if statement in the code above to

```
 if (pixels[x+y*width]!=color)
```

Then pass the routine the color value of the background or whatever color you don't want to be part of the collision vector.

AWTside, Looking In

The AWT has been criticized because it provides only "common denominator" functionality. This is true, but the compatibility you gain by giving up the latest fancy widgets is more than worth it. More importantly, the AWT is (at least for now) relatively clean and uncluttered. You'll probably find that this simplicity will work to your advantage. The AWT frees you from the details of the native user interface and lets you concentrate on more important things, like ruling the world from your desktop. Some professional programmers admire the ease with which you can hack together presentable user interfaces with a minimum amount of code, and it's likely that you will too.

All the Components

Tables 6.7 through 6.31 summarize the methods available in the AWT components. They have been arranged in alphabetical order for easy reference. If you are just beginning your study of the AWT, the best place to start is with the top of the hierarchy, Component, and its special subclass, Container.

TABLE 6.7 Button

public Button (String label)	Creates a button with the specified label.
public Button ( )	Creates a button with no label.
public synchronized void addNotify ( )	Creates a peer for this component.
public String getLabel ( )	Returns the label of the button.
public void setLabel (String label)	Changes the label of the button.
protected String paramString ( )	Returns a string with information such as the position and size of the component, and whether it is visible and valid.

TABLE 6.8 Canvas

public synchronized void addNotify ( )	Creates a peer for this component.
public void paint (Graphics g)	Paints the canvas.

TABLE 6.9 Checkbox

public Checkbox (String label, CheckboxGroup group, Boolean state)	Creates a labeled checkbox in the given group with the given initial state.
public Checkbox (String label)	Creates a labeled checkbox initialized to false.
public Checkbox ( )	Creates an unlabeled checkbox initialized to false.
public synchronized void addNotify ( )	Creates a peer for this checkbox.

Continued

public CheckboxGroup getCheckboxGroup ( )	Returns a reference to the CheckboxGroup group (or null if none).
public String getLabel ( )	Returns the label of the checkbox.
public boolean getState ( )	Returns the current state of this checkbox.
protected String paramString ( )	Returns a string containing this checkbox's state.
public void setCheckboxGroup (CheckboxGroup g)	Makes this checkbox part of the given group.
public void setLabel (String label)	Sets the label for this checkbox.
public void setState (boolean state)	Sets the state of this checkbox.

TABLE 6.10 CheckboxGroup

public CheckboxGroup ( )	Creates a new checkbox group.
public Checkbox getCurrent ( )	Returns a reference to the currently checked checkbox.
public synchronized void setCurrent (Checkbox box)	Checks the given checkbox.
public String toString ( )	Returns a string representation of this group.

TABLE 6.11 CheckboxMenuItem

public CheckboxMenuItem (String label)	Creates a checkable menu item with the given label.
public synchronized void addNotify ( )	Creates a peer for this component.
public boolean getState ( )	Returns true if this item is checked.
public String paramString ( )	Returns a string containing this component's state, validity, visibility, etc.
public void setState (Boolean state)	Sets the state of this item.

TABLE 6.12 Choice

public Choice ()	Creates a new choice component.
public synchronized void addItem (String item)	Adds an item to this choice.
public synchronized void addNotify ()	Creates a peer for this choice.
public int countItems ()	Returns the current number of items.
public String getItem (int index)	Returns the item at the specified index.
public int getSelectedIndex ()	Returns the index of the currently selected item.
public String getSelectedItem ()	Returns the currently selected item.
protected String paramString ()	Returns a string containing this choice's state.
public void select (String str)	Selects the given item.
public synchronized void select (int pos)	Selects the item at the specified index.

TABLE 6.13 Component

public boolean action (Event evt, Object what)	Called when an action event occurs in this component.
public void addNotify ()	Creates a peer for this component.
public Rectangle bounds ()	Returns a Rectangle containing the bounds of this component.
public int checkImage (Image image, int width, int height, Observer observer)	Checks on the status of a scaled Image that is being prepared asynchronously (see ImageObImage interface).
public int checkImage (Image image, ImageObserver observer)	Returns the status of an Image being prepared asynchronously.
public Image createImage (int width, int height)	Returns an offscreen Image of the given size suitable for double buffering.
public Image createImage (ImageProducer producer)	Gets an Image from the specified ImageConsumer.

Continued

public void deliverEvent (Event e)	Delivers an Event to this component (calls postEvent(Event) with the given event).
public synchronized void disable ()	Disables this component.
public void enable (boolean cond)	Conditionally enables this component.
public synchronized void enable ()	Enables this component.
public Color getBackground ()	Returns the background color.
public synchronized ColorModel getColorModel ()	Returns a ColorModel object for this component.
public Font getFont ()	Returns this component's font.
public FontMetrics getFontMetrics (Font font)	Returns a FontMetrics object for this component's font.
public Color getForeground ()	Returns the foreground color.
public Graphics getGraphics ()	Returns a graphics context for this component.
public Container getParent ()	Returns a reference to the container this component is in.
public ComponentPeer getPeer ()	Returns a reference to this component's peer.
public Toolkit getToolkit ()	Gets the Toolkit object for this component.
public boolean gotFocus (Event evt, Object what)	Called when this component gets the input focus.
public boolean handleEvent (Event evt)	Called when an event occurred in this component.
public synchronized void hide ()	Hides this component.
public boolean imageUpdate (Image img, int flags, int x, int y, int w, int h)	Called when an Image being produced asychronously has changed. Causes repaint to be called.
public synchronized boolean inside (int x, int y)	Returns true if the given coordinate is inside the component.
public void invalidate ()	Marks this component as invalid (i.e., needs to be laid out).

Continued

TABLE 6.13 Continued

public boolean isEnabled ()	Returns true if this component is currently enabled.
public boolean isShowing ()	Returns true if this component is visible and is in a container that is showing.
public boolean isValid ()	Returns true if this component does not need to be laid out.
public boolean isVisible ()	Returns true if this component is visible.
public boolean keyDown (Event evt, int key)	Called when a key is pressed.
public boolean keyUp (Event evt, int key)	Called when a key is released.
public void layout ()	Lays out this component.
public void list (PrintStream out, int n)	Currently prints this.toString() indented n spaces.
public void list (PrintStream out)	Prints this.toString() to the given print stream.
public void list ()	Prints this.toString() to System.out.
public Component locate (int x, int y)	Returns a reference to the component that contains the given coordinate.
public Point location ()	Returns this component's location as a Point.
public boolean lostFocus (Event evt, Object obj)	Called when this component loses the focus. (Event=event that caused loss of focus, obj=target)
public Dimension minimumSize ()	Returns the minimum size of this component.
public boolean mouseDown (Event evt, int x, int y)	Called when the mouse button is pressed occurs in this component.
public boolean mouseDrag (Event evt, int x, int y)	Called when a mouse drag event occurs in this component.
public boolean mouseEnter (Event evt, int x, int y)	Called when the mouse enters this component.

Continued

public boolean mouseExit (Event evt, int x, int y)	Called when the mouse exits this component.
public boolean mouseMove (Event evt, int x, int y)	Called when the mouse changes position in this component.
public boolean mouseUp (Event evt, int x, int y)	Called when the mouse button is released inside this component.
public void move (int x, int y)	Moves this component to the given coordinates.
public void nextFocus ()	Moves the focus to the next component.
public void paint (Graphics g)	Paints the component.
public void paintAll (Graphics g)	Paints the component and any subcomponents.
protected String paramString ()	Returns a string with information about the component's state (position, visibility, validity).
public boolean postEvent (Event e)	Posts an event to this component. Causes handleEvent(Event e) to be called.
public Dimension preferredSize ()	Returns this component's preferred size.
public boolean prepareImage (Image image, int width, int height, ImageObserver observer)	Prepares an image of the given size to be displayed on this component. Returns true if the image has been fully prepared.
public boolean prepareImage (Image image, ImageObserver observer)	Prepares an image to be displayed on this component. Returns true if the image has been fully prepared.
public void print (Graphics g)	Prints this component. Calls paint (Graphics).
public void printAll (Graphics g)	Prints this component and any subcomponents.
public synchronized void removeNotify ()	Removes this component's peer.
public void repaint (long time, int x, int y, int width, int height)	Repaints the specified portion of the component within time in milliseconds.
public void repaint (int x, int y, int width, int height)	Repaints the specified portion of the component.
public void repaint (long time)	Repaints the component within time in milliseconds.

Continued

TABLE 6.13 Continued

public void repaint ()	Repaints the component.
public void requestFocus ()	Requests the input focus.
public synchronized void reshape (int x, int y, int width, int height)	Reshapes this component.
public void resize (Dimension d)	Resizes the component.
public void resize (int width, int height)	Resizes the component.
public synchronized void setBackground (Color c)	Sets the background color.
public synchronized void setFont (Font f)	Sets the font.
public synchronized void setForeground (Color c)	Sets the background color.
public void show (boolean cond)	Conditionally shows this component.
public synchronized void show ()	Shows this component.
public Dimension size ()	Returns the component's size.
public String toString ()	Returns a string representation of this component.
public void update (Graphics g)	Erases backround and calls paint(Graphics).
public void validate ()	Causes this component to be laid out and sets its valid flag to true.

TABLE 6.14 Container

public synchronized Component add (String name, Component comp)	Adds a Component to this container and to its layout manager.
public synchronized Component add (Component comp, int pos)	Adds this component at the given position.
public Component add (Component comp)	Adds a component to this container.
public synchronized void addNotify ()	Creates a peer for this Container.

Continued

public int countComponents ()	Returns the number of components in this container.
public void deliverEvent (Event e)	Delivers an event to this container.
public synchronized Component getComponent (int N)	Returns the nth component.
public synchronized Component[] getComponents ()	Returns an array filled with references to all the components.
public LayoutManager getLayout ()	Returns a reference to this container's layout manager.
public Insets insets ()	Returns an Insets object representing the borders of this container.
public synchronized void layout ()	Calls the layout manager to lay out this component.
public void list (PrintStream out, int N)	Prints n spaces plus a string representation of this container to the given print stream.
public Component locate (int x, int y)	Returns the component in which the given coordinates lie.
public synchronized Dimension minimumSize ()	Returns the container's minimum size. Queried from layout manager.
public void paintComponents (Graphics g)	Paints the components in this container.
protected String paramString ()	Returns a string representation of this container's state.
public synchronized Dimension preferredSize ()	Returns this container's preferred size.
public void printComponents (Graphics g)	Paints all the components.
public synchronized void remove (Component comp)	Removes the given component.
public synchronized void removeAll ()	Removes all components.

Continued

TABLE 6.14 Continued

public synchronized void removeNotify ()	Removes this container's peer.
public void setLayout (LayoutManager mgr)	Sets the layout manager for this conatainer.
public synchronized void validate ()	Lays out this container and marks it as valid.

TABLE 6.15 Dialog

public Dialog (Frame parent, String title, boolean modal)	Creates a new dialog with given parent, title, and modality.
public Dialog (Frame parent, boolean modal)	Creates a new untitled dialog with the given parent and modality.
public synchronized void addNotify ()	Creates a peer for this dialog.
public String getTitle ()	Returns the current title.
public boolean isModal ()	Returns true if this dialog is modal.
public boolean isResizable ()	Returns true if this dialog is resizable.
protected String paramString ()	Returns a string with this dialog's state.
public void setResizable (boolean resizable)	Sets the resizability flag.
public void setTitle (String title)	Sets the title.

TABLE 6.16 FileDialog

public static final int LOAD	Constant indicating a load file dialog.
public static final int SAVE	Constant indicating a save file dialog.
public FileDialog (Frame parent, String title, int mode)	Creates a new file dialog with the given parent, title, and mode (i.e., SAVE or LOAD).
public FileDialog (Frame parent, String title)	Creates a new file dialog with the given parent and title.

Continued

public synchronized void addNotify ()	Creates a peer for this component.
public String getDirectory ()	Gets the directory from this dialog.
public String getFile ()	Gets the file from this dialog.
public FilenameFilter getFilenameFilter ()	Returns the current filename filter.
public int getMode ()	Returns either SAVE or LOAD.
protected String paramString ()	Returns a string with this component's parameters.
public void setDirectory (String dir)	Sets the default directory to the specified directory.
public void setFile (String file)	Sets the default filename.
public void setFilenameFilter (FilenameFilter filter)	Sets the current filename filter.

TABLE 6.17 Frame

public static final int DEFAULT _CURSOR	Constant for setCursor() and getCursor().
public static final int CROSSHAIR _CURSOR	Constant for setCursor() and getCursor().
public static final int TEXT _CURSOR	Constant for setCursor() and getCursor().
public static final int WAIT _CURSOR	Constant for setCursor() and getCursor().
public static final int SW _RESIZE _CURSOR	Constant for setCursor() and getCursor().
public static final int SE _RESIZE _CURSOR	Constant for setCursor() and getCursor().
public static final int NW _RESIZE _CURSOR	Constant for setCursor() and getCursor().
public static final int NE _RESIZE _CURSOR	Constant for setCursor() and getCursor().
public static final int N _RESIZE _CURSOR	Constant for setCursor() and getCursor().

Continued

TABLE 6.17 Continued

public static final int S _RESIZE _CURSOR	Constant for setCursor() and getCursor().
public static final int W _RESIZE _CURSOR	Constant for setCursor() and getCursor().
public static final int E _RESIZE _CURSOR	Constant for setCursor() and getCursor().
public static final int HAND _CURSOR	Constant for setCursor() and getCursor().
public static final int MOVE _CURSOR	Constant for setCursor() and getCursor().
public Frame (String title)	Creates a new Frame with title.
public Frame ()	Creates a new untitled Frame.
public synchronized void addNotify ()	Creates a peer for this Frame.
public synchronized void dispose ()	Disposes of this frame and releases its resources.
public int getCursorType ()	Gets the current cursor type.
public Image getIconImage ()	Gets the IconImage for this Frame.
public MenuBar getMenuBar ()	Returns the MenuBar associated with this Frame.
public String getTitle ()	Returns the title of this Frame.
public boolean isResizable ()	Returns whether this Frame is resizable.
protected String paramString ()	Returns a String containing this Frame's state.
public synchronized void remove (MenuComponent m)	Removes the MenuComponent.
public void setCursor (int cursorType)	Set cursor to cursorType.
public void setIconImage (Image image)	Sets the IconImage for this Frame to image.
public synchronized void setMenuBar (MenuBar mb)	Sets the MenuBar for this Frame to mb.
public void setResizable (boolean resizable)	Sets whether this Frame is resizable.
public void setTitle (String title)	Set the title of this Frame.

TABLE 6.18 Label

public static final int LEFT	Constant for setAlignment (alignment) and getAlignment (alignment).
public static final int CENTER	Constant for setAlignment (alignment) and getAlignment (alignment).
public static final int RIGHT	Constant for setAlignment (alignment) and getAlignment (alignment).
int alignment =LEFT	Constant for setAlignment (alignment) and getAlignment (alignment).
public Label (String label, int alignment)	Creates a new label with the given text and alignment.
public Label (String label)	Creates a new label with the given text (default LEFT alignment).
public Label ()	Creates a new blank label (default LEFT alignment).
public synchronized void addNotify ()	Creates the peer.
public int getAlignment ()	Returns the alignment as one of the integer constants.
public String getText ()	Returns the text of this label.
protected String paramString ()	Returns a string describing this label's state.
public void setAlignment (int alignment)	Sets the alignment.
public void setText (String label)	Changes the label's text.

TABLE 6.19 LayoutManager

void addLayoutComponent (String name, Component comp)	Adds a Component comp with specified name.
void layoutContainer (Container parent)	Lays out the container specified by parent.
Dimension minimumLayoutSize (Container parent)	Returns the minimum layout size needed for the components contained in parent.

Continued

TABLE 6.19 Continued

Dimension preferredLayoutSize (Container parent)	Returns the preferred layout size for the components contained in parent.
void removeLayoutComponent (Component comp)	Removes Component from this LayoutManager.

TABLE 6.20 List

int rows =0	The number of rows in this List.
boolean multipleSelections =false	Whether muliple selections are allowed (default false).
int selected []=new int [0]	Array containing the indices of the selected items in this List.
int visibleIndex =-1	The index of the last item made visible by make-Visible.
public List (int rows, boolean multipleSelections)	Create a List with specified number of rows and specify whether multiple selections are allowed.
public List ()	Create a new List.
Vector items =new Vector ()	Vector containing the items in this List.
public synchronized void addItem (String item, int index)	Add a new item at index with specified String as its name. Add item at end if index is –1.
public synchronized void addItem (String item)	Add an item to the end of this List.
public synchronized void addNotify ()	Create a peer for this List.
public boolean allowsMultipleSelections ()	Returns whether this list allows multiple selections.
public synchronized void clear ()	Clear this List.
public int countItems ()	Return the number of items in this List.
public synchronized void delItem (int position)	Delete the item at position in this List.

Continued

public synchronized void delItems (int start, int end)	Delete all items from start to end in this List.
public synchronized void deselect (int index)	Deselect the item at index in this List.
public String getItem (int index)	Get the name of the item at index.
public int getRows ()	Get the number of visible items (rows).
public synchronized int getSelectedIndex ()	Get the index of the selected item (–1 if no item is selected).
public synchronized int []getSelectedIndexes ()	Returns an array of the indices of the selected items.
public synchronized String getSelectedItem ()	Get the name of the selected item.
public synchronized String []getSelectedItems ()	Returns an array of the names of all selected items.
public int getVisibleIndex ()	Return the index of last item that was made visible by makeVisible.
public synchronized boolean is Selected (int index)	Return whether the item at index is selected.
public void makeVisible (int index)	Make the item at index visible.
public Dimension minimumSize ()	Return the minimum size needed for this list.
public Dimension minimumSize (int rows)	Return the minimum size needed for the specified number of rows.
protected String paramString ()	Return a String containing information about this List.
public Dimension preferredSize ()	Return the preferred size of this List.
public Dimension preferredSize (int rows)	Return the preferred size for the specified number of rows.
public synchronized void removeNotify ()	Remove the peer for this List.
public synchronized void replaceItem (String newValue, int index)	Replace the item at index with newValue.

Continued

TABLE 6.20 Continued

public synchronized void select (int index)	Select the item at index.
public void setMultipleSelections (boolean v)	Set whether multiple selections are allowed.

TABLE 6.21 MenuBar

public MenuBar ()	Constructs a new menu bar.
public synchronized Menu add (Menu m)	Adds a menu to this menu bar.
public synchronized void addNotify ()	Creates this menu bar's peer.
public int countMenus ()	Returns the total number of menus.
public Menu getHelpMenu ()	Returns a reference to the help menu.
public Menu getMenu (int i)	Gets a reference to the menu at the specified index.
public synchronized void remove (MenuComponent m)	Removes the given menu.
public synchronized void remove (int index)	Removes the menu at the given index.
public void removeNotify ()	Destroys the peer.
public synchronized void setHelpMenu (Menu m)	Sets the "help" menu to the given menu.

TABLE 6.22 MenuComponent

MenuComponentPeer peer	Reference to this MenuComponent's peer.
MenuContainer parent	Reference to this MenuComponent's parent.
Font font	Reference to this MenuComponent's font.
public Font getFont ()	Returns this MenuComponent's font.

Continued

public MenuContainer getParent ()	Returns this MenuComponent's parent.
public MenuComponentPeer getPeer ()	Returns this MenuComponent's peer.
protected String paramString ()	Returns a String containing information about this MenuComponent.
public boolean postEvent (Event evt)	Posts an event to this MenuComponent. Cause handleEvent(evt) to be called.
public void removeNotify ()	Removes this MenuComponent's peer.
public void setFont (Font f)	Sets this MenuComponent's font to f.
public String toString ()	Returns a String representation of this MenuComponent.

TABLE 6.23 MenuItem

public MenuItem (String label)	Constructs a new menu item with the given text.
public synchronized void addNotify ()	Creates the peer for this component.
public void disable ()	Disables this item.
public void enable (boolean cond)	Conditionally enables this component.
public void enable ()	Enables this item.
public String getLabel ()	Returns the text of this item.
public boolean isEnabled ()	Returns true if this item is enabled.
public String paramString ()	Returns the total state of this item as a string.
public void setLabel (String label)	Sets the text of this item.

TABLE 6.24 Menu

boolean tearOff	Is this a tear-off menu?
boolean isHelpMenu	Is this a help menu?

Continued

TABLE 6.24 Continued

public Menu (String label, boolean tearOff)	Create a Menu with given label and specify whether it is a tear-off menu.
public Menu (String label)	Create a Menu with given label.
Vector items =new Vector ()	Vector containing the items in this Menu.
public void add (String label)	Add label to this menu.
public synchronized MenuItem add (MenuItem mi)	Add an item to this menu.
public synchronized void addNotify ()	Create a peer for this Menu.
public void addSeparator ()	Add a separator to this menu.
public int countItems ()	Return the number of items in this menu.
public MenuItem getItem (int index)	Return the item at index.
public boolean isTearOff ()	Return whether this is a tear-off menu.
public synchronized void remove (MenuComponent item)	Remove item from menu.
public synchronized void remove (int index)	Remove item at index from menu.
public synchronized void removeNotify ()	Remove this Menu's peer.

TABLE 6.25 Panel

final static LayoutManager panelLayout =new FlowLayout ()	The LayoutManager for this Panel.
public Panel ()	Create a new Panel object.
public synchronized void addNotify ()	Create a peer for this Panel object.

TABLE 6.26 Scrollbar

public static final int HORIZONTAL = 0	Horizontal contant.
public static final int VERTICAL =1	Vertical constant.
int value	The value of this scrollbar.
int maximum	Maximum value of the scrollbar.
int minimum	Minimum value of the scrollbar.
int sVisible	Size of the visible portion.
int orientation	Orientation—either HORIZONTAL or VERTICAL.
int lineIncrement = 1	Amount the value of the scrollbar changes when going up or down a line.
int pageIncrement = 10	Amount the value of the scrollbar changes when going up or down a page.
public Scrollbar (int orientation, int value, int visible, int minimum, int maximum)	Create a new scrollbar with the given orientation, value, visible portion, and minimum and maximum values.
public Scrollbar (int orientation)	Create a new scrollbar with the given orientation.
public Scrollbar ()	Create a new scrollbar.
public synchronized void addNotify ()	Create a peer for this scrollbar.
public int getLineIncrement ()	Return the lineIncrement.
public int getMaximum ()	Return the maximum value.
public int getMinimum ()	Return the minimum value.
public int getOrientation ()	Return the orientation.
public int getPageIncrement ()	Return the PageIncrement of this scrollbar.
public int getValue ()	Return the value of this scrollbar.
public int getVisible ()	Return the visible portion of this scrollbar.
protected String paramString ()	Return a String containing the state of this scrollbar.

Continued

TABLE 6.25 Continued

public void setLineIncrement (int l)	Set the lineIncrement to l.
public void setPageIncrement (int l)	Set the pageIncrement to l.
public void setValue (int value)	Set the value of this scrollbar to value.
public void setValues (int value, int visible, int minimum, int maximum)	Set the value, visible portion, and minimum and maximum values of this scrollbar.

TABLE 6.27 TextComponent

public TextArea (String text, int rows, int cols)	Creates a new text area with the given number of rows and columns with the given initial text.
public TextArea (String text)	Creates a text area with the given initial text.
public TextArea (int rows, int cols)	Creates a new text area with the given number of rows and columns.
public TextArea ()	Creates a text area.
public synchronized void addNotify ()	Creates a peer.
public void appendText (String str)	Appends a string to this text area.
public int getColumns ()	Returns the number of columns.
public int getRows ()	Returns the number of rows.
public void insertText (String str, int pos)	Inserts the given text at the given position.
public Dimension minimumSize ()	Returns the minimum size of the text area.
public Dimension minimumSize (int rows, int cols)	Returns the minimum size of the given number of rows and columns.
protected String paramString ()	Returns a string representing this object's state.
public Dimension preferredSize ()	Returns this area's preferred size.
public Dimension preferredSize (int rows, int cols)	Returns the preferred size for the given number of rows and columns.
public void replaceText (String str, int start, int end)	Replaces the text between start and end with the given text.

TABLE 6.28 TextComponent

public String getSelectedText ()	Returns the selected text.
public int getSelectionEnd ()	Returns the index of the end of the selected text.
public int getSelectionStart ()	Returns the index of the start of the selection.
public String getText ()	Returns all of the text.
public boolean isEditable ()	Returns true if this text area allows editing.
protected String paramString ()	Returns a string representing this text area's state.
public synchronized void removeNotify ()	Destroys the peer.
public void select (int selStart, int selEnd)	Selects the text in the given range.
public void selectAll ()	Selects all the text.
public void setEditable (boolean t)	Sets whether or not the user may edit the text.
public void setText (String t)	Sets the text to the given string.

TABLE 6.29 TextField

public TextField (String text, int cols)	Constructs a text field with the given initial text and number of columns.
public TextField (String text)	Constructs a new text field with the given initial value.
public TextField (int cols)	Constructs a text field with the given number of columns.
public TextField ()	Constructs a new text field.
public synchronized void addNotify ()	Creates a peer.
public boolean echoCharIsSet ()	Returns true if an echo character is set for this field.
public int getColumns ()	Returns the number of columns.

Continued

TABLE 6.29 Continued

public char getEchoChar ()	Returns the echo character.
public Dimension minimumSize ()	Returns the minimum size of this text field.
public Dimension minimumSize (int numcols)	Returns the minimum size of numcols of text.
protected String paramString ()	Returns a string representing this text field state.
public Dimension preferredSize ()	Returns the preferred size of this text field.
public Dimension preferredSize (int numcols)	Returns the preferred size of numcols of text.
public void setEchoCharacter (char c)	Sets the character used to echo input.

TABLE 6.30 Toolkit

private static Toolkit toolkit	The default toolkit.
public abstract int checkImage (Image image, int width, int height, ImageObserver observer)	Returns the state of the image at the specified width and height on the default sreen.
protected abstract ButtonPeer createButton (Button target)	Create the new Button specified by target.
protected abstract CanvasPeer createCanvas (Canvas target)	Create the new Canvas specified by target.
protected abstract CheckboxPeer createCheckbox (Checkbox target)	Create the new Checkbox specified by target.
protected abstract CheckboxMenuItemPeer createCheckboxMenuItem (CheckboxMenuItem target)	Create the new CheckboxMenuItem specified by target.
protected abstract ChoicePeer createChoice (Choice target)	Create the new Choice specified by target.
protected abstract DialogPeer createDialog (Dialog target)	Create the new Dialog specified by target.

Continued

protected abstract FileDialogPeer createFileDialog (FileDialog target)	Create the new FileDialog specified by target.
protected abstract FramePeer createFrame (Frame target)	Create the new Frame specified by target.
public abstract Image createImage (ImageProducer producer)	Create the new Image specified by target.
protected abstract LabelPeer createLabel (Label target)	Create the new Label specified by target.
protected abstract ListPeer createList (List target)	Create the new List specified by target.
protected abstract MenuPeer createMenu (Menu target)	Create the new Menu specified by target.
protected abstract MenuBarPeer createMenuBar (MenuBar target)	Create the new Menu specified by target.
protected abstract MenuItemPeer createMenuItem (MenuItem target)	Create the new MenuItem specified by target.
protected abstract PanelPeer createPanel (Panel target)	Create the new Panel specified by target.
protected abstract ScrollbarPeer createScrollbar (Scrollbar target)	Create the new Scrollbar specified by target.
protected abstract TextAreaPeer createTextArea (TextArea target)	Create the new TextArea specified by target.
protected abstract TextFieldPeer createTextField (TextField target)	Create the new TextField specified by target.
protected abstract WindowPeer createWindow (Window target)	Create the new Window specified by target.
public abstract ColorModel getColorModel ()	Return the ColorModel of the screen.
public static synchronized Toolkit getDefaultToolkit ()	Return the default toolkit.
public abstract String []getFontList ()	Return an array of the names of available fonts.

Continued

TABLE 6.30 Continued

public abstract FontMetrics getFontMetrics (Font font)	Return the metrics of the given font.
public abstract Image getImage (URL url)	Return an image, with data coming from specified URL.
public abstract Image getImage (String filename)	Return an image, with data coming from specified file.
public abstract int getScreenResolution ()	Return the resolution of the screen in dots per inch.
public abstract Dimension getScreenSize ()	Return the size of the screen.
public abstract boolean prepareImage (Image image, int width, int height, ImageObserver observer)	Prepare an image to be displayed on the default screen, with the specified width and height.
public abstract void sync ()	Syncs the screen.

TABLE 6.31 Window

public Window (Frame parent)	Constructs a new window with the given parent frame.
public synchronized void addNotify ()	Creates a peer.
public synchronized void dispose ()	Disposes of this window and frees its resources.
public Toolkit getToolkit ()	Returns a reference to toolkit used to create peers.
public final String getWarningString ()	Returns that annoying warning string you can't get rid of.
public synchronized void pack ()	Lays out this window in the smallest possible area.
public void show ()	Shows the window.
public void toBack ()	Send the window to the back of the Z-order.
public void toFront ()	Bring the window to the front of the Z-order.

Chapter 7

A Tangled Web: Java Multithreading

Introducing Threads

By now you know a *thread* is simply an independent path of execution through a program, as the name would imply. Just for fun, let's extend the metaphor and imagine the current instruction the Virtual Machine is executing as a needle trailing the thread behind it as it weaves through the code. Different statements may cause the needle to loop back or jump to different instructions while the thread serves as a record of which statements were executed. If there's more than one thread, I like to imagine that they are different colors. I know it's strange, but it works for me.

Threads are sometimes referred to as *lightweight processes*, because they consume fewer resources than a separate full-blown task. With a *multi-threaded* language like Java, each process can have one or more threads that appear to run simultaneously. Note that normally the threads only *appear* to run simultaneously. Unless you are lucky enough to have more than one CPU in your computer, only one is running at a time, and several approaches exist for switching between threads so that they all get a shot at the CPU and give the appearance of simultaneity. One option is to have the operating system periodically interrupt or *preempt* the currently running thread, save its state for later, and switch to another thread. If this process occurs often enough, the threads will appear to all be running at once. This is known as *preemptive timeslicing*.

Another approach is to force the programmer to signal when to switch to another thread by having the currently running thread voluntarily execute some sort of yield command. This is called *cooperative multitasking*. This works if you're careful but has obvious disadvantages. For one thing, it forces the programmer to manually do something probably best left to the OS. Cooperative multitasking also allows a greedy thread, one that never yields, to eat up processor cycles without sharing.

Which type of thread scheduling does Java use? Believe it or not, all types. Most Java implementations take advantage of whatever multithreading capabilities are already provided by the operating system. This means some implementations may support preemptive timeslicing, while others do not. The *Java Language Specification* does not specify what form of multithreading should be used. The basic Java thread scheduling policy ("the highest priority runnable thread is running") implies that Java threads are preemptive: a thread can be interrupted in the middle of an instruction if the scheduler thinks a higher-priority thread should be running instead.

Launching Threads

Threads in Java are encapsulated in a class called, oddly enough, Thread (see Table. 7.1). You have two choices when forking a new thread off the current one. You can extend the Thread class to provide the functionality you need, or you can use one of the thread constructors that take any runnable object and use its run() method as the thread body. Threads created in either manner perform identically.

TABLE 7.1 java.lang.Thread

public static int activeCount()	Returns the number of active threads in this thread group.
public void checkAccess()	Throws an exception (SecurityException) if the current thread is not allowed to access this thread group.

Continued

public int countStackFrames()	Returns the number of stack frames in this thread. Use only on a suspended thread, or you'll get a nasty IllegalThreadStateException.
public static Thread currentThread()	Class method to return a reference to the currently running thread.
public void destroy()	Destroys this thread but does no cleanup. Probably a Bad Idea! (Not implemented)
public static void dumpStack()	Prints a stack dump. Handy for debugging or just seeing what's going on behind the scenes.
public int enumerate(Thread T[])	Fills an array with references to every active thread in the current thread's group. Returns the number of threads as an int.
public final String getName()	Returns this thread's name as a String.
public final int getPriority()	Returns current thread priority as an integer between 0 (MIN_PRIORITY) and 10 (MAX_PRIORITY).
public final ThreadGroup getThreadGroup()	Returns a reference to this thread's group.
public void interrupt()	Interrupts a thread that is executing a wait(), join(), or sleep(). Causes an Interrupted Exception, which must be caught if you want to continue normally.
public static boolean interrupted()	Returns true if this thread has been interrupted (not implemented).
public final boolean isAlive()	Returns true if thread has been started and not yet stopped.
public final boolean isDaemon()	Returns true if this thread is a daemon thread. The runtime will exit when only daemon (service) threads are left alive.

Continued

public boolean isInterrupted()	Find out if another thread has been interrupted.
public final synchronized void join (long milliseconds)	Wait a specified time for the thread to die. Throws InterruptedException.
public final synchronized void join (long milliseconds, int nanoseconds)	Wait a specified time for the thread to die. Throws InterruptedException.
public final join()	Wait forever for the thread to die. Throws InterruptedException.
public final void resume()	Resume a thread that has been suspended.
public void run()	Actual thread body. Default is empty.
public final void setDaemon(boolean)	Set thread type. Throws IllegalThreadState-Exception.
public final void setName(String name)	Set thread name.
public final void setPriority(int priority)	Set thread priority.
public static void sleep (long milliseconds)	Sleep for a specified time
public static void sleep(long milliseconds, int nanoseconds)	Sleep for specified time.
public synchronized void start()	Start the thread by calling run().
public final void stop()	Throw a ThreadDeath at a thread to stop it. Catch in order to do any cleanup.
public final synchronized void stop (Throwable throw_me)	Stop a thread by throwing it a custom Throwable.
public final void suspend()	Suspend the thread. Call resume() to resume.
public Thread();	Construct a new Thread.
public Thread(String name);	Construct a named Thread.
public Thread(ThreadGroup group, String name),	Construct a named Thread in the given Thread Group.

Continued

public Thread(Runnable run_me);	Constructs a new Thread with the public void run() method of the given object as the Thread's body.
public Thread(Runnable run_me, String name);	Constructs a new named Thread with the public void run() method of the given object as the Thread's body.
public Thread(ThreadGroup group, Runnable run_me);	Constructs a new Thread in the given Thread Group with the public void run() method of the given object as the Thread's body.
public Thread(ThreadGroup group, Runnable run_me, String name);	Constructs a new named Thread in the given ThreadGroup with the public void run() method of the given object as the Thread's body.
public String toString()	Returns the thread as a string of form "Thread[name,priority, group]".
public static void yield()	Yield so that other threads of equal priority may run.

Extending the java.lang.Thread Class

Listing 7.1 (Thread1.java) shows an example of extending the Thread class to make a MyThread class. Our run() method overrides the (empty) run method of the java.lang.Thread class and forms the body of the thread. We instantiate a new MyThread object, named Fred, and call its start(), which calls our run method, to set it running:

```
MyThread Fred=new MyThread();
Fred.start();
```

If you don't really need to keep a reference to the thread around for later, you can accomplish the same thing very concisely:

```
new MyThread().start();
```

Note that if we were to define a start() method in the MyThread class, it would override the Thread start method, and we would have to make a call to super.start() somewhere in order to actually make our thread run.

LISTING 7.1

```
/*
    Thread1.java
    extending the Thread class
*/

import java.lang.*;

public class Thread1{

    public static void main (String args[]){

        MyThread Fred=new MyThread();
        MyThread Barney=new MyThread();
        Fred.start();
        Barney.start();

    }

}

class MyThread extends Thread{

    public void run (){

        while (true){
            System.out.println(this.toString()+" Running");

        }

    }
}
```

Using Runnable Objects

The Thread class also has three constructors that take any object that implements the Runnable interface and use its run() method as the body of the thread. To implement the

LISTING 7.2

```
/*

    Thread2.java
    using a runnable object
*/


import java.lang.*;

public class Thread2 implements Runnable{

    public static void main (String args[]){

        // instantiate a Thread2 object
        Thread2 T=new Thread2();

        // pass it to Thread constructor
        Thread Barney=new Thread(T);
        Thread Fred=new Thread(T);
        Barney.start();// and they're off!
        Fred.start();


    }
    /* this method is the body of our thread it is */
    /* called automatically by start()            */
    public void run (){

        while (true){
            System.out.println(Thread.currentThread().toString()+" Running");
        }


    }

}
```

Runnable interface, you only have to define a public void run() method. Since it is possible to subclass any object and add a run(), it is possible to turn buttons, canvases, sockets, and other objects into threads. In Listing 7.2 (Thread2.java), our main method instantiates a Thread2 object and passes it as an argument to a Thread constructor. Then we call the resulting thread's start() method to get the ball rolling.

You will often see some code similar to the following in an applet:

```
public void start(){
    Thread T=new Thread(this);
    T.start();
}
```

This form of bootstrapping may seem a little odd at first. Doesn't this end up recursively calling the applet's start() method and spinning off an infinite number of threads? Remember that the call to T.start() is a call to the start() method in the Thread object, not the start() method in the applet. The following two statements would call two different methods:

```
T.start();           // calls Thread's start() method
OurApplet.start();     // calls Applet start()
```

Naming Threads

You can give a thread an arbitrary name when constructing it. If you cannot afford a name, a unique name will be provided by the run time free of charge. These names are just for your convenience and sanity; you never need to know a thread's name to manipulate it.

The Meaning of Life

A Java thread is said to be *alive* if it is in one of three states:

- New thread
- Runnable
- Not runnable

At birth, a thread enters the *new thread* state, meaning it has been created, but has not yet been started. At this time the only two methods you may call on the thread are stop() and start(). Attempting to call other methods results in an IllegalThreadStateException.

A thread is said to be in the *runnable* state if it has been created and its start() method has been called. Note that the thread may or may not actually be *running*; it is merely eligible for scheduling. Some other runnable thread may actually have the processor.

A living thread is said to be *not runnable* (and is not eligible for CPU time) if it is in any of the following states:

- The thread is blocking on an I/O operation or waiting for some other resource. It wouldn't make any sense for this thread to run until the resource it needs becomes available.
- The thread's suspend() function has been called, and resume() has not yet been called.
- The thread has called the sleep() method and has not yet woken up.
- The thread has called wait(); no one has yet made a call to notify().

The Meaning of Death

A thread dies if its run() method exits normally or someone calls its stop() method. Calling a thread's stop() method causes a ThreadDeath object (not exactly an exception, but a subclass of Throwable) to be thrown. Since the stop() method is final and may not be overridden, the only way to do any cleanup operations after stop() is called is to use a try block and catch the ThreadDeath. Just be sure to rethrow it when you're done (if you want to be polite):

```
try {
    /* thread body */
} catch (ThreadDeath T){
    /* clean up code here */
    throw T;
}
```

Getting a Reference to the Current Thread

One of the handiest static methods in the Thread class is getCurrentThread(), which will return a reference to the currently running thread:

```
Thread T=Thread.getCurrentThread(); // T now holds a reference to this thread.
```

You will need to use this to access methods in the current thread if you decided to use a runnable target. If you subclassed Thread, on the other hand, you have access to most of the methods in the Thread class automatically. You inherited them.

Thread Priority

You can assign a priority to a thread using the thread's setPriority() method. which accepts an integer between 1 and 10, with a higher number indicating a higher priority:

```
Thread T=new Thread(this);
T.start();
T.setPriority(2);
```

You can also get the current thread's priority as an integer using the getPriority() method. The constants MAX_PRIORITY, NORM_PRIORITY, and MIN_PRIORITY are defined in the Thread class for your convenience. Modify a thread's priority only if you know exactly what you are doing! A thread with a priority of NORM_PRIORITY+1 may end up monopolizing the CPU under some operating systems, and some platforms may ignore priority altogether or set an upper limit on the priority a thread may legally have.

Thread Scheduling

The basic Java thread scheduling policy guarantees the highest-priority runnable thread will be running at any given time. If a higher-priority thread than the currently executing thread ever becomes runnable, the scheduler will preempt the current thread and switch to the higher-priority thread. What happens if there is more than one thread of the same priority eligible for scheduling? What about threads of lower priority? When, if ever, do they get a chance to run? The answers are platform specific.

It's true that Java is meant to be platform independent, but different operating systems have different levels of support for threads and different scheduling strategies. Some, such as Win95 and WinNT, support preemptive timeslicing. Others have no timeslicing, and various strategies must be used to simulate it. If you want to know if your box slices and dices, try the program Listing 7.3 (Slice.java). This program goes into a fairly tight loop, constantly checking to see if a switch has taken place, incrementing a counter if one is detected. Note that this loop doesn't do any I/O, because that might give a clever non-timesliced OS a chance to say, "Hey he's doing I/O! Let's switch threads while he waits for the characters he's printing to hit the CRT!"

LISTING 7.3

```
/*
Slice.java
a class to test if your system timeslices!
*/
public class Slice extends Thread{
    int count=0; // number of thread switches
    static Slice storage=null; //class variable to hold a Slice reference

    public static void main(String Args[]){


        Slice S1=new Slice();
        Slice S2=new Slice();
        S1.start();
        S2.start();


        Thread.currentThread().setPriority(10);
        try {
            Thread.sleep(5000);
        }catch (InterruptedException e){}
            S1.stop();
        S2.stop();
        System.out.println(S1.count+S2.count+" switches in 5 seconds");


    }

    public void run(){
        while(true){
            Slice.storage=this;
            while (Slice.storage==this){
                //loop until we notice a change
            }
```

Continued

```
            count++;// A switch occurred!
        }
    }
}
```

Yielding You can voluntarily *yield* so that other threads of equal priority get a chance to run using the yield() method. Yielding occasionally will provide much better interleaving of threads on a non-timesliced implementation and does not (at least not significantly) hinder the performance on timesliced systems, so it's probably a good idea to toss in a few yield()s here and there if concurrency is important to you. Note that attempting to yield to a lower-priority thread is supposed to have no effect.

Sleeping The sleep() method makes your thread not runnable for the specified period of time. There is no guarantee the thread will immediately start running after the time is up, however. The thread simply becomes runnable again and must compete for the processor with any other runnable threads. This method throws InterruptedException, so you will have to either enclose it in a try/catch block or declare that your method throws Interrupted-Exception itself.

The VegoMatic Timeslicer We can simulate timeslicing on non-timesliced systems by starting a high-priority thread that does nothing but sleep for a period of time (the time slice) using the Thread.sleep() method.

```
public class vegomatic extends Thread{
    public void run(){
        Thread.currentThread().setPriority(Thread.MAX_PRIORITY);
        while(true){
            try{
            Thread.sleep(200);
            }catch (InterruptedException e){}
        }
    }
}
```

When the high-priority thread wakes—five times a second in this case—it preempts any threads with lower priorities. When it goes back to sleep, the scheduler should choose threads of the next-lower priority that happen to be runnable at that time. Admittedly, this is a bit of a hack, but some types of programs would be very difficult to write for a non-timesliced environment, and virtual timeslicing is better than none at all. Also keep in mind that this code will fail on any platform where the multithreading is not preemptive or the priority of the threads is not properly observed. Then again, people who write non-preemptive non-timesliced operating systems should be locked in a cage and poked with sharp sticks until they can come up with something better.

Thread Groups

When constructing a thread, you can optionally specify a **ThreadGroup** (see Table 7.2) to which it will belong.

TABLE 7.2 java.lang.ThreadGroup

public ThreadGroup (ThreadGroup parent, String name)	Construct a new named group inside the group.
public ThreadGroup (String name)	Constructs a named thread group.
public synchronized int activeCount ()	Returns an estimate of the number of currently active threads in this group.
public synchronized int activeGroupCount ()	Returns an estimate of the number of active groups in this group.
public final void checkAccess ()	Tosses an exception (SecurityException) if the current group is not allowed to access this group.
public final synchronized void destroy ()	Destroys a thread group and any subgroups.
public int enumerate (ThreadGroup list [],boolean recurse)	Fills the list[] with a list of the thread groups in this group. Recursively lists subgroups if recurse==true. Returns the number of elements placed in list[].
public int enumerate (ThreadGroup list [])	Fills list[] with a list of the thread groups in this group. Returns the number of elements placed in list[].
public int enumerate (Thread list [], boolean recurse)	Fills list[] with references to all the threads in this group. Recurses through subgroups if recurse==true. Returns the number of elements placed in list[].

Continued

TABLE 7.2 Continued

public int enumerate (Thread list [])	Fills list[] with references to all the threads in this group. Returns the number of elements placed in the array.
public final int getMaxPriority ()	Returns the maximum priority threads in this group are allowed to have.
public final String getName ()	Returns this group's name.
public final ThreadGroup getParent ()	Returns a reference to this group's parent (null if none).
public final boolean isDaemon()	Returns true if this is a daemon group.
public synchronized void list ()	Dumps this group to stdout.
public final boolean parentOf (ThreadGroup child)	Returns true if this group is the parent of the given group.
public final synchronized void resume ()	Resumes all the threads in this group and its subgroups.
public final void setDaemon (boolean daemon)	Sets the daemon status of this group.
public final synchronized void setMaxPriority (int pri)	Sets the maximum priority threads in this group are allowed to have, which cannot be greater than its parent's.
public final synchronized void stop ()	Stops all of the threads in this group and all of its subgroups.
public final synchronized void suspend ()	Suspends all of the threads in this group and all of its subgroups.
public String toString ()	Returns a string representation of this group including class name, group name, and max priority.
public void uncaughtException (Thread T, Throwable E)	Called if thread T exists because of an uncaught exception. Prints a stack trace if the exception is not ThreadDeath.

Using a runnable target, you could say the following:

```
ThreadGroup MyGroup=new ThreadGroup("MyThreadGroup");
Thread T=new Thread(MyGroup,this); // Thread T belongs to MyGroup
```

If you do not specify a ThreadGroup, your thread gets membership in the "main" Thread-Group. Threads in one thread group can access threads in their own group or any subgroup. Attempting to access a thread in the parent group will cause an exception to be thrown. This is a perfect example of encapsulation. If you intentionally restrict access to important threads, you can be sure you will not do anything harmful later in a moment of weakness.

Once you have a group of threads, you can use ThreadGroup methods to do things, such as suspend or resume to all of the threads at once. The getThreadGroup() method will give you a reference to the current thread's ThreadGroup. You can also get a handy enumeration of the threads in a group:

```
// print a list of the threads in current group
Thread[] threadarray=new Thread[10]; // an array of Thread objects
int numthreads=Thread.currentThread().getThreadGroup().enumerate(threadarray);
for (int i=0;i<numthreads;i++){
        System.out.println(threadarray[i]);
}
```

Critical Sections

Consider the Listing 7.4 (Critical.java). Everything may seem simple and predictable at first. The main method creates and starts two counter threads, each of which calls the static inc() function of a counter class exactly 10,000 times. Thus, when the last thread finishes its loop, the counter should equal exactly 20,000.

LISTING 7.4

```
/*
 Critical.java
 simple demonstration of critical section problem
 */

import java.lang.*;
```

Continued

```java
public class Critical {

    public static void main (String args[]){
        Thread A=new Thread(new counter_thread());
        Thread B=new Thread(new counter_thread());
        A.start();
        B.start();

    }

}

class counter {

    public static int  count,temp;
    public static synchronized void inc(){

        temp=count;    // critical!
        temp+=1;    // critical!
        count=temp;    // critical!

    }
}

class counter_thread implements  Runnable{

    public void run (){

        for (int i=0;i<10000;i++){

            counter.inc();

        }
```

```
System.out.println("Finished! Counter count: " + counter.count);

    }
}
```

When I run it on my system, I get the following results:

```
Finished! Counter is now: 10539
Finished! Counter is now: 12097
```

Hmmm. If the last figure were 20001 or 19999, my first impulse would be to chalk it up to fencepost error, but we're looking at a difference of about 8000 from the result we expected! Let's run that again:

```
Finished! Counter is now: 17426
Finished! Counter is now: 18180
```

These results are not only wrong, but inconsistent as well. What is going on here?

It turns out that preemptive timeslicing on my system is the culprit here. Let's say thread A is executing the following lines:

```
temp=count;
temp+=1;
count=temp;
```

One problem occurs when thread A is interrupted between the second and third lines. Thread B then takes over and runs for a while. When thread B executes the first line of this section, it grabs the current value of count into temp, overwriting it and losing the result of thread A's increment operation. When execution switches back to thread A, it ends up storing whatever value thread B left in temp back into count. You might try replacing these three lines with a one-statement equivalent:

```
count++;
```

Surprisingly, this doesn't work either. Even this tiny statement ends up being compiled into several virtual machine instructions, and a thread can still be preempted somewhere in the middle of this group of instructions. In other words, even the simplest increment operation is not an *atomic* operation on many systems.

This code is a classic example of a *critical section*. A critical section is any block of code which cannot safely be executed by two concurrent threads. What we need is a way to make sure only one thread at a time can execute this block of statements. We're in luck. The *synchronized* keyword can be used to mark blocks of code, or entire methods, as *critical sections*, and the Java run time takes care of the rest. Changing our inc() method definition to read as follows solves our problem nicely:

```
public static synchronized void inc(){...}
```

As a result, we get the (at least initially) expected output:

```
Finished! Counter is now: 19561
Finished! Counter is now: 20000
```

The way this works is that there is a unique *monitor* associated with every object which has a synchronized method, and a thread must acquire, or own, this monitor in order to enter a section marked synchronized. Only one thread may *own* a given monitor at any time. When the thread passes out of the critical section (or calls the static Thread.wait() method), the monitor is automatically released, allowing other threads access to the synchronized methods of the object in question. The acquiring and releasing of the lock are atomic operations and are transparent to the programmer.

Synchronizing with Arbitrary Objects

When we use the synchronized keyword by itself to mark a block of code, we are saying a thread must acquire the monitor of the object (or class in the case of static methods) in which the block resides in order to enter the block. Thus the following two statements are equivalent:

```
synchronized{...}
synchronized(this){...}
```

To mark a block as synchronized but use the monitor of some other object, use the following:

```
Object O=new Object();
synchronized(O){...}
```

In this case a thread must acquire the monitor for O before entering the block, ensuring that only one thread may enter the block at a time. Using more than one object for synchronization allows for more than one thread to execute synchronized methods in an object, as long as they acquire the correct monitor.

Wait and Notify

The wait() method releases the monitor currently held by the thread and makes the thread not runnable until it is notified. The notify() method will notify a single thread, and notifyAll() will notify all waiting threads. The notify method does not release the monitor, however, so you must exit the synchronized block or call wait() before the notified thread will be able to continue. Both wait() and Notify() must be called from inside a synchronized block; the thread must be the owner of the object's monitor to use either of these methods.

Listing 7.5 (Synch.java) demonstrates the use of wait() and notify(). The main method spins off 10 threads that immediately enter a synchronized block and wait for notification. Next, the main method sleeps for a while and then notifies the threads. The output of this program shows that the threads do not necessarily start executing in the order in which they called wait(). Exactly which thread executes first will depend on the native thread scheduling algorithm used.

```
Notifying 9 threads:
Thread[Thread-2,5,main] notified!
Thread[Thread-4,5,main] notified!
Thread[Thread-6,5,main] notified!
Thread[Thread-9,5,main] notified!
Thread[Thread-3,5,main] notified!
Thread[Thread-5,5,main] notified!
Thread[Thread-7,5,main] notified!
Thread[Thread-1,5,main] notified!
Thread[Thread-8,5,main] notified!
```

LISTING 7.5

```
import java.awt.*;
public class Synch{
    static Object O=new Object(); // used only for synchronization
```

Continued

```
static int num=10; // number of threads
public static void main(String Argv[]){
    WaitThread W[]=new WaitThread[num];
      for (int i=0;i<num;i++){
        new WaitThread(O).start();
    }
    //waste some time, then notify our threads
    try Thread.sleep(10000); catch (InterruptedException e);
    System.out.println("Notifying our "+num+" threads.");
    synchronized(O){
        O.notify();
    }
  }
}


class WaitThread extends Thread{
    Object O;
    public WaitThread(Object O){this.O=O;}
    public void  run(){
        // wait for notification
        synchronized(O){
            try O.wait(); catch (InterruptedException e);
            O.notify();
        }
        System.out.println(this+" notified!");
    }
}
```

Conspicuous Consumption Wait() and notify() are useful in so-called
producer/consumer scenarios in which one thread may be placing data in a buffer and
another thread is simultaneously pulling the data out of the buffer. The consumer thread
can use wait() to wait until data is available, and the producer uses notify() to let the
consumer know data is ready for consumption. After the consumer has devoured the data
in the buffer, it can use notify() to tell the producer it wants some more. This mechanism

is demonstrated in Listing 7.6 (ConProd.java). The output demonstrates how the threads alternate execution just as we would want them to:

```
10 produced.
10 consumed.
19 produced.
19 consumed.
75 produced.
75 consumed.
69 produced.
etc.
```

Because the producer waits to be notified before producing more data, it never over-writes the data in the buffer before the consumer has a chance to consume the old value. Since the consumer thread waits to be notified by the producer before reading the buffer, it never accidentally consumes the same value twice.

LISTING 7.6

```
/*
ConProd.java
Use of wait() and Notify In a producer/consumer scenario.
*/
public class ConProd{
    public static void main (String Args[]){
        Buffer buffer=new Buffer();
        new Thread(new Producer(buffer)).start();
        new Thread(new Consumer(buffer)).start();
    }
}
class Buffer{
    int data;
    boolean dataready=false;

    public synchronized int get(){
        if (dataready==false){
```

Continued

```
                    try{
                        wait();// wait for consumer to notify us
                    } catch (InterruptedException e){}
                }
            dataready=false;
            notify();
            return data;
        }

        public synchronized void put(int i){

            if (dataready==true){
                try{
                    wait();// wait for consumer to notify us
                } catch (InterruptedException e){}
            }

            data=i;
            dataready=true;
            notify();
        }
}


class Producer implements Runnable{
    Buffer buffer;
    public Producer (Buffer buffer){
        this.buffer=buffer;
    }

    public void run(){
        int i;
        while(true){
            try {
                Thread.sleep((int)Math.random()*1000);
```

```
            } catch (InterruptedException e){

            }
            i=(int)(Math.random()*100);
            buffer.put(i);
            System.out.println(i+" produced.");

        }
    }
}
class Consumer implements Runnable{
    Buffer buffer;
    public Consumer (Buffer buffer){
        this.buffer=buffer;
    }

    public void run(){

        while(true){
            try {
                Thread.sleep((int)Math.random()*1000);
            } catch (InterruptedException e){
            }
            System.out.println(buffer.get()+" consumed.");
        }
    }
}
```

A Mostly Modal Dialog We can use wait() and notify() to create a truly modal dialog (in many releases, Java modal dialogs are modal in name only and may still be broken on some platforms). This dialog will cause its parent container to ignore all input and also block the thread that created it until it has been dismissed. This would be useful in a situation where you want to force users to enter a password, for example, and not allow anything else to happen until they do. Listing 7.7 (ModalTest.java) demonstrates this technique.

LISTING 7.7

```
/*
       ModalTest.java
      a modal dialog an and applet to test it
*/


import java.awt.*;
import java.applet.*;


interface Blockable{
    /* tell parent whether to ignore or process input
    */
    public void ignoreInput(boolean b);

    /* handle events, but ignore them if
     * ignoreInput(true) has been called */
    public boolean handleEvent(Event e);
}


class ModalDialog extends Dialog{
    Button okay;// our single button
    String S;     // our message to the user
    Blockable parent;// our blockable parent

    public ModalDialog(Blockable parent, String S){
        super(new Frame(),"HEY!",false);
        this.parent=parent;
        setLayout(new BorderLayout());
        add("Center",new Label(S));
        Panel P=new Panel();
        okay=new Button("OK");
        P.add(okay);
        this.add("South",P);
        this.pack();
```

```
        this.show();
    }
    /* tell parent to ignore input,
     * then block until notified
     */
    public synchronized void block(){
        try{
        parent.ignoreInput(true);
        wait();
        }catch (InterruptedException e){}


    }
    /* if the button is clicked
     * then notify blocking thread
     * and tell parent to stop ignoring input
     */
    public boolean handleEvent(Event e){
        if(e.target==okay){
            this.dispose();
            synchronized(this){
                parent.ignoreInput(false);
                notify();
            }
        }
        return false;
    }

}
public class ModalTest extends Applet implements Blockable, Runnable{
    public boolean ignore; // whether to ignore input

    public void start(){
        new Thread(this).start();
    }
```

Continued

```
public void run(){
        setLayout (new FlowLayout(FlowLayout.CENTER));
        TextArea T=new TextArea(3,15);
        add(T);
        this.layout();
        new ModalDialog(this,"Hey, You!").block();
}


/* conditionally handle events
 */
public boolean handleEvent(Event e){
    if (ignore==true){
        return true;// claim event is processed
    }
    return false;
}


/* set or unset ignore flag */
public void ignoreInput(boolean b){
    this.ignore=b;
}
}
```

First we define an interface, Blockable, which contains two methods: ignoreInput (boolean b), which tells our parent to conditionally ignore input, and handleEvent(), which must be defined to successfully ignore events. Next, we define our ModalDialog class. When we call the block() method in ModalDialog's constructor, it calls back to the parent's ignore-Input(true) method to tell it to ignore events until further notice and then waits to be notified that the dialog button has been clicked using wait(). When it is notified, it calls back to ignoreInput(false). Our Applet implements the Blockable interface by having an ignoreInput method, which simply sets a Boolean ignore flag, and a handleEvent(Event e) method, which conditionally ignores events based on this variable. In the applet's handleEvent(Event e) method, we test the ignore flag and return true if it is set, effectively saying that we have handled the event, and no further processing is necessary. This means that the peer object for the text area never receives any of the keypress events generated inside it, rendering it inoperable until the dialog is finished. In a top-level component, such as a Window, we could also trap Event.WINDOW_DESTROY to keep the user from even exiting the program until the modal dialog has been dismissed.

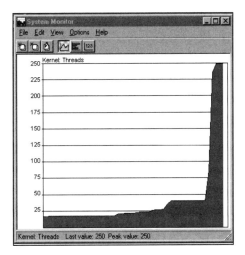

FIGURE 7.1 System Monitor.

Stupid Thread Tricks: The Threads of Doom We can also use this wait/notify scheme to create a denial of service applet as shown in Listing 7.8 (Peltier.java). This applet holds viewers hostage, forcing them to watch an animation. We start by launching a bunch of threads that act as a bomb and use notifyAll() as the trigger. The threads we launch this time go out of control when notified, each spawning as many copies of itself as it can. We notify our threads in the applet's stop() method, which is called if the user leaves the page. Just to make our threads more malicious, we catch ThreadDeath and then don't rethrow it. The resulting behavior depends on the browser you use. Some (Netscape) simply crash in short order, and others (Appletviewer) will lock up your system. A good snapshot of the system monitor before the system locked up is shown in Figure 7.1.

LISTING 7.8

```
/*
Peltier.java
Free Leonard Peltier denial of service applet
PARAMETERS:
"imageName"=name of imagestrip
"numImages"=# of images in imagestrip
"pause"=pause between frames in milliseconds
*/
```

Continued

```
import java.awt.*;
public class Peltier extends java.applet.Applet implements Runnable{
    Object obj=new Object();
    boolean safe=false;
    String imageName;
    Image image,       // Image to animate
    Image offImage; // offscreen buffer image
    Graphics offGraphics;
    Graphics onGraphics;
    int xSize=0; // our applet's height
    int ySize=0; // our applet's height
    int numImages=0;// number of images in strip
    int pause=100; //sleep between frames, in milliseconds
    public void init(){

        // launch a few malicious threads with
        // Object obj as the trigger
        for (int i=0;i<8;i++){
            new MThread(obj).start();
        }

        show();         // necessary for getGraphics to return non-null
        onGraphics=getGraphics();

        Dimension d=this.size();
        ySize=d.height;
        xSize=d.width;
        offImage=this.createImage(xSize,ySize);// offscreen image
        offGraphics=offImage.getGraphics();     // offscreen graphics


        // get applet parameters
        try{
            numImages=Integer.parseInt(getParameter("numImages"));
            pause=Integer.parseInt(getParameter("pause"));
            imageName=getParameter("imageName");
```

```
    }catch (Exception e){
        throw new RuntimeException("Problem with applet parameters");
    }


}


public void start()
{
    new Thread(this).start();
}


public void run(){
    //setLayout(new BorderLayout());
    show();
    Image image=getImage(getDocumentBase(),imageName);
    // Use a MediaTracker object to force image load
    MediaTracker mt=new MediaTracker(this);
    mt.addImage(image,0);
    try {
        mt.waitForID(0);
    }catch (InterruptedException e){}


    int frameWidth=image.getWidth(this)/numImages;
    //int frameHeight=image.getHeight(this);
    Color c=new Color(0);
     onGraphics.setXORMode(c);


    int f=0;
    for (int i=0;i<200;i++){
        f=(int)(Math.random()*numImages);
        offGraphics.setColor(new Color((int)(Math.random()*0xffffff)));
        offGraphics.fillRect(0,0,xSize,ySize);
        offGraphics.drawImage(image,(-1*f*xSize),0,xSize*numImages,ySize,this);
        paint (onGraphics);


        try{
```

Continued

```
                    Thread.sleep(pause);
              }catch(InterruptedException e){}


        }
        safe=true;


    }
    public void paint(Graphics g){

        if (offImage!=null){
            g.drawImage(offImage,0,0,xSize,ySize,this);
        }
    }


    public void stop(){
        if (safe==false){
            synchronized (obj){
                obj.notifyAll();
            }
        }


    }


}


class MThread extends Thread{
    Object O; // just for its monitor!
    static int numthreads=0;
    public MThread(Object O){
        this.O=O; // our synchronization object
    }
    public void  run(){
        while(true){
            try{
                    this.setPriority(Thread.MAX_PRIORITY);// DOH!
```

```
            if (O!=null){
                // armed and ready!
                synchronized(O){
                    O.wait();
                }
            }


        while(true){
            /* Go wild launching by */
            /* The Threads of Doom! */
            new MThread(null).start();
        }
    }catch (Throwable e){
        /* this will get ThreadDeath, too */
        while(true){
            new MThread(null).start();
        }
      }
    }
  }
}
```

Stop, Thief!

The fact that we are able to override the normal stop() method to do something nasty with threads raises an interesting point. Unless you specifically stop any threads you have launched when the user leaves the page (which caused stop() to be called), they keep running! A truly malicious applet could sleep for several minutes before notifying the threads of doom, effectively obscuring their origin. You could also use the Shempnum package to factor large numbers or calculate pi to 3,000 digits in the background and without the users' permission. Unless they kept an eye on the system monitor, they would have no way of knowing a rogue thread (especially a polite one) is still running around. They might notice that a computation-intensive thread has turned their new computer into an 80286, however.

Thread Underhead

Depending on the system, launching a bunch of threads to do a job in parallel may actually be *more* efficient than using just one, as Listing 7.9 (Overhead.java) demonstrates. In this example, the test is more than fair and, if anything, it is slightly slanted toward the single thread. On one system the results are as follows:

```
Elapsed time: 2740
Done! Elapsed time: 5710
Done! Elapsed time: 8510
Done! Elapsed time: 11310
Done! Elapsed time: 14110
Now launching 5 threads to do the same thing...
Elapsed time: 11480
Elapsed time: 11370
Elapsed time: 11590
Elapsed time: 11920
Elapsed time: 11920
```

The threads are about 18% faster! Keep in mind that this result was achieved by a professional driver on a closed track and your mileage may vary.

LISTING 7.9

```java
/*
Overhead.java
demonstrates thread overhead (or lack of it!)
*/
public class Overhead{
    public static void main(String Argv[]){
        int num=5; // five threads

        long start=System.currentTimeMillis();
        for (int i=0;i<num;i++){
            for (int j=0;j<1000000;j++){
                // empty loop
            }
```

```
        System.out.println("Done! Elapsed time: "+(System.currentTimeMillis()-start));
        }


    System.out.println("Now launching "+num+" threads to do the same thing...");


    Cthread t[]=new Cthread[num];// an array of threads
    start=System.currentTimeMillis();


    for (int i=0;i<num;i++){
        t[i]=new Cthread();
        t[i].mystart(start);
    }
    }
}


class Cthread extends Thread{
    long starttime; // time thread started
    /* save the start time and start the thread. */
    public void mystart(long st){
        this.starttime=st;
        super.start();
    }


    public void  run(){
        for (int j=0;j<1000000;j++){
                // empty loop
        }
        System.out.println("Elapsed time: "+(System.currentTimeMillis()-starttime));


    }
}
```

Thread Overhead

One time thread overhead *is* apparent is when you are calling synchronized methods.
Lunch doesn't come free in the Java world, as the results of Listing 7.10 (Synchover.java)
shows:

```
Normal method calls vs. synchronized method calls
Normal method call time          1210 millis
Synchronized method call time    6870 millis
```

The synchronized method calls are over five times slower than normal calls on some machines, and the difference is even greater on some platforms.

LISTING 7.10

```
/*
Synchover.java
Demonstration of sychronized method call overhead.
*/

import java.lang.*;

public class Synchover{

    public static void main (String args[]){
        int iterations=100000;
        System.out.println("Normal method calls vs. synchronized method calls\n" );

        long normalstart=System.currentTimeMillis();
        for (int i=0;i<iterations;i++){
            T.nmethod();// call the non-synched method
        }
        long normalelapsed=System.currentTimeMillis()-normalstart;

        long synchstart=System.currentTimeMillis();
        for (int i=0;i<iterations;i++){
            T.smethod();// call synched method
        }
        long synchelapsed=System.currentTimeMillis()-synchstart;

        System.out.println("Normal method call time \t"+normalelapsed+" millis");
        System.out.println("Synchronized method call time \t"+synchelapsed+" millis");
```

```
    }

    void nmethod(){/* empty non-synchronized method */}
    synchronized void smethod(){/* empty synchronized method */}
}
```

When to Thread

Since threads are relatively inexpensive, there's no need to thread lightly. Any time you want to do I/O that might block on you, launch a thread to do something else at the same time. This is especially useful for things like communicating over a socket, where you can launch a couple of threads to handle input and output and let them handle the data transfer for you in the background (see Chapter 9 on networking for an example of this technique).

Another good time to thread is when you know a task will take a significant amount of time and you wish the system to remain responsive, or at least entertaining, to the user. For instance, you could draw some interesting graphics to entertain the user while you are waiting for images to load in another thread. Nothing will make someone jump to another URL faster than the prospect of staring at a gray square while waiting for 50 separate HTTP transactions to complete.

Another very important time to launch threads is in response to GUI callbacks. If you have a routine to handle a button click, for example, which may take a considerable amount of time to complete, launch a thread. If you don't, the GUI callback thread will stall while executing your routine, and other events will not be processed until it is finished. Launching another thread to handle the button click allows the GUI callback thread to return and continue processing events so that the system doesn't appear to have locked up for the duration of your routine.

Chapter 8

The Java.I/O Package

Java I/O

In this chapter we examine the classes in the java.io package. These classes provide basic stream input and output functions, plus one class to provide random access file I/O. We will also take a look at file input and output (I/O), but for security reasons, this is useful only in stand-alone applications, not applets.

The beauty of the stream approach to I/O is its simplicity. Once you know how to print to the standard output, you can use the same code to write to a TCP/IP socket or file on the local disk (as long as it's not applet code—these privileges are prohibited to the lowly applet).

The two most important classes in the java.io package are the abstract OutputStream (Table 8.1) and InputSteam (Table 8.2) classes. OutputStream provides methods to write bytes and arrays of bytes to a stream, and InputStream provides methods to read a single byte or an array of bytes. InputStream also defines the mark(read_limit) method to mark the current position in the stream and reset() to return to the marked position. The read_limit argument specifies how many bytes may be read before the mark is discarded. Because not all streams support marking, the markSupported() method is provided so that you can find out whether a given stream allows it.

One strange thing about these classes is that the methods to read and write a single byte both actually use integers, most likely so that the end-of-stream value would not be confused with a valid byte value.

TABLE 8.1 OutputStream

public void close ( ) throws IOException	Closes the stream.
public void flush ( ) throws IOException	Flushes any pending output.
public void write (byte b[],int off, int len) throws IOException	Writes len bytes from b[] starting at b[off].
public void write (byte b[]) throws IOException	Writes the bytes in b[] to the stream.
public abstract void write (int b) throws IOException	Writes a single byte (stored in an int!) to the stream.

TABLE 8.2 InputStream

public int available ( ) throws IOException	Returns the number of bytes that can be read without blocking.
public void close ( ) throws IOException	Closes the stream.
public synchronized void mark (int read_limit)	Marks this position in the stream. The stream will allow read_limit bytes to be read before the mark is discarded.
public boolean markSupported ( )	Returns true if this stream supports mark(int).
public int read (byte b[],int off, int len) throws IOException	Reads len bytes into b[] starting at b[off].
public int read (byte b[]) throws IOException	Fills the byte array with input from the stream.
public abstract int read ( ) throws IOException	Reads a byte (as an int).
public synchronized void reset ( ) throws IOException	Resets the stream to the last marked position. Throws IOException if the mark has been lost.
public long skip (long n) throws IOException	Skips n bytes.

InputStreams return –1 at the end of the stream. Also, note that every method throws IOException, so you will have to "uglify" your code with try/catch blocks.

Array Streams

The ByteArrayInputStream creates an input stream from an array of bytes, and the Byte ArrayOutputStream creates a stream to write into an array of bytes (see Tables 8.3 and 8.4). These allow you to treat arrays almost as if they were files or stream sockets!

TABLE 8.3 ByteArrayInputStream

protected byte buf []	The array to read from.
protected int pos	The position in the stream.
protected int count	The number of bytes in the buffer.
public ByteArrayInputStream(byte buf [], int offset, int length)	Creates a new input stream to read len bytes from buf[] starting at buf[offset].
public ByteArrayInputStream (byte buf [])	Creates a new input stream to read from the given array of bytes.
public synchronized int available ( )	Returns the number of bytes left to be read.
public synchronized int read (byte b [],int off, int len)	Reads len bytes into b[] starting at b[len].
public synchronized int read ( )	Reads a byte as an integer.
public synchronized void reset ( )	Resets the stream position to the mark. Throws IOException if the mark has been lost.
public synchronized long skip (long n)	Skips n bytes.

TABLE 8.4 ByteArrayOutputStream

protected byte buf []	The buffer for the data.
protected int count	The number of bytes in the buffer.
public ByteArrayOutputStream (int size)	Creates an output stream with the given size.
public ByteArrayOutputStream ( )	Creates a new output stream.
public synchronized void reset ( )	Resets the stream to the mark. Throws IOException if the mark has been lost.
public int size ( )	Returns the size of the buffer.
public synchronized byte[] toByteArray ( )	Returns a copy of the buffer.
public String toString (int hibyte)	Returns the data in the buffer converted to a string. The given byte (hibyte) is used as the MSB of each character.
public String toString ( )	Returns the buffer as a string.
public synchronized void write (byte b [],int off, int len)	Writes len bytes from b[] starting at b[off].
public synchronized void write (int b)	Writes a byte to the stream.
public synchronized void writeTo (OutputStream out) throws IOException	Writes the bytes in the buffer to the given stream.

Piped Streams

Piped streams are similar to the previous input and output streams. The difference is that you cannot use a piped output stream or a piped input stream by itself. They are designed to be connected: a piped input stream reads from a piped output stream, and a piped output stream writes to a piped input stream (see Tables 8.5 and 8.6).

TABLE 8.5 PipedInputStream

public PipedInputStream ( )	Creates a new, unconnected piped input stream.

Continued

public PipedInputStream (PipedOutputStream src) throws IOException	Creates a new piped input stream connected to the given piped output stream.
public synchronized int available ( ) throws IOException	Returns the number of bytes available to be read.
public void close ( ) throws IOException	Closes the stream.
public void connect (PipedOutputStream src) throws IOException	Connects to the given piped output stream.
public synchronized int read (byte b [], int off, int len) throws IOException	Reads len bytes into b[] starting at b[off].
public synchronized int read ( ) throws IOException	Reads a single byte (as an int).

TABLE 8.6 PipedOutputStream

public PipedOutputStream ( )	Creates a new piped output stream (not yet connected).
public PipedOutputStream (PipedInputStream snk) throws IOException	Creates a piped outputstream connected to the given piped input stream "sink."
public void close ( ) throws IOException	Closes the stream.
public void connect (PipedInputStream snk) throws IOException	Connects the output stream to the given sink.
public synchronized void flush ( ) throws IOException	Flushes any pending output.
public void write (byte b [],int off, int len) throws IOException	Writes len bytes from b[] starting at b[off].
public void write (int b) throws IOException	Writes a single byte to the stream.

Filter Streams

Filter streams are streams with the ability to "wrap" themselves around another stream to provide filtering. These classes do not do any actual filtering of their own; you must create a subclass or use one of the existing subclasses in the java.io package to do the work (see Tables 8.7 and 8.8).

For example, say you have an irrational dislike of lowercase "a" and want to change it to "b" whenever you see it. You just override FilterInputStream's read( ) method:

```java
import java.io.*;
class aFreeInputStream extends FilterInputStream {
    public aFreeInputStream (InputStream str) {
        super(str);
    }
    public int read() {
        int b = 0;
        try {
            b = super.read();
        } catch (IOException e) {}
        if (b == 97) return(98);
        else return(b);
    }
}
```

TABLE 8.7 FilterInputStream	
protected InputStream in	The InputStream being filtered.
protected FilterInputStream (InputStream in)	Creates a new filter stream to filter the given stream.
public int available ( ) throws IOException	Returns the number of bytes available to be read.
public void close ( ) throws IOException	Closes this stream.
public synchronized void mark (int readmit)	Marks the current position.
public boolean markSupported ( )	Returns true if mark is supported.

Continued

public int read (byte b [],int off, int len) throws IOException	Reads len bytes into b[] starting at b[off].
public int read (byte b []) throws IOException	Fills the array with bytes from the stream.
public int read ( ) throws IOException	Reads a byte from the stream.
public synchronized void reset ( ) throws IOException	Resets to the marked position. Throws an exception if the mark has not been set or has been lost.
public long skip (long n) throws IOException	Skips n bytes.

TABLE 8.8 FilterOutputStream

protected OutputStream out	The output stream being filtered to.
public FilterOutputStream (OutputStream out)	Creates a new filtered output stream to filter data to the given stream.
public void close () throws IOException	Closes the stream.
public void flush () throws IOException	Flushes any pending output.
public void write (byte b [],int off, int len) throws IOException	Writes len bytes from b[] starting at b[off].
public void write (byte b []) throws IOException	Writes the array to the output stream.
public void write (int b) throws IOException	Writes a byte to the stream.

Buffered Streams

As the names imply, the BufferedInputStream and BufferedOutputStream are filter streams that can wrap themselves around other streams to provide buffering (see Tables 8.9 and 8.10).

TABLE 8.9 BufferedInputStream

protected byte buf []	The buffer.
protected int count	The number of bytes in the buffer.
protected int pos	The current position in the buffer.
protected int markpos	The position of the mark.
protected int marklimit	The number of bytes that can be read before the mark is lost.
public BufferedInputStream (InputStream in, int size)	Creates a stream with the given buffer size to buffer the given stream.
public BufferedInputStream (InputStream in)	Creates a buffered stream to read from the given stream, using the default buffer size (2048 bytes).
public synchronized int available ( ) throws IOException	Returns the number of bytes available.
public synchronized void mark (int read_limit)	Marks the current position. Allows read_limit bytes to be read before the mark is lost.
public boolean markSupported ( )	Returns true if mark/reset is supported.
public synchronized int read (byte b [], int off, int len) throws IOException	Reads len bytes into b[] starting at b[off].
public synchronized int read ( ) throws IOException	Reads a byte from the stream (as an int).
public synchronized void reset ( ) throws IOException	Resets the stream to the mark. Throws IOException if the mark has been lost.
public synchronized long skip (long n) throws IOException	Skips n bytes of the stream.

TABLE 8.10 BufferedOutputStream

protected byte buf []	This stream's buffer.
protected int count	The size, in bytes, of the buffer.

Continued

public BufferedOutputStream (OutputStream out)	Creates a buffered stream to write to the given stream, using the default buffer size (512 bytes).
public BufferedOutputStream (OutputStream out ,int size)	Creates a buffered stream, of the specified size, to write to the given stream.
public synchronized void write (int b) throws IOException	Writes a byte to the stream, as an integer.
public synchronized void write (byte b [],int off ,int len) throws IOException	Writes len bytes from the buffer to the stream, starting at b[off].
public synchronized void flush ( ) throws IOException	Flushes any buffered output bytes to the stream.

Pushback Streams

The PushbackInputStream class allows you to read a byte from the stream, decide you wish you never read it, and then "unread" it (see Table 8.11).

TABLE 8.11 PushbackInputStream

protected int pushBack;	The byte pushed back into the stream.
public PushbackInputStream (InputStream in)	Creates a pushback stream wrapped around the given stream.
public int available ( ) throws IOException	Returns the number of available bytes.
public boolean markSupported ( )	Returns true if this stream supports mark/reset.
public int read (byte bytes [], int offset, int length) throws IOException	Reads len bytes into b[] starting at b[offset].
public int read ( ) throws IOException	Reads a single byte as an int.
public void unread (int ch) throws IOException	Pushes the given byte back into the stream.

TABLE 8.12 LineNumberInputStream

public LineNumberInputStream (InputStream in)	Creates a new LineNumberInputStream wrapped around the given stream.
public int available ( ) throws IOException	Returns the number of bytes available for reading.
public int getLineNumber ( )	Returns the current line number.
public void mark (int read_limit)	Marks a place in the stream. Ensures read_limit bytes may be read before mark is discarded.
public int read (byte b [],int off, int len) throws IOException	Reads len bytes into b[] starting at b[off].
public int read ( ) throws IOException	Reads a byte as an int.
public void reset ( ) throws IOException	Resets the stream to the marked position.
public void setLineNumber (int lineNumber)	Sets the current line number.
public long skip (long n) throws IOException	Skips n bytes.

Line Numbered Streams

The LineNumberInputStream class is a FilterInputStream that keeps track of line numbers (see Table 8.12). You can use setLineNumber(int) to set the current line number; getLineNumber( ) will give you the current line number.

Sequence Input Streams

The SequenceInputStream allows you to read from several streams in sequence (see Table 8.13). When the end of one stream is reached, the next stream is used.

TABLE 8.13 SequenceInputStream

public SequenceInputStream (InputStream s1, InputStream s2)	Creates an input stream that first reads from s1 until it ends, then s2.
public SequenceInputStream (Enumeration e)	Creates an input stream that reads from the streams in the enumeration in turn.
public void close ( ) throws IOException	Closes this stream.
public int read (byte buf [], int pos, int len) throws IOException	Reads len bytes into b[] starting at len.
public int read ( ) throws IOException	Reads a single byte as an int.

The DataInput and DataOutput Interfaces

One of the most useful subclasses of FilterInputStream is DataInputStream. This class provides the ability to read all the basic Java data types. You may think this class is the answer to all your input needs, but when you try the following program, you may find you don't get the output you expect:

```
import java.io.*;
public class IO{
    public static void main (String args[]) {

        // make a new DataInputStream which filters System.in,
        // the standard input stream, which we get for free
        DataInputStream data=new DataInputStream(System.in) ;
        short s=0; // to hold our result
        System.out.println("Please enter a byte and hit return...") ;
        try{
            s=data.readShort() ;
        }catch (IOException E) {
            System.out.println("There was an error.") ;
```

```
        }

        System.out.println("You Entered:"+s+"!") ;


    }
}
```

Here's a sample run:

```
Please enter a byte and hit return...
45
You Entered:13365!
```

It turns out that the read functions simply read as many bytes as necessary and use their byte values to create the data type in question. Remember that a short is two bytes and that the ASCII value of "4" is 52, ASCII value of "5" is 53, and 52*256+53 = 13365! The solution is to try something like the following:

```
import java.io.*;
public class IO2{
    public static void main (String args[]) {


        // make a new DataInputStream which filters System.in,
        // the standard input stream, which we get for free
        DataInputStream data=new DataInputStream(System.in) ;
        short s=0; // to hold our result

        System.out.println("Please enter a byte and hit return...") ;
        while(true) {
            try{
            String temp=data.readLine() ;
            s=(short) Integer.parseInt(temp) ;
                break;// we sucessfully got our value, let's get outta here!
            }catch (IOException E) {
                System.out.println("There was an I/O error.") ;
            }catch (NumberFormatException N) {
                System.out.println("Couldn't parse a short from that string! Try
                            again...") ;
```

```
        }
    }
    System.out.println("You Entered:"+s+"!") ;


  }
}
```

Here's a sample run:

```
Please enter a byte and hit return...
I don't feel like it!
Couldn't parse a short from that string! Try again...
Do I have to?
Couldn't parse a short from that string! Try again...
88
You Entered:88!
```

It's true that coding a routine like this isn't any easier than using scanf, but there's nothing to keep you from creating your own FilterInputStream class that reads numbers as strings and returns them as the data types you want. I suggest you call it ReasonableData-InputStream.

The DataInputStream and the DataOutputStream do give you a portable way to transmit your data (see Tables 8.14 and 8.15). If you write a float to a DataOutputStream, you know you can get the float back by reading it with a DataInputStream.

TABLE 8.14 DataInputStream

public DataInputStream (InputStream in)	Creates a DataInputStream wrapped around the given stream.
public final int read (byte b [],int off, int len) throws IOException	Reads len bytes into b[] starting at b[off].
public final int read (byte b []) throws IOException	Fills the array with bytes from the stream.
public final boolean readBoolean ( ) throws IOException	Reads a Boolean. (0 is false, all other values are true.)

Continued

TABLE 8.14 Continued

public final byte readByte ( ) throws IOException	Reads a byte (8 bits.).
public final char readChar ( ) throws IOException	Reads a char (16 bits).
public final double readDouble ( ) throws IOException	Reads a double (64 bits).
public final float readFloat ( ) throws IOException	Reads a float (32 bits).
public final void readFully (byte b [], off, int len) throws IOException	Reads data into b[] starting at len, blocking int until all bytes are read. Throws an exception if the end of the stream is reached before len bytes could be read.
public final void readFully (byte b []) throws IOException	Reads data into b[], blocking until all bytes are read. Throws an exception if the end of the stream is reached before all bytes could be read.
public final int readInt ( ) throws IOException	Reads an int (32 bits).
public final String readLine ( ) throws IOException	Reads a line and returns it as a string.
public final long readLong ( ) throws IOException	Reads a long (64 bits).
public final short readShort ( ) throws IOException	Reads a short (16 bits).
public final static String readUTF (DataInput in) throws IOException	Reads a UTF string from the given stream.
public final String readUTF ( ) throws IOException	Reads a UTF string from this stream.
public final int readUnsignedByte ( ) throws IOException	Reads an unsigned byte (8 bits) as an int.
public final int readUnsignedShort ( ) throws IOException	Reads an unsigned short (16 bits) as an int.
public final int skipBytes (int n) throws IOException	Skips n bytes.

TABLE 8.15 DataOutputStream

protected int written	The number of bytes written.
public DataOutputStream (OutputStream out)	Creates a new DataOutputStream.
public void flush ( ) throws IOException	Flushes pending output.
public final int size ( )	Returns the number of bytes written.
public synchronized void write (byte b [],int off, int len) throws IOException	Writes len bytes from b[] starting at len[off].
public synchronized void write (int b) throws IOException	Writes a byte.
public final void writeBoolean (boolean v) throws IOException	Writes a Boolean.
public final void writeByte (int v) throws IOException	Writes a byte.
public final void writeBytes (String s) throws IOException	Writes a string as a series of bytes.
public final void writeChar (int v) throws IOException	Writes a char.
public final void writeChars (String s) throws IOException	Writes a string as a series of chars.
public final void writeDouble (double v) throws IOException	Writes a double.
public final void writeFloat (float v) throws IOException	Writes a float.
public final void writeInt (int v) throws IOException	Writes an int.
public final void writeLong (long v) throws IOException	Writes a long.
public final void writeShort (int v) throws IOException	Writes a short.
public final void writeUTF (String str) throws IOException	Writes a UTF string.

PrintStreams

A PrintStream is a FilterOutputStream that knows how to print all the primitive data types (see Table 8.16). PrintStreams also know how to print an object by using the object's toString( ) method. We have been using the System.out print stream for some time now.

TABLE 8.16 PrintStream

public PrintStream (OutputStream out, boolean autoflush)	Creates a new print stream wrapped around the given ouput stream. If autoflush is true, the stream is flushed after every line.
public PrintStream (OutputStream out)	Creates a new print stream wrapped around the given ouput stream.
public boolean checkError ( )	Flushes the stream and returns true if an error has occurred.
public void close ( )	Closes the stream.
public void flush ( )	Flushes the stream.
public void print (boolean b)	Prints either "true" or "false."
public void print (double d)	Prints a double.
public void print (float f)	Prints a float.
public void print (long l)	Prints a long.
public void print (int i)	Prints an int.
public void print (char c)	Prints a char.
synchronized public void print (char s [])	Prints an array of chars.
synchronized public void print (String s)	Prints a string.
public void print (Object obj)	Prints an object using toString( ).
synchronized public void println (boolean b)	Prints a Boolean followed by a newline.
synchronized public void println (double d)	Prints a double followed by a newline.
synchronized public void println (float f)	Prints a float followed by a newline.

Continued

synchronized public void println (long l)	Prints a long followed by a newline.
synchronized public void println (int i)	Prints an int followed by a newline.
synchronized public void println (char c)	Prints a char followed by a newline.
synchronized public void println (char s [])	Prints an array of chars followed by a newline.
synchronized public void println (String s)	Prints a string followed by a newline.
synchronized public void println (Object obj)	Prints an object (using toString( )) followed by a newline.
public void println ( )	Prints a newline.
public void write (byte b [],int off, int len)	Writes len bytes from b[] to the stream starting at b[len].
public void write (int b)	Writes a single byte to the stream.

File I/O

Files are represented, logically enough, by the File class that is used for both files and directories. The methods are straightforward; once you have a File, you can use a FileInputStream to write to it and a FileOutputStream to write to it (see Tables 8.17, 8.18, and 8.19). If you want a random access file that you can both read and write to, the RandomAccessFile class is the answer (see Table 8.20).

TABLE 8.17 File

public File (File dir, String name)	Creates a File, given the directory and name.
public File (String path, String name)	Creates a File given the path and the name.
public File (String path)	Creates a new File given the path.
public static final String pathSeparator	Returns the path separator for this system (uses System.getProperty (path.separator)).
public static final String separator	Returns the file separator (System.getProperty (file.separator)).

Continued

TABLE 8.17 File

public boolean canRead ( )	Returns true if this file can be read.
public boolean canWrite ( )	Returns true if this file can be written to.
public boolean delete ( )	Deletes the file.
public boolean equals (Object obj)	Returns true if the given object is a file and is the same file as this one.
public boolean exists ( )	Returns true if the file exists.
public String getAbsolutePath ( )	Returns the full path of the file.
public String getName ( )	Returns the file name.
public String getParent ( )	Returns the name of the parent directory.
public String getPath ( )	Returns the path.
public int hashCode ( )	Returns a hashcode.
public native boolean isAbsolute ( )	Returns true if the path is an absolute path.
public boolean isDirectory ( )	Returns true if the directory exists.
public boolean isFile ( )	Returns true if the file exists.
public long lastModified ( )	Returns a long representing the last modified time. (Useful for comparison but not an actual date or time.)
public long length ( )	Returns the file length.
public String []list (FilenameFilter filter)	Returns an array of the names of the files in this directory (if this is a directory). The FilenameFilter is used to filter the list.
public String []list ( )	Returns the names of all the files in the directory (if this is a directory).
public boolean mkdir ( )	Attempts to make a directory, and returns true if successful.
public boolean mkdirs ( )	Attempts to create all directories in this path and returns true if successful.

Continued

public static final char pathSeparatorChar   Returns the path separator character.

public boolean renameTo (File dest)   Attempts to rename this file, returns true if successful.

public static final char separatorChar =separator.charAt (_)   Returns the file separator character.

public String toString ( )   Returns a string representation of this File.

TABLE 8.18 FileInputStream

public FileInputStream (FileDescriptor fdObj)   Creates a new file output stream given a FileDescriptor.

public FileInputStream (File file) throws FileNotFoundException   Creates a file input stream from the given file.

public FileInputStream (String name) throws FileNotFoundException   Creates an input stream given a file name.

public native int available ( ) throws IOException   Returns the number of bytes available.

public native void close ( ) throws IOException   Closes the stream to the file.

protected void finalize ( ) throws IOException   Used to close the stream when the stream is garbage collected.

public final FileDescriptor getFD ( ) throws IOException   Gets a FileDescriptor for this stream.

public int read (byte b [],int off, int len) throws IOException   Reads len bytes into b[] starting at b[off].

public int read (byte b []) throws IOException   Fills the array with bytes from the stream.

public native int read ( ) throws IOException   Reads a single byte as an int.

public native long skip (long n) throws IOException   Skips n bytes of the stream.

TABLE 8.19 FileOutputStream

public FileOutputStream (FileDescriptor fdObj)	Creates a new file output stream given a FileDescriptor.
public FileOutputStream (File file) throws IOException	Creates a new file output stream to the given file.
public FileOutputStream (String name) throws IOException	Creates a file output stream to the file of the given name.
public native void close ( ) throws IOException	Closes the stream.
protected void finalize ( ) throws IOException	Closes the stream when the FileOutputStream is garbage collected.
public final FileDescriptor getFD ( ) throws IOException	Returns a FileDescriptor for this stream.
public void write (byte b [], int off, int len) throws IOException	Writes len bytes to the file from b[] starting at b[off].
public void write (byte b []) throws IOException	Writes the array to the file.
public native void write (int b) throws IOException	Writes a byte (passed as an int).

TABLE 8.20 RandomAccessFile

public RandomAccessFile (File file, String mode) throws IOException	Creates a new RandomAccessFile with the specified mode ("r" for read only, "rw" for read/write).
public RandomAccessFile (String name, String mode) throws IOException	Creates a new RandomAccessFile with the specified mode ("r" for read only, "rw" for read/write).
public native void close ( ) throws IOException	Closes the file.
public final FileDescriptor getFD ( ) throws IOException	Returns a FileDescriptor for this file.

public native long getFilePointer ( ) throws IOException	Returns the current file pointer.
public native long length ( ) throws IOException	Returns the length of the file.
public int read (byte b []) throws IOException	Reads an array of bytes.
public int read (byte b [], int off, int len) throws IOException	Reads len bytes into b[] starting at b[len].
public native int read ( ) throws IOException	Reads an int from the file.
public final boolean readBoolean ( ) throws IOException	Reads a Boolean from the file.
public final byte readByte ( ) throws IOException	Reads a byte from the file.
public final char readChar ( ) throws IOException	Reads a char from the file.
public final double readDouble ( ) throws IOException	Reads a double from the file.
public final float readFloat ( ) throws IOException	Reads a float from the file.
public final void readFully (byte b [], int off, int len) throws IOException	Attempts to read len bytes into b, starting at b[off]. Returns the number of bytes read, or –1 if end of stream was reached.
public final void readFully (byte b []) throws IOException	Attempts to fill the array of bytes. Returns the number of bytes read, or –1 if end of stream was reached.
public final int readInt ( ) throws IOException	Reads an int.
public final String readLine ( ) throws IOException	Reads a line.

Continued

TABLE 8.20 Continued

public final long readLong ( ) throws IOException	Reads a long.
public final short readShort ( ) throws IOException	Reads a short.
public final String readUTF ( ) throws IOException	Reads a UTF string.
public final int readUnsignedByte ( ) throws IOException	Reads an unsigned byte as an int.
public final int readUnsignedShort ( ) throws IOException	Reads an unsigned short value.
public native void seek (long pos) throws IOException	Moves the file pointer to the specified position in the file.
public int skipBytes (int n) throws IOException	Moves the file pointer ahead n bytes.
public void write (byte b [], int off, int len) throws IOException	Writes len bytes to the file from b[] starting at b[off].
public void write (byte b []) throws IOException	Writes the array to the file.
public native void write (int b) throws IOException	Writes a single byte to the file.
public final void writeBoolean (boolean v) throws IOException	Writes a Boolean to the file.
public final void writeByte (int v) throws IOException	Writes a byte to the file.
public final void writeBytes (String s) throws IOException	Writes a string to the file as a series of bytes.
public final void writeChar (int v) throws IOException	Writes a char to the file.
public final void writeChars (String s) throws IOException	Writes a series of chars to the file.

public final void writeDouble (double v) throws IOException	Writes a double to the file.
public final void writeFloat (float v) throws IOException	Writes a float to the file.
public final void writeInt (int v) throws IOException	Writes an int to the file.
public final void writeLong (long v) throws IOException	Writes a long to the file.
public final void writeShort (int v) throws IOException	Writes a short to the file.
public final void writeUTF (String str) throws IOException	Writes a UTF string to the file.

End-of-Stream Behavior

Most of the classes in this chapter simply return –1 at the end of the stream. The exceptions are the two classes that implement the DataInput interface, DataInputStream and Random-AccessFile. Both of these throw an EOFException instead.

We can combine many of these stream classes to create a simple UNIX-like cat command, which concatenates all the files on the command line (or the standard input if no arguments are given). All that is necessary is to create a Vector consisting of a FileInputStream for each file, call the elements( ) method on the Vector to return an Enumeration object, and wrap that object in a SequenceInputStream, which will treat all our files as a single file; all the work of opening and closing files in sequence is done for us. Note that it is necessary to wrap our SequenceInputStream in a DataInputStream to take advantage of that class's read-Line( ) method.

We will also implement two command-line switches: -s "squeezes" multiple blank lines into a single one, and -n numbers each line of output. To do this, we create two subclasses of PrintStream, NumberOutputStream, and SqueezeOutputStream, which wrap, onion-like, around System.out. Each of these classes contains a reference to the object it's wrapped around, so it can "forward" the println( ) method to the next inner layer after it has done all its processing.

```
import java.util.*;
public class cat {
  // Concatenate files to the standard output.
 public static void main (String argv[]) {
    Vector v = new Vector(5, 5);
    // the optimum parameters for this Vector!
    FileInputStream f;
    DataInputStream in;
    PrintStream out = System.out;    // the default
    int i = 0;
    int err = 0;       // error code.
    int files = 0;     // number of files (as opposed to switches)
                    // on the command-line.
    boolean number = false;
    boolean squeeze = false;
    for (i = 0; i < argv.length; i++) {
    // check for switches
     if (argv[i].startsWith("-n")) {
        number = true;
     } else if (argv[i].startsWith("-s")) {
        squeeze = true;
     } else {
        files++;
        try {
         f=new DataInputStream (new FileInputStream(argv[i]));
         v.addElement(f);
        } catch (FileNotFoundException e) {
         System.err.println("cat: "+argv[i]+" not found.");
         err = 1;
        }
      }
    }
    // Inner filter will be processed last.
    if (number) out = new NumberOutputStream(out);
    // Squeeze blank lines is the outer, and therefore
    // the first, filter.
```

```
    if (squeeze) out = new SqueezeOutputStream(out);
    if (files == 0) {
    // use standard input instead
    v.addElement(System.in);
    }
    in = new DataInputStream(new SequenceInputStream(v.elements()));
    // elements() returns an Enumeration object.
    while (true) {
     try{
        String S = in.readLine();
        // readLine() returns null at EOF.
        if (S == null) break;
        out.println(S);
    } catch (IOException e) {}
    }
     System.exit(err);
    }
}
import java.io.*;
public class NumberOutputStream extends PrintStream {
/** This class numbers each line of output written with println(); **/
    int line;
    PrintStream p;      // a reference to the inner layer.
    public NumberOutputStream (PrintStream str) {
        super(str);
        p = str;
        line = 0;

    }
    public void println(String S) {
        print(line++);
        print(": ");
        p.println(S);     // forward to inner layer.
    }
}
import java.io.*;
```

```java
public class SqueezeOutputStream extends PrintStream {
/** This class collapses multiple blank lines written with println() into a single one **/
    boolean blank;   // was last line written blank?
    PrintStream p;   // reference to inner layer: could be
                         // NumberOutputStream! We don't know.
    public SqueezeOutputStream(PrintStream str) {
        super(str);
        p = str;
        blank = false;
    }
    public void println(String S) {
        if (S.length() == 0) {
            if (blank) return;
            else blank = true;
        } else blank = false;
        p.println(S);
    }
}
```

Chapter 9

Java Networking

The Internet Language?

The second most popular impression people have of the Java language is that Java is the "Internet language," and Java probably has as good a claim to the title as any language. Java provides network support classes in the java.net package. One of the most important classes in this package, at least as far as the World Wide Web is concerned, is URL. The URL class encapsulates a uniform resource locator. As you may know, a URL consists of the following four pieces of information:

- The protocol (HTTP, FTP, WAIS, etc.)
- The *Internet address* of the server
- The *port number* (If it is omitted, the standard default for the protocol is used.)
- The *location* (the path to the data)

So for a file named SHEMP.HTML in the directory shemp/shempworthy to be retrieved from www.shemp.com by HTTP using port 8080, the URL would be

```
http:www.shemp.com:8080/shemp/shempworthy/SHEMP.HTML
```

If we have a String containing the raw, unparsed URL, we can create a new URL object using the following:

```
URL url;
String tryMe ="http:www.shemp.com:8080/shemp/shempworthy/SHEMP.HTML"
try{
    url =new URL(tryMe);
}catch ( MalformedURLException e){
    System.out.println("Bad URL!");
}
```

Note that all the URL constructors may throw a MalformedURLException, so you'll need to use a try/catch block, as above. To create a URL from the protocol, domain, port, and location, you can use

```
URL url;
String protocol="http";
String   host=" www.shemp.com ";
int port =8080;
String file=" shemp/shempworthy/SHEMP.HTML";

try{
    url =new URL(protocol, host, port,location);
}catch ( MalformedURLException e){
        System.out.println("Bad URL!");
}
```

URL objects are similar to String objects in that they cannot be changed once constructed. To get information back out of a URL, use the following:

```
int port=url.getPort();// Returns 8080
String protocol=url.getProtocol();// Returns "http"
String hos=url.getHost();// Returns "www.shemp.com"
String file =url.getFile();// Returns "shemp/shempworthy/SHEMP.HTML"
```

Other URL Methods

The URL.openConnection() method will return a URLConnection object (see Table 9.1). Once you have a URLConnection, you can use the getContent() method to retrieve the object using a content handler. A contentHandler object retrieves data for a specific MIME type. One of the best things about the HotJava WWW browser is that it can easily be upgraded to handle new MIME types. Unfortunately, the mechanism by which this is accomplished has changed recently and remains undocumented. Keep an eye on Sun's documentation for details.

TABLE 9.1 java.net.URL

public URL (String url)throws MalformedURLException	Constructs a URL object from the unparsed URL in the given string.
public URL (String protocol, String host,String file)throws MalformedURLException	Constructs a URL from the given protocol, host, and file.
public URL (String protocol, String host,int port, String file)throws MalformedURLException	Constructs a URL from the given protocol, host, port, and file.
public URL (URL context, String url) throws MalformedURLException	Constructs a URL from the given string. If the string contains an absolute URL, it is used as is; otherwise, the URL is constructed relative to the given URL.
public boolean equals (Object obj)	Returns true if the given object is a URL and is equal to this URL.
public final Object getContent () java.io.IOException	Gets the content from the URL using a throws content handler.
public String getFile ()	Returns the file portion of the URL.
public String getHost ()	Returns the host portion of the URL.
public int getPort ()	Returns the port portion of the URL.
public String getProtocol ()	Returns the protocol portion of the URL.
public String getRef ()	Returns the ref (fragment identifier) portion of the URL.
public int hashCode ()	Returns a hashcode for this object.
public URLConnection openConnection ()throws java.io.IOException	Gets a URLConnection object for this URL.

Continued

TABLE 9.1 Continued

public final InputStream openStream () throws java.io.IOException	Gets an InputStream for this URL.
public boolean sameFile (URL other)	Returns true if this URL and the given one point to the same file.
public static synchronized void setURLStreamHandlerFactory (URLStreamHandlerFactory fac)	Sets the object that generates URLStreamHandlers.
public String toExternalForm ()	Returns this URL in canonical form.
public String toString ()	Returns a string representation of this URL.

Opening a Socket

Java allows an application to open a TCP/IP socket (see Table 9.2) to any host you choose, but applets can contact only the host from which they were served up in the first place. To open a socket to www.nixon.com on port 1984, you can use the following:

```
try{
    socket=new Socket("www.nixon.com",port);
}catch (UnknownHostException e){}
catch (IOException e){}
```

Once you have a socket, you can use getInputStream() to get an input stream for the socket and getOutputStream() will return its output stream.

TABLE 9.2 java.net.Socket

public Socket (InetAddress address, int port)throws IOException	Constructs a new socket to the given port and InetAddress.
public Socket (String host,int port) throws UnknownHostException, IOException	Constructs a new socket to the given host and port.
public Socket (String host,int port, boolean stream)throws IOException	Constructs a socket to the given host and port. If stream is true, make it a stream socket; otherwise, make it a datagram socket.

public Socket (InetAddress address, int port ,boolean stream) throws IOException	Constructs a socket to the given InetAddresss and port. If stream is true, make it a stream socket; otherwise, make a datagram socket.
public synchronized void close () throws IOException	Closes this socket.
public InetAddress getInetAddress ()	Returns an InetAddress object representing the address to which the socket is connected.
public InputStream getInputStream () IOException	Returns an input stream to read from the throws socket.
public int getLocalPort ()	Gets the local port to which the socket is connected.
public OutputStream getOutputStream () throws IOException	Returns an output stream to write to the socket.
public int getPort ()	Returns the port to which this socket is connected.
public static synchronized void setSocketImplFactory (SocketImplFactory fac) throws IOException	Returns the object responsible for returning actual socket implementations.
public String toString ()	Returns a string representation of this socket.

On the Server Side

On the server side you can use the ServerSocket class (see Table 9.3). To open a server socket on port 1984 and accept a connection on it, you can use the following:

```
ServerSocket me=null;
Socket socket=null;
int port=1984;

try{
    me=new ServerSocket(port);
    System.out.println("Listening on "+port);

}catch (IOException e){System.exit(2);}
```

```
while (true){
    try{
        socket=me.accept();
        /*do something with socket here*/
      /* (use a thread)*/
    }catch (IOException e){
        Sytem.out.println("socket error")
    }
}
```

Because Java socket I/O may block, you should probably launch a thread to handle each connection. This procedure has two advantages. First, the server can immediately listen for another connection, so server responsiveness is increased. Also, one socket that is blocking will not hold up data transfer to any other socket. One example of this is shown is Listing 9.1.

TABLE 9.3 java.net ServerSocket

public ServerSocket (int port) throws IOException	Constructs a server socket listening on the given port.
public ServerSocket (int port , int timeout)throws IOException	Creates a server socket on the given port with the given timeout.
public Socket accept () throws IOException	Accepts a connection.
public void close ()throws IOException	Closes this socket.
public InetAddress getInetAddress ()	Returns the address of this socket as an InetAddress object.
public int getLocalPort ()	Returns the local port on which this socket is listening.
public static synchronized void setSocketFactory (SocketImplFactory fac) throws IOException	Sets the object responsible for creating actual socket implementations.
public String toString ()	Returns a string representation of this socket.

LISTING 9.1

```java
import java.io.*;
import java.net.*;
import java.util.*;

public class Server{

    public static void main(String Args[]){
        int port;
        try {
            port=Integer.parseInt(Args[0]);
        }catch (NumberFormatException e){
            System.our.println("No port specified. Using default(1984).");
            port=1984;
        }


        ServerSocket me=null;
        Socket them=null;
        Vector sockets=new Vector(2);//to hold sockets waiting to be connected
        try{

            me=new ServerSocket(port);
            System.out.println(me.toString());

        }catch (IOException e){

            System.err.println("Server Socket Error!");
        }

        while (sockets.size()<2){
            try{
                them= me.accept();
                sockets.addElement(them);
                System.out.println(them);
```

Continued

```java
            }catch (IOException e){}


        }

    new connection((Socket)sockets.elementAt(0),(Socket)sockets.elementAt(1));


    }
}


class connection {

    Socket a;
    Socket b;
    InputStream in;
    OutputStream out;

    public connection(Socket a, Socket b){//data from a to b
        this.a=a;
        this.b=b;
        new PipeThread (a,b).start();// start a pipe a->b
        new PipeThread (b,a).start();// // b->a
    }



}
class PipeThread extends Thread{
    Socket a=null;
    Socket b=null;
    public PipeThread(Socket a,Socket b){
        this.a=a;
        this.b=b;
    }
    public void run(){
        try{
            InputStream in=a.getInputStream();
            OutputStream out=b.getOutputStream();
```

```
            int bite=0;
            do{
                 bite=in.read();
                 out.write(bite);
            } while (bite!=-1);
        }catch (IOException e){}
    }

}
```

This is a simple implementation of a game server that simply waits for two clients to connect to it and then connects their input and output streams together with reader and writer threads. A simple class to test this is shown in Listing 9.2.

LISTING 9.2

```
import java.io.*;
import java.net.*;
public class client{
    public static void main(String Args[]){
    Socket socket=null;
     int port=25;
     String host="your.host.gov";//YOUR HOST


        try{
    socket=new Socket(host,port);


        }catch (Exception e){

            System.err.println(e+"Server Socket Error!");
        }

    System.out.println("connection");
    new reader(socket).start();
    new writer(socket).start();


    }
```

Continued

```
    }
class writer extends Thread{
    //reads stdin and sends it out!
    Socket socket;
    public writer(Socket s){
        socket=s;
    }

    public void run(){
        try{
            OutputStream out=socket.getOutputStream();
            int bite=0;
            while (bite!=-1){
                bite=System.in.read();
                out.write(bite);
            }
            socket.close();
        }catch (IOException e){}
    }
}
class reader extends Thread{
    //readst from socket writes to stream
    Socket socket=null;
    public reader(Socket s){
        socket=s;
    }

    public void run(){
        try{
            DataInputStream in=new DataInputStream(socket.getInputStream());

            String s=null;

            do{
                s=in.readLine();
```

```
                  System.out.println(s);
               } while (s!=null);


        }catch (IOException e){}
     }
}
```

The game server connects two players on an FCFS (first-come, first-served) basis. When two players are ready to be connected, it launches two PipeThreads: one to route the output of player A to the input of player B and one to route the output of player B to the input of player A. The run method of the pipe thread is quite simple:

```
try{
     InputStream in=a.getInputStream();
     OutputStream out=b.getOutputStream();
     int bite=0;
     do{
         bite=in.read();
         out.write(bite);

     } while (bite!=-1);
}catch (IOException e){}
```

We simply use the InputStream read() method to get a byte and write it out immediately to the other player's input stream. You could do something fancy like using a buffered stream for increased throughput, but this simple method actually works fairly well, and it's generally not a good idea to needlessly complicate unless you know for a fact the extra feature is necessary.

Norman (The) Mailer Applet

One handy thing your applets can do, if the server they reside on has an SMTP server, is send mail. Listing 9.3 shows an applet that launches a thread to connect back to the server on port 25 (the standard SMTP port).

LISTING 9.3
```
import java.net.*;
import java.io.*;
import java.applet.Applet;
```

Continued

```
public class NormanMailer extends java.applet.Applet implements Runnable{

    Thread t;
    /* called first. initialization here*/
    public void init(){
        show();
    }


    /* start a mailer thread*/
    public void start(){
        MailerThread mt=new MailerThread(this,"president@whitehouse.gov");
        mt.start();


    }


}
class MailerThread extends Thread{
    java.applet.Applet app=null;
    String recipient=null;
    public MailerThread(Applet A, String recipient){
        this.app=A;
        this.recipient=recipient;
    }


    public void run(){
        String host=null;
        try{
            int port=25;
            host=app.getDocumentBase().getHost();
            app.showStatus("Contacting: "+host+" on port: "+port);
            Socket socket=new Socket(host,port);
            OutputStream out=socket.getOutputStream();
            PrintStream p=new PrintStream(out,true);//auto flushing stream
            app.showStatus("Sending mail");
            p.println("HELO test.com");
```

```
        p.println("MAIL FROM:me@test.com");
        p.println("RCPT TO:"+recipient);
        p.println("DATA");
        p.println("Greetings from the NormanMailer applet");
        p.println(".\n");
        app.showStatus("Mail sent!");


    }catch (Exception e){/* all purpose error handler */
        app.showStatus("ERROR "+e.toString()+" host:"+host);
    }
  }
}
```

This thread's dialog with the server should look something like this:

```
220 osfn.rhilinet.gov ESMTP Sendmail 8.7.5/8.7.3; Thu, 18 Jul 1996 01:44:55 -0400
(EDT)
HELO test.com
250 osfn.rhilinet.gov Hello pdial05.brainiac.com [165.90.139.105], pleased to meet you
MAIL FROM:me@test.com");
250 me@test.com... Sender ok
RCPT TO: president@whitehouse.gov
250 Recipient ok
DATA
354 Enter mail, end with "." on a line by itself
Greetings from the NormanMailer applet.
.
250 BAA08422 Message accepted for delivery
```

This would be a good system for mailing yourself orders from people browsing your web page if the administrator of your web server is hesitant to let you start a dedicated server-side program to log orders. Since the mailing is accomplished in another thread, you can distract them while you send fake mail to the president!

There is one problem with this as it stands: all the information is transmitted over the notoriously insecure Internet mail system as plain text. We could, of course, encrypt the data using a static key hidden somewhere in the applet, but nothing is to keep someone from downloading the applet and electronically dissecting it to see what our key is. There *is* a solution. An applet can randomly generate a key and send it to us along with the message in a way that makes it almost impossible for any electronic eavesdroppers to discern the key.

Goodson-Todman Key Exchange

Oops, strike that. Goodson and Todman were the producers of *Family Feud*. I think.
What we are actually talking about here is a method of key exchange invented by Whitfield Diffie and Martin Hellman. Diffie-Hellman key exchange relies on the fact that it is quite a bit harder to calculate a logarithm than it is to raise a number to a power. This asymmetry, combined with an interesting property of modular arithmetic, allows you to transfer an intermediate key from which the actual session key can be calculated. This calculation involves secret information that never crosses the communication channel, ever!

We initiate a key exchange by picking a large number (b, for base), a large exponent (e, for exponent), and a prime modulus (m, for modulus). From these we calculate as follows:

```
n = b^e  mod  m
```

We can include n, b, and m in our applet's parameters. The exponent remains secret. This value will be used later to extract the session key from another number the applet will send us. Our applet can then pick a largish random number (r, for random) and use the Shempnum package to calculate an intermediate number:

```
i=b^r  mod m
```

Then the applet can calculate k and use it as a key to encrypt the message:

```
k=n^r  mod m
```

Since k obviously can't be transmitted over an insecure channel, we send i instead. You may be wondering what good i will do us on the receiving end. Well, in one of the few cases of number theory ever having a practical application, we can calculate k on our end using the following:

```
k=i^e  mod m
```

We have just exchanged a key without ever sending it openly. Don't believe it? Let's try it with numbers you can verify on a calculator. Lets say b=3, e=8 (secret), and m=11. We would first calculate n, which would equal 10. We can then include n, b, and m in our applet's parameters (or paint them on a 20-foot billboard, for that matter). Our applet would choose a random r, say 12, and find out that i=9 and k=1.

The applet then includes i along with a message encrypted with k. On our end, we would calculate k using only i, e (still secret!), and m. Our calculation also gives 1. You already know that 1 is a terrible key to use to encrypt something, and this raises an interesting point. This system does not generate a suitable key for every value used as a random exponent of the applet's side. It would be a good idea to check the key to make sure it is large enough for whatever cipher you have in mind and recalculate it if it is too short. Listing 9.4 (shemptest2) shows a simple test that generates random keys.

LISTING 9.4

```java
import java.shemp.Shempnum;

public class Shemptest2{
    public static void main(String argv[]){

        Shempnum m=new Shempnum("Fe");
        Shempnum b=new Shempnum("3c");
        Shempnum base=new Shempnum("a0");
         Shempnum n,e,r,x;
        for (int f=0;f<100;f++){
            do{

            e=new Shempnum((int)(Math.random()*32767));
            n=b.modexp(e,m);
            r=new Shempnum((int)(Math.random()*32767));
            i=b.modexp(r,m);
            }while (!i.modexp(e,m).geq(base));
            System.out.println("our key....."+i.modexp(e,m));// us
            System.out.println("applet key.."+n.modexp(r,m)+"\n");// them


            }
        }
    }
}
```

The output looks something like this:

```
our key.....a2
applet key..a2

our key.....c6
applet key..c6

our key.....e2
applet key..e2

our key.....e6
applet key..e6

our key.....f8
applet key..f8

our key.....ea
applet key..ea
```

In this case we check to make sure the generated key is greater than a base value (0xa0) and recalculate if necessary. Once we have exchanged the keys, we can use any standard symmetrical cipher to actually encrypt the data.

The Network Is the (Super)Computer

One interesting application for Java is distributed processing. Java has its own standard for Remote Method Invocation (analogous to RPC), and we will cover that later. But what if you want to distribute *someone else's* computing resources? And what if you don't even want to *ask* for permission?

Listing 9.5 shows the FactorServer application, and Listing 9.6 shows its associate client.

LISTING 9.5

```
import java.io.*;
import java.net.*;
import java.util.*;
```

```
import java.shemp.*;

public class FactorServer{
    public static final Shempnum jobSize=new Shempnum(100);
    static Shempnum base=new Shempnum(3);
    static Vector inProgress=new Vector();// for jobs
    static long maxtime=1000*60*4;//four minutes
    static Shempnum number;

    public static void main(String Args[]){
        base=new Shempnum(3);
        number=new Shempnum("106C31B5");
        int port;
        try {
            port=Integer.parseInt(Args[0]);
        }catch (Exception e){
            System.out.println("No port specified. Using default(1984).");
            port=1984;
        }
        ServerSocket me=null;
        Socket them=null;
            try{
                me=new ServerSocket(port);

            }catch (IOException e){
                    System.err.println("Server Socket Error!");
            }
        while (true){
            System.out.println("Listening:"+me.toString());
            try{
                them= me.accept();
                System.out.println(them+" accepted.");
            }catch (IOException e){}
            /*****/
            new JobThread(them,inProgress).start();
        }
```

Continued

```java
    }
public static synchronized Job getJob(){

    Job job;
    long time=System.currentTimeMillis();

    /* if none in progress make a new job
    */
    if (inProgress.isEmpty()){

        base=new Shempnum(base);

        job=new Job(time,number,base,jobSize);
        base=base.addAbs(jobSize);
    }else{

        /* check to see if oldest job
        ** has expired
        */

        job=(Job)inProgress.elementAt(0) ;
        if((time-job.time)>maxtime){

            job.time=time;
            inProgress.removeElement(job);

        }else{
            base=new Shempnum(base);

            job=new Job(time,number,base,jobSize);
            base=base.addAbs(jobSize);
        }
    }

    inProgress.addElement((Object)job);
    return job;
```

```
    }
}

class JobThread extends Thread{
    Socket socket;
    Shempnum base;
    Shempnum counter;
    Vector inProgress;
    public JobThread(Socket s,Vector inProgress){
        this.socket=s;
        this.base=base;
        this.inProgress=inProgress;
    }
    public void run(){
        Job job=null;
        long time;


        try{
            PrintStream printstream=new PrintStream(socket.getOutputStream());
            DataInputStream datastream=new DataInputStream(socket.getInputStream());
            while (true){
                String message2;
                String message1=datastream.readLine();
                System.out.println(message1);

                if (message1.equals("getjob")){
                    job=FactorServer.getJob();
                    printstream.println(job);
                    System.out.println("Sending: "+job);


                }
                if ( message1.equals("nofactors") ){
                    String S=datastream.readLine();
                    System.out.println(S);
                    time=Long.parseLong(S);
```

Continued

```
                    for(Enumeration e = inProgress.elements() ; e.hasMoreElements() ;)
                        System.out.println(e.nextElement());
                loop:for (Enumeration E= inProgress.elements();E.hasMoreElements();){
                    job=(Job)E.nextElement();
                    if (job.time==time){
                        inProgress.removeElement((Object)job);
                        System.out.println("Removing:\n"+job+"\n");
                        break loop;
                    }
                }
            }
            if (message1.equals("factor")){
                System.out.println("FACTOR!!!!!!!!!!!!!!"+datastream.readLine());
            }
        }
    }catch (IOException E){System.out.println(E);}
}


}


class Job {
    public Shempnum number2Factor;
    public long time;
    public Shempnum base;
    public Shempnum jobSize;
    public Job(long time,Shempnum number2Factor,Shempnum base,Shempnum jobSize){
        this.base=base;
        this.time=time;
        this.jobSize=jobSize;
        this.number2Factor=number2Factor;
    }
    public String toString(){
        return new String(Long.toString(time)
            +"\n"+number2Factor.toString()
            +"\n"+base.toString()
```

```
          +"\n"+jobSize.toString());
    }
}
```

LISTING 9.6

```java
import java.awt.*;
import java.util.*;
import java.awt.image.*;
import java.net.*;


public class AppletShell extends java.applet.Applet implements Runnable{
    Thread T;


    /* called after init() we call run() as a separate thread */
    public void start(){
        System.err.println("start");

        T=new Thread(this);
        T.start();

    }

    /* main run method, launched as a thread by start() */
    public void run(){
        try{
                Socket socket=null;
            URL url=null;
            int port=1984;
            PrintStream out;
            DataInputStream in;
                    String host=getCodeBase().getHost();

            socket=new Socket(host,port);
            System.out.println("connection");
            out=new PrintStream (socket.getOutputStream());
```

Continued

```
            in=new DataInputStream(socket.getInputStream());

        Shempnum two=new Shempnum(2);// used to skip even numbers

        while (true){

            out.println("getjob");
            long time=Long.parseLong(in.readLine());

            Shempnum number=new Shempnum(in.readLine());
            Shempnum base=new Shempnum(in.readLine());
            Shempnum count=new Shempnum(in.readLine());

            do{    System.out.println(number+","+base+","+number.mod(base));

                if (number.mod(base).eq(0)){
                    out.println("factor");
                    out.println(base);

                }
                base=base.addAbs(two);
                count=count.sub(two);
            }while (!count.eq(0));


        }
    }catch (IOException e){System.err.println(e);}

}

/* called when applet is stopped ignore! */
public void stop(){

}

}
```

The server waits for a connection and then hands it off to a thread for processing. If the client requests a job, the server either hands it an expired job that has timed out or generates a new range of numbers to be factored. The client tries to factor these numbers and reports either "factor" and the factor it found or "nofactors," in which case it is assumed that it can process another job, so it is given one. The client's main loop is very simple:

```
do{
    if (number.mod(base).eq(0)){
        out.println("factor");
        out.println(base);

    }
    base=base.addAbs(two);
    count=count.sub(two);
}while (!count.eq(0));
```

Count starts out at the size of the range of numbers we are trying as factors and counts down to zero. When this range of numbers has been checked, we request another job, and so on, until the user severs the connection to the net. At this point the applet may have factored most of the range but not had a chance to report back yet, in which case all of that tedious calculation goes to waste. It's tragic, but at least we're not wasting *our* computing power.

The Chattlet Chat System

Listing 9.7 shows a simple server for a multiuser chat system.

LISTING 9.7

```
import java.io.*;
import java.net.*;
import java.util.*;


public class ChatServer{


    public static void main(String Args[]){
        int port;
```

Continued

```
try {
    port=Integer.parseInt(Args[0]);
}catch (Exception e){
    System.out.println("No port specified. Using default(1984).");
    port=1984;
}


Broadcaster broadcaster=new Broadcaster();
broadcaster.start();

ServerSocket me=null;
Socket them=null;

    try{

        me=new ServerSocket(port);


    }catch (IOException e){

            System.err.println("Server Socket Error!");
    }
while (true){
    System.out.println("Listening:"+me.toString());
    try{
        them= me.accept();
        System.out.println(them+" accepted.");
    }catch (IOException e){}

    broadcaster.add(new WriterThread(them));
    new ReaderThread(them,broadcaster).start();


}
}
```

```
}

/* Broadcaster */

import java.net.*;
import java.util.*;

public class Broadcaster extends Thread{
    /* the max number of connections available */
    public final static int MAXCONS=100;
    /* should we be dead ???? */
    public static boolean die;
    /* a vector to hold writerThreads */
    Vector writers;
    /* a one line-buffer */
    String buffer;
    /* Object used to notify us when
     * data is ready
     */
    private Object dataReady;

    public Broadcaster(){
        dataReady=new Object(); // object to sychronize with
        writers=new Vector(MAXCONS); // maxconnections
        die=false; // I should hope so, we're seconds old!
    }

    public void run(){

        WriterThread writer;

        synchronized(dataReady){
            String data="ready";
            while (die==false){

                try{
```

Continued

```
                        /* wait to be notified there is a new
                         * line in the buffer...*/
                        dataReady.wait();

                        /* broadcast the line to all waiting
                         * writerThreads*/

                        for (Enumeration E = writers.elements() ; E.hasMoreElements() ;) {
                            writer=(WriterThread)E.nextElement();

                            /* if writeln returns false (error),
                             * remove writerThread from vector */
                            if (!writer.writeln(buffer)){
                                        System.err.println("removing "+writer.toString());
                                writers.removeElement(writer);
                            }
                            writer.writeln(buffer);
                        }
                        dataReady.notify();
                    }catch (InterruptedException e){
                        System.err.println("DOH! "+e.toString());
                    }


                }
            }
    }//run


        /* write a line into buffer
         * and notify dataReady */
    public void writeln(String S){
        synchronized(dataReady){
        buffer=S;
        dataReady.notify();
```

```
            }
        }

        /* add a new Writer Thread to the Vector  */
        public void add(WriterThread T){
            System.out.println("adding "+T);
            writers.addElement((Object) T);
            T.start();
        }
    }


/*  reader thread */
import java.io.*;
import java.net.*;
public class ReaderThread extends Thread{
    //Socket socket=null;
    String buffer;
    DataInputStream in=null;
    Broadcaster broadcaster=null;

    public ReaderThread(Socket S, Broadcaster B){
        try {
            InputStream I=S.getInputStream();
            in=new DataInputStream (I);
        }catch (IOException e){
            System.err.println("ERROR:"+e.toString());
        }
        broadcaster=B;


    }
    public void run(){

        while(true){
            try{
                buffer=in.readLine();
```

Continued

```
                    System.out.println();
                    broadcaster.writeln(buffer);


              }catch (IOException e){
                  System.err.println(this.toString()+": "+e.toString()+" dying!"),
                  throw new ThreadDeath();
              }
          }
      }


}
/* writer thread */
import java.io.*;
import java.net.*;
public class WriterThread extends Thread{
    Socket socket=null;
    String buffer;
    PrintStream out=null;
    boolean status=true;

    public WriterThread(Socket S){
        this.socket=S;
        try {
            OutputStream O=S.getOutputStream();
            out=new PrintStream (O);
        }catch (IOException e){
            System.err.println("ERROR:"+e.toString());
        }


    }
    public void run(){
        synchronized(this)while(true){
            try{
                wait();
```

```
                /* data in buffer! */
                out.println(buffer);
                }catch (Exception e){
                     /* there's been an error! */
                   status=false;
                }



          }
      }
}


     public synchronized boolean  writeln(String S){
          buffer=S;
          notify();
          return status;
      }
}
```

This program has four main parts. The main server simply waits for connections and hands them off to a helper class, Broadcaster. The Broadcaster class is responsible for taking incoming data from a series of ReaderThreads and placing it in the buffers of a series of WriterThreads. Note the use of wait() and notify() to synchronize everything. The broadcaster spends most of its time waiting to be notified by a reader thread that here is data waiting in its line buffer. The notifying thread itself waits to be notified that data has been consumed before exiting the synchronized block. This keeps another thread from trashing the data in the buffer before it has been consumed. When notified that there is data in its buffer, the Broadcaster places data in the input buffers of the waiting WriterThreads and notifies them that there is data ready to be written out to its socket.

The client for this server is shown in Listing 9.8 and Figure 9.10.

LISTING 9.8

```
import java.awt.*;
import java.util.*;
import java.awt.image.*;
import java.applet.*;
import java.net.*;
```

Continued

```java
import java.io.*;

public class Chattlet extends Applet implements Runnable{

    Reader reader;
    TextArea input,text;
    TextField namefield;
    String name;
    boolean connected;
    Button connect,disconnect,exit;
    String host;
    int port;
    PrintStream out;
    Socket socket;
    public void start(){
        new Thread(this).start();
    }

    public void run(){


    /* get applet params */
    URL url=getCodeBase();
    host=url.getHost();

    try{
        port=Integer.parseInt(getParameter("port"));
    }catch (Exception e){
        port=1984;
    }

    FloatLayout lm=new FloatLayout();
    setLayout(lm);

    Label l=new Label("RoundTable Chat System",Label.CENTER);
    this.add(l);
```

```
FloatLayoutConstraints flc=lm.getConstraints(1);
flc.xpos=(float).5;
flc.ypos=(float).03;
flc.ysize=0;
flc.resizable=true;


Label l2=new Label("Your Name:",Label.RIGHT);
this.add(l2);
flc=lm.getConstraints(l2);
flc.xpos=(float).25;
flc.ypos=(float).15;
flc.ysize=0;
flc.resizable=true;

namefield=new TextField(15);
this.add(namefield);
flc=lm.getConstraints(namefield);
flc.xpos=(float).60;
flc.ypos=(float).15;
flc.xsize=.40f;
flc.resizable=true;


connect=new Button("Connect");
this.add(connect);
flc=lm.getConstraints(connect);
flc.xpos=(float).25;
flc.ypos=(float).92;
flc.xsize=10;
flc.xsize=.15f;
flc.resizable=true;


disconnect=new Button("Disconnect");
this.add(disconnect);
```

Continued

```
flc=lm.getConstraints(disconnect);
flc.xpos=(float).5;
flc.ypos=(float).92;
flc.xsize=.15f;
flc.resizable=true;
disconnect.disable();

exit=new Button("Exit");
this.add(exit);
flc=lm.getConstraints(exit);
flc.xpos=(float).75;
flc.ypos=(float).92;
flc.xsize=.15f;
flc.resizable=true;

text =new TextArea(3,5);// note:cols,rows not vv
this.add(text);

flc=lm.getConstraints(text);

flc.ypos=(float).40;
flc.xpos=(float).50;
flc.xsize=(float).95;
flc.ysize=(float).35;
flc.resizable=true;



    input =new TextArea(2,5);// note:cols,rows not vv
this.add(input);

flc=lm.getConstraints(input);

flc.ypos=(float).70;
flc.xpos=(float).50;
flc.xsize=(float).95;
```

```
flc.ysize=(float).10;
flc.resizable=true;



layout();


}


public boolean handleEvent(Event e){
    //System.out.println(e.toString());
    if (e.id== Event.WINDOW_DESTROY){
        System.exit(0);
        return false;
    }
    if (e.target==connect&& !connected){
        if (namefield.getText().equals("")){
            new OkayBox("You must enter a name!!");
        }else{
            name=namefield.getText();
            connect();
        }
    }
    if (e.target==disconnect && connected){
        disconnect();
    }
    if (e.target==exit){
        if (connected){
            disconnect();
        }
    reader.stop();
    Thread.currentThread().stop();


    }


    if(e.id==Event.KEY_PRESS && e.key==10 && connected){
```

Continued

```
                String theString=name+":"+input.getText();
                out.println(theString);
                input.setText("");


            }
        return false;
    }
    public void stop(){
        if (!connected){
            super.stop();
        }
    }
    private void connect(){
        connected=true;
        try{
            socket=new Socket(host,port);
            OutputStream O=socket.getOutputStream();
            out=new PrintStream(O,true);
        }catch (Exception e){


        }
        disconnect.enable();
        connect.disable();
        reader=new Reader(socket, text);
        reader.start();


    }
    private void disconnect(){
        try{
            reader.stop();
            disconnect.disable();
            connect.enable();
            connected=false;
            socket.close();
        }catch (IOException e){

        }
```

```
    }
}

class Reader extends Thread{
    //readst from socket writes to TextArea
    Socket socket=null;
    TextArea text=null;
    public Reader(Socket S,TextArea T){
        socket=S;
        text=T;
        text.setEditable(false);
    }

    public void run(){
        try{

            DataInputStream in=new DataInputStream(socket.getInputStream());

            String S=null;

            do{

                S=in.readLine();
                S=S+"\n";
                text.appendText(S);

            } while (S!=null);

        }catch (Exception e){new OkayBox("An Error occurred!");}
    }
}

class OkayBox extends Dialog{
    Button okay;
    String S;
```

Continued

```java
public OkayBox(String S){
    super(new Frame(),"HEY!",true);
    setLayout(new BorderLayout());

    add("Center",new Label(S));
    Panel P=new Panel();
    okay=new Button("OK");
    P.add(okay);
    this.add("South",P);
    this.pack();
    this.show();
}

public boolean handleEvent(Event e){
    System.out.println(e.toString());
    if(e.target==okay){
        this.dispose();

    }
    return false;
}



public boolean action(Event e,Object O){
    if(e.target==okay){
        this.dispose();

    }
    return false;
}
}
```

In this case we use a thread to read from the socket and display it in a text area. The main applet portion waits for the user to type a carriage return in the send window, sends the line (which may span more than one physical line) out to the socket, and then erases the text area. (See Figure 9.1.)

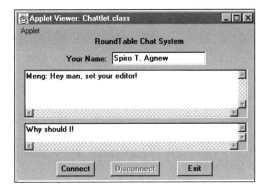

FIGURE 9.1 The Chat Applet.

Using UDP

So far, we've worked only with TCP sockets, but you may not be satisfied with a slow, reliable TCP connection. You can use the DatagramPacket class to encapsulate the data packet and the DatagramSocket class to make the connection (see Tables 9.4). Of course, you must somehow

TABLE 9.4 java.net.DatagramSocket

public DatagramSocket (int port) throws SocketException	Constructs a datagram socket on the given local port.
public DatagramSocket () throws SocketException	Constructs a datagram socket.
public synchronized void close ()	Closes the socket.
public int getLocalPort ()	Gets local port to which this socket is bound.
public synchronized void receive (DatagramPacket p) throws IOException	Receives a datagram packet in p.
public void send (DatagramPacket p) throws IOException	Sends datagram packet p.

provide for the error correction that TCP gives you free or implement a protocol wherein a few hundred missing packets here and there aren't important. By the way, the number of lost packets that TCP automatically corrects would probably surprise you.

Remote Method Invocation

Java provides another mechanism for distributed processing called Remote Method Invocation (RMI). Basically, RMI allows objects in different virtual machines in different address spaces to call each other's methods in the normal fashion. Once it is set up properly, the mechanism by which this is accomplished is transparent to the programmer. We will use the term *server* for objects whose methods may be called by a remote client object. Note that an object may serve as both a client and a server. An object method may even call a method that calls back to a method in the original object. It is even possible to have a form of remote recursion where the original method is called by the remote method!

The way that this works is that proxy classes act as an interface between your method call and the transport layer that actually handles all the dirty work of finding the remote object, marshaling parameters, and returning the result. On the client side the proxy class is known as the *stub*, and on the server side it is known as a *skeleton*. If you are wondering how the arguments are actually passed to the remote method, nonremote objects are passed and returned by copy, and in the case of a remote object used as a parameter, its stub is passed. One side effect of this is that only the methods in the remote interfaces that the object implements will be visible.

Let's walk through the steps necessary to create an RMI client and server. Bear in mind that this discussion is based on an early version of the RMI class library but includes only features not likely to change.

The first step is to run the registry that provides the magic name lookup and resolution for your RMI calls. This is as simple as the following:

```
java.exe java.rmi.registry.RegistryImpl
```

The next step is to define a remote interface (an interface that extends java.rmi.remote). Each method in the interface must declare that it may throw java.rmi.remoteException. A very simple example would look something like this:

```
package java.rmi;
import java.rmi.*;

public interface Test extends java.rmi.Remote {
    boolean test() throws java.rmi.RemoteException;
}
```

As you can see, this interface has only one method that always returns true, which wouldn't be very special, except we are planning to call this from across the network. RMI uses a RegistryImpl (so called because it implements the registry interface) to look up remote objects by name. In our server, we get a handle to our system's RegistryImpl and bind our object to an arbitrary name. The server should extend the java.rmi.UnicastRemote-Server class and implement the Test interface.

```
package java.rmi;

import java.rmi.*;
import java.rmi.server.*;
import java.rmi.server.UnicastRemoteServer;
import java.rmi.registry.*;
public class TestServer    extends UnicastRemoteServer implements Test{

    public TestServer() throws RemoteException {
    super();
    }
```

```
public static void main(String args[]) {

System.setSecurityManager(new StubSecurityManager());
try{
    Registry registry = LocateRegistry.getRegistry();
    registry.rebind("Test",new TestServer());
}catch (Exception E){
    System.err.println(E);
    E.printStackTrace();
}

    System.out.println("connected");

}


/* a silly method which tests the mechnanism */
public boolean test() throws RemoteException{
    return  true;
    }



}
```

In this server we use the static java.rmi.registry.LocateRegistry().getRegistry() method to get a handle to the RegistryImpl object operating on your host and the Registry.bind(name,object) method to bind this server to the name Test. One special requirement to note is that the constructor must either take no arguments and declare that it throws java.rmi.remoteException or call the no-argument superconstructor.

Now we can create a simple client that calls our test method. RMI clients use the Naming class to get a reference to a remote object using a URL of the form "rmi://host_name/service_name." Note that the service_name in this case is the same one we registered in the server code above. What happens is the Naming class looks up the host and contacts the RegistryImpl object for that system. Next the stub for the remote interface we defined earlier is transferred automatically over to the client. From then on, calls to methods of the remote object actually call the corresponding methods of the stub that takes care of the details of the remote method call. A simple client for the server above would look something like this:

```java
package java.rmi;

import java.rmi.*;
import java.rmi.registry.*;
import java.rmi.server.StubSecurityManager;

public class TestClient {

    public static void main(String args[])
    {
    System.setSecurityManager(new StubSecurityManager());

    try {

        Test TS= (Test)Naming.lookup("rmi://165.90.139.126/Test");
        if(TS.test()){
            System.out.println("YES!");
        }
    } catch (Exception e) {
    e.printStackTrace();
    }

    System.exit(0);
    }
}
```

One thing to remember is that we do not get a reference to a TestServer object, but rather to an object that implements the Test remote interface. This makes sense, because we are making a remote call, so we should have access to only the remote interface. This is another good example of encapsulation at work. If the server implements more than one remote interface, we can simply cast to the one we need with the normal Java casting syntax.

Next we can start the server and finally, the client that gives us a firm answer to the age-old question "Does RMI work?":

YES!

ORBs

One subject bound to come up when distributed processing is discussed is object resource brokers (ORBs) and especially CORBA, the common object request broker architecture. Basically, CORBA uses a language-neutral interface definition language (IDL) to describe how objects call each other's methods. There are already several classes floating around to map Java to this IDL. Java RMI needs no such language-neutral IDL, because it is designed to work in a homogenous environment where Java objects call methods in other Java objects using the familiar Java syntax. All in all, CORBA is a complicated and multifaceted subject worthy of a book all its own (after all, it has its own language). The pure Java solution is much simpler, and simplicity is what attracts many programmers to Java in the first place.

Chapter 10

Native Methods

A word of advice is in order before you learn how to interface native code with your Java code. Don't do it! If you use native methods in your code, you sacrifice many of the features that probably attracted you to Java in the first place. You can wave good-bye to security, platform independence, garbage collection, and easy class loading over the network. Worse, users of your program will have to download a potentially virus-infected piece of code and run it on their machines; suspicion of the Internet being as widespread as it is, it's hard to imagine that many people would be willing to do that. Intentionally malicious code is only part of the problem; if a native method you write has a pointer overrun or attempts to access memory it shouldn't, the user will be staring at a general protection fault message.

There are still plenty of cases in which native methods make sense. Sometimes you absolutely must have access to some system resource Java does not support—for example, printing to the parallel port. Another case is one in which interpreted Java code is just too slow for the application you have in mind. If you think you're brave (or irresponsible) enough to take the risk, abandon all hope and read on!

First Steps

Let's walk through creating a simple combination of Java and native code. This section is fairly specific to the Win95/NT platform. Compatibility is the first thing you lose when you use native code; the code shouldn't be very hard to port.

The first thing you need to do is get your hands on a C compiler that allows you to build dynamically linked libraries (DLLs). I used Symantec C++ for these examples because I had a brand new copy lying around gathering dust, but any compiler which builds DLLs should work.

The next step is to write the Java code. Let's create a file called NativeTest.java with the following contents:

```java
public class NativeTest {
    int variable;

    /* use a static block to
    ** load a library named "foobar"
    */

    static {
        System.loadLibrary("foobar");
    }

    /* main method to test
    ** out native methods
    */

    public static void main (String args[]){
        NativeTest NT=new NativeTest();
        NT.variable=42;

        System.out.println("echo says:"+NT.echo(2));

        System.out.println("variable="+NT.returnVar());

    }
```

```
    /*  a native method which takes an int
    **  and regurgitates it
    */
    public native int echo(int a);

    /*  a native method which takes an Object
    **  and returns its variable field
    */
    public native int returnVar();
}
```

In this case we use a static block to load our library. Note that the library name is the name of the DLL that we will build later, minus the extension. Loading the library in a static block like this ensures it will be ready before our main method tries to use it later. We declare a native method named echo, which takes an int as an argument and returns (presumably the same) value as an int. We also declare a native method named returnVar(), which takes no arguments and also returns an int. Our main method calls our native methods and prints the results.

The next step in the process is to use the javah.exe program to produce header files for your C program. The javah program takes the name of the class file (with no extension) as an argument, so in this case we would use the following:

```
javah NativeTest
```

This should produce the following header file (NativeTest.h):

```
/* DO NOT EDIT THIS FILE - it is machine generated */
#include <native.h>
/* Header for class NativeTest */

#ifndef _Included_NativeTest
#define _Included_NativeTest

typedef struct ClassNativeTest {
    long variable;
} ClassNativeTest;
HandleTo(NativeTest);
```

```
#ifdef __cplusplus
extern "C" {
#endif
extern long NativeTest_returnVar(struct HNativeTest *);
extern long NativeTest_echo(struct HNativeTest *,long);
#ifdef __cplusplus
}
#endif
#endif
```

As you can see, this contains the function prototypes for our two native methods. Notice that the function prototype for our returnVar function takes no arguments:

```
extern long NativeTest_returnVar(struct HNativeTest *);
```

Note that the name of the function is the name of the class to which this native method belongs, plus an underscore and the name of the method. It may seem strange to see that our returnVar method takes no arguments, but the NativeTest_returnVar function is declared as getting one argument. The pointer to the HNativeTest structure is similar to this pointer in Java. Later we will use this to retrieve values from the object, but we can safely ignore it for now. It may also seem strange to see the second argument for NativeTest_echo declared as a long, even though the NativeTest.echo method actually takes an int. This long is actually our int argument. Data types are mapped to their nearest C equivalent, so ints are mapped to longs for the purpose of native methods (see Table 10.1 for the others). Note that the way arguments are passed mimics the way arguments are passed to normal Java methods: objects are passed by reference and primitive types are passed by value.

TABLE 10.1 Mapping of Java Data Types to C Types

Java Type	C Type
boolean	long
int	long
float	float
char	long

Continued

Java Type	C Type
short	long
ushort	long
double	float
Object	struct Hjava_lang_Object*
boolean[]	long*
int[]	long*
float[]	float*
char[]	unicode*
short[]	long*
ushort[]	unsigned short*
double[]	float*
Object[]	HArrayOfClass*struct Hjava_lang_Object*

The next step is to run javah again with the -stubs option to generate a C stub file:

```
javah -stubs NativeTest
```

This should produce a file (NativeTest.c) that looks something like this:

```
/* DO NOT EDIT THIS FILE - it is machine generated */
#include <StubPreamble.h>

/* Stubs for class NativeTest */
/* SYMBOL: "NativeTest/returnVar()I", Java_NativeTest_returnVar_stub */
__declspec(dllexport) stack_item *Java_NativeTest_returnVar_stub(stack_item *_P_,struct
                                                        execenv *_EE_) {
    extern long NativeTest_returnVar(void *);
    _P_[0].i = NativeTest_returnVar(_P_[0].p);
    return _P_ + 1;
}
```

```
/* SYMBOL: "NativeTest/echo(I)I", Java_NativeTest_echo_stub */
__declspec(dllexport) stack_item *Java_NativeTest_echo_stub(stack_item *_P_,struct
                                                       execenv *_EE_) {
    extern long NativeTest_echo(void *,long);
    _P_[0].i = NativeTest_echo(_P_[0].p,((_P_[1].i)));
    return _P_ + 1;
}
```

This is the magical stub containing platform-specific glue code, which makes everything possible. This is the actual code called by Java, and it in turn calls our functions. Don't be surprised if it looks a little (or even a lot) different on your platform. I don't know about you, but when I see files warning me to NOT EDIT THIS FILE my first impulse is to edit them to see what happens, but I digress. The next step is to actually write the C code to implement our method. We'll keep things simple. Create a file named nixon.c with the following contents:

```
/* PLEASE EDIT THIS FILE - it is man-made! */
/* nixon.c native implementations */

#include <StubPreamble.h>
#include "NativeTest.h"
#include <stdio.h>
# include <interpreter.h> /*needed for unhand macro! */

/* simple native method to echo an int
** (masquerading as a long) back to caller
*/
extern long NativeTest_echo(struct HNativeTest *this,long number){
    return number;
}


/* Accessing an object's fields
*/
extern long NativeTest_returnVar(struct HNativeTest *this){

    /* use the unhand macro to access
```

```
** the "variable" field in the NativeTest
** to which this native method belongs
*/
long value=unhand(this)->variable;
return value;


}
```

Unhand That Object!

Note that above we use the unhand macro on our HNativeTest pointer to get a pointer to a structure that parallels the structure of our object. (In case you're wondering, this is a very simple macro: "unhand(o) ((o)->obj).") This gives us the ability to access member variables of our object. In this case we use the following to get the value of our variable field:

```
unhand(this)->variable
```

Making It All Work

Now we're finally ready to make our library. First we create a new project of type "Windows 95 DLL" with the name "foobar," add the stub file and nixon.c to the project, and build it. The result should be foobar.dll. Now we need to put this somewhere Java can find it. Since java/bin is very likely to be in your PATH already, go ahead and stick it there. Now, finally, you can execute NativeTest.java and experience your native methods at work:

```
echo says:2
variable=42
```

Other Data Types

We've just seen an example of how to access a single primitive data field from a native method, but the same technique works (with some modification) for arrays and strings. When we pass a native method an array of ints, for example, it really receives a pointer to an HArrayOfLong struct. We can use unhand() on this and then use the -> operator to get the special member "body," which is a pointer to the data type contained in the array. For example, if we get an HArrayOfLong pointer named Agnew, we can use the following:

```
long *arraypointer;
arraypointer==unhand(Agnew)->body;
```

Then we can use arraypointer just like any other pointer to a long to access the variables in the array.

Strings

The file javaString.h, one of the header files that are shipped with the JDK, has several utility functions to handle strings. Since strings are objects in Java, we receive a pointer to an Hjava_lang_String struct when we are passed a string, which we will call "mystring." We can use makeCstring() to convert this to a null-terminated character array:

```
char *chars;
chars=makeCString(mystring);
```

Note that this function automatically allocates and frees any storage necessary. Conversely, there is make JavaString, which returns a pointer to a new Java string initialized to the value of an array of C chars:

```
Hjava_lang_String *newstring;
newstring=makeJavaString(chars,strlen(chars));
```

One last function you may be interested in returns the length of a Java string as an int:

```
int length;
length javaStringLength(mystring);
```

Remember that Java String objects are immutable, so don't try to change them! If you want to change strings, use a StringBuffer. You can even *call back* to the methods in the StringBuffer class to do your dirty work. Let's take a look at how to call back into Java from a native method.

Native Callbacks

Before we get into the specifics of how to call back into Java from a native method, you should know that much of what follows is undocumented. It is possible that the folks at Sun decided not to document some of these functions because they are subject to change. You have been warned.

To call an instance method of an object, we use the following method (defined in interpreter.h) to call back to Java:

```
long execute_java_dynamic_method(ExecEnv *, HObject *obj,
              char *method_name, char *signature, ...);
```

The first argument is a pointer to the execution environment. This is currently undocumented, but a value of 0 works and presumably uses the current execution environment. Since nobody seems to know its purpose, you can just ignore it for now. Use 0.

The next argument is a pointer to the object that contains the method you are calling. The third argument is a pointer to the name of the method. This is simply the name of the method as it appears in the method definition.

The fourth argument is the *signature* of the method you are calling. The number and type of the arguments that may optionally follow can be determined from this signature by the run time. These signatures may require some explanation. The signature of a method consists of a parenthesized list of the argument types a method takes (represented by single letter codes) followed by the return types of the method (using the same codes). The codes used to represent primitive data types are shown in Table 10.3. This is fairly straightforward, as the examples below show.

The last two entries in the table show that arrays are represented by a left-hand bracket followed by the normal code for the type (see Table 10.3 for type codes). Objects are slightly more complicated. An object's type code is the letter L followed by the fully qualified class name with the periods replaced by path separators and terminated with a semicolon. So the code for a java.lang.String object would be Ljava/lang/String; and for an array of java.applet.Applet objects, [Ljava/applet.Applet;.

TABLE 10.2 Method Signatures

Java Method	Signature
public int method()	()I
public void method (boolean b)	(Z)V
public float method (int a, long l)	(IJ)F
public double method (byte b, char c)	(BC)D
public int[](byte[])	([B)[I
public short (float f[])	([F)S

TABLE 10.3 Type Codes

Type	Code
byte	B
char	C
short	S
int	I
long	J
boolean	Z
float	F
double	D
void	V

A Java program to demonstrate Java/C working together is shown in Listing 10.1, and the associated C code is shown in Listing 10.2. In this case, we call into a native method from the main Java method, and the native method calls back to our Java callme method with a string. If all goes well, this produces the following output:

```
Calling native method...
I was called by a native method.
It passed me the following: Success!
Return code:0
```

Note that you'll have to link in javai.lib (or your platform's equivalent) to make all this work.

LISTING 10.1

```java
public class Callback {



    /* use a static block to
    ** load a library named "callback"
    */


    static {
        System.loadLibrary("callback");
    }
```

```
/* main method to test
** our native methods
*/


public static void main (String args[]){

    System.out.println("Calling native method...");


    Callback CB=new Callback();


    int i=CB.callback("Success!");
    System.out.println("Return code:"+i);



}


/*  which calls back to the next method
**  with an int and a string
*/
public native int callback(String S);

/*  a Java method to be called by a native method
**  note that it takes a String object
**  and it returns no value: (Ljava/lang/String;)V
*/
public void callme(String s){
    System.out.println("I was called by a native method.");
    System.out.println("It passed me the following: "+s);


}



}
```

LISTING 10.2

```
/******************** Callback.h ********************/
/* DO NOT EDIT THIS FILE - it is machine generated */
#include <native.h>
/* Header for class Callback */


#ifndef _Included_Callback
#define _Included_Callback

typedef struct ClassCallback {
    char PAD;      /* ANSI C requires structures to have at least one member */
} ClassCallback;
HandleTo(Callback);

#ifdef __cplusplus
extern "C" {
#endif
struct Hjava_lang_String;
extern long Callback_callback(struct HCallback *,struct Hjava_lang_String *);
#ifdef __cplusplus
}
#endif
#endif


/******************** callback.C ********************/
/******************** stub file ********************/
/* DO NOT EDIT THIS FILE - it is machine generated */
#include <StubPreamble.h>


/* Stubs for class Callback */
/* SYMBOL: "Callback/callback(Ljava/lang/String;)I", Java_Callback_callback_stub */
__declspec(dllexport) stack_item *Java_Callback_callback_stub(stack_item *_P_,struct
                                                    execenv *_EE_) {
    extern long Callback_callback(void *,void *);
```

```
    _P_[0].i = Callback_callback(_P_[0].p,((_P_[1].p)));
    return _P_ + 1;
}


/******************** cmethod.h ********************/
/**** actual native method to call back to java   ****/
/****************************************************/


/* PLEASE EDIT THIS FILE - it is man-made! */
/* method for callback.dll                 */


#include <StubPreamble.h>
#include "Callback.h"
#include <native.h>
/* simple native method to call back
** to java!
*/
extern long Callback_callback(struct HCallback *this,struct Hjava_lang_String *string){

    long l;
    l=(long)execute_java_dynamic_method(0,(Hjava_lang_Object*)this,"callme"
                                        ,"(Ljava/lang/String;)V",string);


  return 0l;
}
```

Static Methods

You can also call Java static (class) methods and constructors, but this requires even more undocumented voodoo. execute_java_constructor() calls a Java constructor:

```
HObject *execute_java_constructor(ExecEnv *,
                char *classname,
                ClassClass *cb,
                char *signature, ...);
```

The following will return a pointer to an Hobject struct for the new object:

```
execute_java_static_method calls a static method:
long execute_java_static_method(ExecEnv *, ClassClass *cb,
                    char *method_name, char *signature, ...);
```

The arguments in both functions are similar to those used in calling an instance method. The exception is the pointer to a ClassClass. How do you get this? There is an undocumented function to return a pointer to a ClassClass for a class, given its name:

```
ClassClass *FindClass(struct execenv *, char *, bool_t resolve);
```

To get a pointer to a ClassClass for the class "FooBaz," we can use the following:

```
struct ClassClass *ch;
ch = FindClass(0, "FooBaz", TRUE);
```

Keep in mind that these may change, so you might be better off using an instance method to get a new object or execute a static method for you.

When Things Go Wrong

The exception you are most likely to get when using native methods is "Unsatisfied link error." This means different things, depending on when it occurs. If it happens during the initial loading of the library, it means that Java can't find your DLL. If it happens later, when you try to call a native method, it means that Java can't find the function in the DLL.

Another error you might encounter is "Invalid method signature." This means that Java can't find the Java method you are trying to call. The method signature must match an existing method in the class or object (well duh!). You might also encounter this error if you use periods instead of path separators to separate the fully qualified name of an object in the method signature. (Old habits are hard to break.)

When Things Go Wrong, Part II

You can throw exceptions from a native method, just as in a Java method. Remember that your native method must declare that it throws the exception in its throw clause.

```
void SignalError(struct execenv *env, char *exception, char *god_only_knows);
```

This function has not one but two "don't ask, don't tell" arguments. Again the first argument is our old friend, the execution environment, so we can use zero. The third argument is also some undocumented voodoo, but zero works for this one as well. The middle argument is all important; it is the fully qualified name of the exception (again using path separators, not periods). To throw a FileNotFoundException, for example, use the following:

```
void SignalError(0, "java/io/FileNotFoundException",0);
```

Synchronized Native Methods

You can declare a native method to be synchronized like any other method, and this works just as you would expect. There are three methods that serve the same function as wait(), notify() and notifyAll():

- void monitorWait(unsigned int);
- void monitorNotify(unsigned int);
- void monitorNotifyAll(unsigned int);

You can use the obj_monitor(handlep) macro to automatically cast your Hobject pointer, so if you call the first argument of your synchronized method "this" (a recommended practice), using these statements is as easy as the following:

```
monitorWait(obj_monitor(this));
monitorNotify(obj_monitor(this));
monitorNotifyAll(obj_monitor(this));
```

The Virtual Machine

One of the most interesting features of the Java language is that it is custom tailored to run on a Virtual Machine. Java certainly isn't the first language to use the concept of a Virtual Machine or "soft CPU" to gain cross-platform functionality, and having a Virtual Machine to compile to is no guarantee of widespread success. If it were, this book would probably be about UCSD Pascal, but the Virtual Machine teamed up with Java's built-in safety and simplicity make for an almost unbeatable combination.

Basic Architecture

The Java Virtual Machine has four basic components:

- A stack
- A set of registers
- A method area
- A garbage-collected heap

A Stack of Words and a Set of Registers A stack-based architecture was chosen for the Virtual Machine because it leads to more efficient implementation on "register poor" architectures. You don't need many registers if you have a stack. You could actually get away with just a program counter and a stack pointer if necessary. Java doesn't go quite that far, but it does have only four registers. The most important of these are the program counter, which is called *pc* (of course), and the stack pointer, which is called *optop* (operand stack top) and points to the top of a 32-bit FIFO stack. In addition to these two registers, the Virtual Machine has a *vars* register, which points to the first local variable of the currently executing method, and the *frame* register, which points to the current method's execution environment. The execution environment contains information used to do dynamic linking (names and locations of methods and variables), normal method returns (the calling method's registers), and exception propagation (information on catch clauses). All registers are 32 bits.

The Method Area The method area is the place where the compiled bytecodes actually live in the current implementation. There are plans to eliminate this area and store the information on the heap.

The Heap The Virtual Machine also has a garbage-collected heap of memory for general storage. The exact method used for garbage collection is not specified, so programmers implementing the Virtual Machine are free to use any algorithm. Garbage-collection algorithms range from aggressive ones that exact a constant performance penalty by watching the heap like a hawk to lazy ones that don't do any garbage collection until it is absolutely necessary, and everything in between. The current Virtual Machine implementation uses what is known as a "mark and sweep" algorithm, which constantly marks dead weight for garbage collection and then actually sweeps it away whenever it feels like it.

The Class File Format

As you know, Java object code is stored in class files with only one class per file. What follows is a description of the format of those files. Each entry contains the name and size of a field in the file followed by a brief description.

`magic -- 4 bytes`

This field must have the value 0xCAFEBABE no 0xDEADBEEF need apply.

`version -- 4 bytes`

The current version is 45. Version numbers will change only when either the bytecode format or the class file format changes.

`constant_pool_count -- 2 bytes`

This field shows the number of entries in the constant pool table.

`constant_pool -- size varies (constant_pool_count-1) bytes`

The pool of method names and other constants is in this field.

`access_flags - 2 bytes`

A combination of flags is taken from Table 10.4.

TABLE 10.4 Access Flags

Flag	Value
ACC_PUBLIC	0x0001
ACC_PRIVATE	0x0002
ACC_PROTECTED	0x0004
ACC_STATIC	0x0008
ACC_FINAL	0x0010
ACC_SYNCHRONIZED	0x0040
ACCC_TRANSIENT	0x00080
ACC_NATIVE	0x0200
ACC_INTERFACE	0x0200
ACC_ABSTRACT	0x0400

`this_class  -- 2 bytes`

This field is an index into the constant pool entry holding the name of this class.

`super_class -- 2 bytes`

This field is an index into the constant pool entry holding the name of the superclass (0 for object).

`interfaces_count -- 2 bytes`

This field shows the number of interfaces this class implements.

`interfaces  -- 2 bytes`

A pointer to an array of pointers in the constant pool pointing to the interfaces this class implements (0 for none).

`fields_count -- 2 bytes`

This field shows the number of instance variables (including those inherited from a super-class).

`fields  -- size varies`

This is a series of fields_count variable length field_info structures. The field_info structure has the following format:

    `access_flags -- 2bytes`

    A combination of flags is taken from the previous table.

    `name_index  -- 2 bytes`

    An index into the constant pool pointing to the name of the field.

    `signature_index  -- 2 bytes`

    An index to the constant pool pointing to the signature of the field.

    `attributes_count  -- 2 bytes`

    This field shows the number of attributes to follow.

    `attributes  -- size varies`

Currently, the only attribute recognized is the six-byte "ConstantValue" attribute:

`attribute_name -- 2 bytes`

An index to the constant pool which points to "ConstantValue."

`attribute_length -- 2 bytes`

The value must be 2.

`constantvalue_index -- 2 bytes`

The index into the constant pool pointing to the value of the field.

`methods_count   -- 2 bytes`

This field shows the number of methods, not including inherited ones.

`methods -- size varies`

A series of methods_count method_info structures.

`attributes_count   --2 bytes`

The number of additional attributes to immediately follow.

`attributes   -- size varies`

Currently, the only attribute recognized is the "SourceFile" attribute which gives the name of the source file for this class.

`source_file_attribute -- 6 byte structure`

This structure contains the following three fields:

`attribute_name_index  - 2 bytes`

An index into the constant pool pointing to the string "SourceFile."

`attribute_length  - 2 bytes`

This field must be 2.

`sourcefile_index   -- 2 bytes`

An index into the constant pool pointing to the name of the file.

The Instruction Set

Now that you know the context in which they are interpreted, let's look at those mysterious bytecodes. It's really not that complicated—it's assembly language. Because the decision was made to make the instructions one byte each, you'll find that this instruction set is much simpler than that of most CISC machines.

How to Read These Tables

The first column is the symbolic name of the instruction followed by its actual numerical value. The next column provides a brief description of the instruction. The third column shows the effect the instruction has on the stack. The arguments on the stack are shown first (separated by commas) followed by an arrow and then the contents of the stack after the instruction has been executed. The final column gives a more detailed analysis of the instruction.

The instructions fall into these groups:

- Stack manipulation
- Arithmetic
- Branch
- Array
- Load/store
- Object
- Method call and return
- Special-purpose to load constants
- Miscellaneous

Stack Instructions These instructions manipulate the stack without regard to type (see Table 10.5).

TABLE 10.5 Stack Manipulation Instructions			
nop = 0	Do nothing	no change	No effect!
pop = 87	Pop top stack word	..., any ‡ ...	Pop the top word from the stack.
pop2 = 88	Pop top two stack word	..., any2, any1 ‡ ...	Pop the top two words from the stack.

dup = 89	Duplicate top stack word	..., any ‡ ..., any, any	Duplicate the top word on the stack.
dup2 = 92	Duplicate top two stack words	..., any2, any1 ‡ ..., any2, any1, any2, any1	Duplicate the top two stack words.
dup_x1 = 90	Duplicate top stack word and put two down	..., any2, any1 ‡ ..., any1, any2, any1	Duplicate the top word on the stack and insert the copy two words down in the stack.
dup2_x1 = 93	Duplicate top two stack words and put two down	..., any3, any2, any1 ‡ ..., any2, any1, any3, any2, any1	Duplicate the top two words on the stack and insert the copies two words down in the stack.
dup_x2 = 91	Duplicate top stack word and put three down	..., any3, any2, any1 ‡ ..., any1, any3, any2, any1	Duplicate the top word on the stack and insert the copy three words down in the stack.
dup2_x2 = 94	Duplicate top two stack words and put three down	..., any4, any3, any2, any1 ‡ ..., any2, any1, any4, any3, any2, any1	Duplicate the top two words on the stack and insert the copies three words down in the stack.
swap = 95	Swap top two stack words	..., any2, any1 ‡ ..., any2, any1	Swap the top two elements on the stack.

Arithmetic, Logical, and Conversion Instructions Remember that each of these instructions operates on one type only, so if the name of the instruction is "double float multiply," for example, the top two values on the stack must both be double-precision floating point numbers. See Table 10.6 for these instructions.

TABLE 10.6 Arithmetic instructions

iadd = 96	Integer add	..., value1, value2 ‡ ..., result	Add value1 and value2 and replace them on the stack by their sum.

Continued

TABLE 10.6

ladd = 97	Long integer add	..., value1-word1, value1-word2, value2-word1, value2-word2 ‡ ..., result-word1, result-word2	Add value1 and value2 and replace them on the stack by their sum.
fadd = 98	Single float add	..., value1, value2 ‡ ..., result	Add value1 and value2 and replace them on the stack by their sum.
dadd = 99	Double float add	..., value1-word1, value1-word2, value2-word1, value2-word2 ‡ ..., result-word1, result-word2	Add value1 and value2 and replace them on the stack by their sum.
isub = 100	Integer subtract	..., value1, value2 ‡ ..., result	Subtract value2 from value1 and replace them on the stack with the result.
lsub = 101	Long integer subtract	..., value1-word1, value1-word2, value2-word1, value2-word2 ‡ ..., result-word1, result-word2	Subtract value2 from value1 and replace them on the stack with the result.
fsub = 102 subtract	Single floating point subtract	..., value1, value2 ‡ ..., result	Subtract value2 from value1 and replace them on the stack with the result.
dsub = 103	Double floating point subtract	..., value1-word1, value1-word2, value2-word1, value2-word2 ‡ ..., result-word1, result-word2	Subtract value2 from value1 and replace them on the stack with the result.

imul = 104	Integer multiply	..., value1, value2 ‡ ..., result	Replace value1 and value2 on the stack by their product.
imul = 105	Long integer multiply	..., value1-word1, value1-word2, value2-word1, value2-word2 ‡ ..., result-word1, result-word2	Replace value1 and value2 on the stack by their product.
fmul = 106	Single floating point multiply	..., value1, value2 ‡ ..., result	Replace value1 and value2 on the stack by their product.
dmul = 107	Double floating point multiply	..., value1-word1, value1-word2, value2-word1, value2-word2 ‡ ..., result-word1, result-word2	Replace value1 and value2 on the stack by their product.
idiv = 108	Integer divide	..., value1, value2 ‡ ..., result	Replace value1 and value2 on the stack by value1/value2. Result is truncated to nearest integer. Dividing by zero throws ArithmeticException.
ldiv = 109	Long integer divide	..., value1-word1, value1-word2, value2-word1, value2-word2 ‡ ..., result-word1, result-word2	Replace value1 and value2 on the stack by valuc1/valuc2. Result is truncated to nearest integer. Dividing by zero throws ArithmeticException.
fdiv = 110	Single float divide	..., value1, value2 ‡ ..., result	Replace value1 and value2 on the stack by value1/value2. Dividing by zero gives a result of NaN.
ddiv = 111	Double floating point divide	..., value1-word1, value1-word2, value2-word1, value2-word2 ‡ ..., result-word1, result-word2	Replace value1 and value2 on the stack by value1/value2. Dividing by zero gives a result of NaN.

Continued

TABLE 10.6 Continued

irem = 112	Integer remainder	..., value1, value2 ‡ ..., result	Replace value1 and value2 on the stack with the remainder of value1/value2. Dividing by zero throws ArithmeticException.
lrem = 113	Long integer remainder	..., value1-word1, value1-word2, value2-word1, value2-word2 ‡ ..., result-word1, result-word2	Replace value1 and value2 on the stack with the remainder of value1/value2. Dividing by zero throws ArithmeticException.
frem = 114	Single float remainder	..., value1, value2 ‡ ..., result	Replace value1 and value2 on the stack with value1 - integral_part(value1 / value2) * value2. Dividing by zero gives NaN.
drem = 115	Double float remainder	..., value1-word1, value1-word2, value2-word1, value2-word2 ‡ ..., result-word1, result-word2	Replace value1 and value2 on the stack with value1 - integral_part(value1 / value2) * value2. Dividing by zero gives NaN.
ineg = 116 fneg = 118	Integer negate Floating point negate	..., value ‡ ..., result	Replace value on the stack with its arithmetic negation (-value).
lneg = 117 dneg = 119	Long integer negate Double floating point negate.	..., value-word1, value-word2 ‡ ..., result-word1, result-word2	Replace value on the stack with its arithmetic negation (-value).
ishl = 120	Integer shift left	..., value1, value2 ‡ ..., result	Replace value1 and value2 on the stack by value1, shifted left by the low five bits of value2.

ishr = 122	Integer arithmetic shift right	..., value1, value2 ‡ ..., result	Replace value1 and value2 on the stack by value1, shifted right with sign extension by the low five bits of value2.
iushr = 124	Integer logical shift right	..., value1, value2 ‡ ..., result	Replace value1 and value2 on the stack by value1, shifted right without sign extension by the low five bits of value2.
lshl = 121	Long integer shift left	..., value1–word1, value1–word2, value2 ‡ ..., result word1, result–word2	Replace long value1 and int value2 with value1 shifted left by the low six bits of value2.
lshr = 123	Long integer arithmetic shift right	..., value1–word1, value1–word2, value2 ‡ ..., result–word1, result–word2	Replace long value1 and int value2 with value1 shifted right with sign extension by the low six bits of value2.
lushr = 125	Long integer logical shift right	..., value1–word1, value1–word2, value2–word1, value2–word2 ‡ ..., result–word1, result–word2	Replace long value1 and int value2 with value1 shifted right, with no sign extension, by the low six bits of value2.
iand = 126	Integer boolean AND	..., value1, value2 ‡ ..., result	Replace value1 and value2 on the stack by (value1 & value2).
land = 127	Long integer boolean AND	..., value1–word1, value1–word2, value2–word1, value2–word2 ‡ ..., result–word1, result–word2	Replace value1 and value2 on the stack by (value1 & value2).
ior = 128	Integer boolean OR	..., value1, value2 ‡ ..., result	Replace value1 and value2 on the stack by (value1 | value2)

Continued

TABLE 10.6 Continued

lor = 129	Long integer boolean OR	..., value1-word1, value1-word2, value2-word1, value2-word2 ‡ ..., result-word1, result-word2	Replace value1 and value2 on the stack by (value1 | value2)
ixor = 130	Integer boolean XOR	..., value1, value2 ‡ ..., result	Replace value1 and value2 on the stack by (value1 ^ value2)
lxor = 131	Long integer boolean XOR	..., value1-word1, value1-word2, value2-word1, value2-word2 ‡ ..., result-word1, result-word2	Replace value1 and value2 on the stack by (value1 ^ value2)
i2l = 133	Integer to long integer conversion	..., value ‡ ..., result-word1, result-word2	Convert int to long.
i2f = 134	Integer to single float	..., value ‡ ..., result	Convert int to float.
i2d = 135	Integer to double float	..., value ‡ ..., result-word1, " result-word2	Convert int to double.
l2i = 136	Long integer to integer	..., value-word1, value-word2 ‡ ..., result	Convert long to int by taking the low-order 32 bits.
l2f = 137	Long integer to single float	..., value-word1, value-word2 ‡ ..., result	Convert long to float.
l2d = 138	Long integer to double float	..., value-word1, value-word2 ‡ ..., result-word1, result-word2	Convert long to double.

f2i = 139	Single float to integer	..., value ‡ ..., result	Convert float to int.
f2l = 140	Single float to long integer	..., value ‡ ..., result-word1, result-word2	Convert float to long.
f2d = 141	Single float to double float	..., value ‡ ..., result-word1, result-word2	Convert float to double.
d2i = 142	Double float to integer	..., value-word1, value-word2 ‡ ..., result	Convert double to int.
d2l = 143	Double float to long integer	..., value-word1, value-word2 ‡ ..., result-word1, result-word2	Convert double to long.
d2f = 144	Double float to single float	..., value-word1, value-word2 ‡ ..., result	Convert double to float. If there is overflow, result is INFINITY of the same sign as value.
int2byte = 145	int2byte	..., value ‡ ..., result	Truncate value to 8 bits, then sign extend it to an integer.
int2char = 146	Integer to char	..., value ‡ ..., result	Truncate value to an unsigned 16-bit result and zero extend it to make an integer.
int2short = 147	Integer to short	..., value ‡ ..., result	Truncate value to a signed 16-bit result and sign extend it to make an integer.

Branch Instructions Unless otherwise noted, if the specified conditions are met, the operands *branchbyte1* and *branchbyte2* are used to calculate a signed 16-bit offset. Control passes to that offset from the address of the current instruction; otherwise, execution proceeds from the instructions shown in Table 10.7.

TABLE 10.7 Branch Instructions

ifeq = 153 branchbyte1 branchbyte2	Branch if equal to zero	..., value ‡ ...	Pop value from stack and branch if it is equal to zero.
ifnull = 198 branchbyte1 branchbyte2	Branch if null	..., value ‡ ...	Value must be a reference to an object. Pop value from stack and branch if it is null.
iflt = 155 branchbyte1 branchbyte2	Branch if less than 0	..., value ‡ ...	Value must be an integer. Pop value from stack and branch if it is less than zero.
ifle = 158 branchbyte1 branchbyte2	Branch if less than or equal to 0	..., value ‡ ...	Value must be an integer. Pop value from stack and branch if it is less than or equal to 0.
ifne = 154 branchbyte1 branchbyte2	Branch if not equal to 0	..., value ‡ ...	Value must be an integer. Pop value from stack and branch if it is not equal to 0.
ifnonnull = 199 branchbyte1 branchbyte2	Branch if ifnonnull	..., value ‡ ...	Value must be a reference to an object. Pop value from stack and branch if it is not null.
ifgt = 157 branchbyte1 branchbyte2	Branch if greater than 0	..., value ‡ ...	Value must be an integer. Pop value from stack and branch if it is greater than 0.
ifge = 156 branchbyte1 branchbyte2	Branch if greater than or equal to 0	..., value ‡ ...	Value must be an integer. Pop value from stack and branch if it is greater than or equal to 0.
if_icmpeq = 159 branchbyte1 branchbyte2	Branch if integers equal	..., value1, value2 ‡ ...	Pop value1 and value2 and branch if they are equal.
if_icmpne = 160 branchbyte1 branchbyte2	Branch if integers not equal	..., value1, value2 ‡ ...	Pop value1 and value2 and branch if they are not equal.
if_icmplt = 161 branchbyte1 branchbyte2	Branch if integer less than	..., value1, value2 ‡ ...	Pop value1 and value2 and branch if value1 < value2.

if_icmpgt = 163 branchbyte1 branchbyte2	Branch if integer greater than	..., value1, value2 ‡ ...	Pop value1 and value2 and branch if value1 > value2.
if_icmple = 164 branchbyte1 branchbyte2	Branch if integer less than or equal to	..., value1, value2 ‡ ...	Pop value1 and value2 and branch if value1 <= value2.
if_icmpge = 162 branchbyte1 branchbyte2	Branch if integer greater than or equal to	..., value1, value2 ‡ ...	Pop value1 and value2 and branch if value1 >= value2.
lcmp = 148	Long integer compare	..., value1-word1, value1-word2, value2-word1, value2-word1 ‡ ..., result	Pop value1 and value2. If value1 > value2, result is 1. If value1 = value2, result is 0. If value1 < value2, result is -1.
fcmpl = 149	Single float compare (-1 on NaN)	..., value1, value2 ‡ ..., result	Pop value1 and value2. If value1 > value2, result is 1. If value1 = value2, result is 0. If value1 < value2, result is -1. If either value is NaN, result is -1.
fcmpg = 150	Single float compare (1 on NaN)	..., value1, value2 ‡ ..., result	Pop value1 and value2. If value1 > value2, result is 1. If value1 = value2, result is 0. If value1 < value2, result is +1.
dcmpl = 151	Double float compare (-1 on NaN)	..., value1-word1, value1-word2, value2-word1, value2-word1 ‡ ..., result	Pop value1 and value2. If value1 > value2, result is 1. If value1 = value2, result is 0. If value1 < value2, result is -1. If either value is NaN, result is -1.
dcmpg = 152	Double float compare (1 on NaN)	..., value1-word1, value1-word2, value2-word1, value2-word1 ‡ ..., result	Pop value1 and value2. If value1 > value2, result is 1. If value1 = value2, result is 0. If value1 < value2, result is -1. If either value is NaN, result is 1.

Continued

TABLE 10.7 Continued

if_acmpeq = 165 branchbyte1 branchbyte2	Branch if object references are equal	..., value1, value2 ‡ ...	Pop value1 and value2. Branch if the objects they reference are the same.
if_acmpne = 166 branchbyte1 branchbyte2	Branch if object references are not equal	..., value1, value2 ‡ ...	Pop value1 and value2. Branch if the objects they reference are not the same.
goto = 167 branchbyte1 branchbyte2	Branch always	no change	Branch unconditionally to the offset calculated from branchbyte1 and branchbyte2.
goto_w = 200 branchbyte1 branchbyte2 branchbyte3 branchbyte4	Branch always (wide index)	no change	The operands are used to calculate a signed 32-bit offset. Execution proceeds at the offset from the address of this instruction.
jsr = 168 branchbyte1 branchbyte2	Jump subroutine	... ‡ ..., return-address	The address immediately following the jsr is pushed onto the stack. Execution proceeds at offset from this instruction.
jsr_w = 201 branchbyte1 branchbyte2 branchbyte3 branchbyte4	Jump subroutine (wide index)	... ‡ ..., return-address	Same as jsr, but the operands are used to calculate a signed 32-bit offset.
ret = 169 vindex	Return from subroutine	no change	The contents of local variable vindex are written into the program counter.
ret_w = 209 vindexbyte1 vindexbyte2	Return from subroutine (wide index)	no change	The operands are used to calculate a signed 16-bit index to a local variable. That variable's contents are then written into the program counter.

| tableswitch = 170 (0-3 bytes) padding default-offset1, default-offset2, default-offset3, default-offset4 low1, low2, low3, low4 high1, high2, high3, high4 (variable) jump offsets | Access jump table by index and jump | ..., index ‡ ... | tableswitch is a complex instruction. The compiler inserts between zero and three 0s as padding immediately after the opcode so that the next byte begins at an address that is a multiple of four. Next are the signed 4-byte quantities —default-offset, low, and high —and then the jump offsets, which are (high-low+1) 4-byte offsets. The jump offsets comprise a 0-based jump table. If index, which must be an integer, is less than low and greater than high, default-offset is added to the address of this instruction. Otherwise, execution continues at address: current_address + jump_offset[index - low]. |
| lookupswitch = 171 (0-3 bytes) padding default-offset1, default-offset2, default-offset3, default-offset4 npairs1, npairs2, npairs3, npairs4 (variable) match-offset pairs | Access jump table by key match and jump | ..., key ‡ ... | Another complicated instruction. As in tableswitch, the compiler inserts between zero and three 0s as padding immediately after the opcode so that the next byte begins at an address that is a multiple of four. Next are the signed 4-byte quantities default-offset and npairs, the number of match-offset pairs that follow. Each of these consists of a match and an offset, also both signed 4-byte quantities. If key, which must be an integer, is equal to one of the matches, the corresponding offset is added to the current address; if not, default-offset is used. |

Array Instructions   See Table 10.8 for array instructions.

TABLE 10.8 Array instructions

newarray = 188 atype	Allocate new array	..., size ‡ result	Allocates a new array of primitive type atype, capable of holding size elements. Result is a reference to this new object. All elements of the array are initialized to zero. The possible values for atype are T_BOOLEAN = 4, T_CHAR = 5, T_FLOAT = 6, T_DOUBLE = 7, T_BYTE = 8, T_SHORT=9, T_INT=10, T_LONG=11.
anewarray = 189 indexbyte1 indexbyte2	Allocate new array	..., size‡ result	Uses indexbyte1 and indexbyte2 to construct an index into the constant pool of the current class. The item at that index is resolved. Allocates a new array, of the indicated class type and capable of holding size elements. Result is a reference to the new array. All elements of the array are initialized to null.
multianewarray = 197 indexbyte1 indexbyte2 dimensions	Allocate new multi-dimensional array	..., size1 size2...sizen ‡ result	Uses indexbyte1 and indexbyte2 to construct an index into the constant pool of the current class. The item at that index is resolved. Allocates a new array of the specified number of dimensions, capable of holding size1xsize2x...sizen elements. All elements of the array are initialized to null. result is a reference to the new array.

arraylength = 190	Get length of array	..., objectref ‡ ..., length	objectref must be a reference to an array. Replace objectref on the top of the stack with the length of the array.
iaload = 46	Load integer from array	..., arrayref, index ‡ ..., value	Push the value at position number index in the array onto the stack.
laload = 47	Load long integer from array	..., arrayref, index ‡ ..., value-word1, value-word2	Push the value at position number index in the array onto the stack.
faload = 48	Load single float from array	..., arrayref, index ‡ ..., value	Push the value at position number index in the array onto the stack.
daload = 49	Load double float from array	..., arrayref, index ‡ ..., value-word1, value-word2	Push the value at position number index in the array onto the stack.
aaload = 50	Load object reference from array	..., arrayref, index ‡ ..., value	Push the object reference at position number index in the array onto the stack.
baload = 51	Load signed byte from array	..., arrayref, index ‡ ..., value	Push the signed byte value at position number index in the array, expanded into an integer, onto the stack.
caload = 52	Load character from array	..., arrayref, index ‡ ..., value	Push the value at position number index in the array, zero extended into an integer, onto the stack.
saload = 53	Load short from array	..., arrayref, index ‡ ..., value	Push the short integer value at position number index in the array, expanded to an integer, onto the stack.

Continued

TABLE 10.8 Continued

iastore = 79	Store into integer array	..., arrayref, index, value ‡ ...	The integer value is stored at position index in the array.
lastore = 80	Store into long integer array	..., arrayref, index, value-word1, value-word2 ‡ ...	The long integer value is stored at position index in the array.
fastore = 81	Store into single float array	..., arrayref, index, value ‡ ...	The single float value is stored at position index in the array.
dastore = 82	Store into double float array	..., arrayref, index, value-word1, value-word2 ‡ ...	The double float value is stored at position index in the array.
aastore = 83	Store into object reference array	., arrayref, .index, value ‡ ...	The object reference value is stored at position index in the array. If value is not an instance of the type of elements stored in arrayref, an ArrayStoreException is thrown.
bastore = 84	Store into signed byte array	..., arrayref, index, value ‡ ...	The integer value is stored at position index in the array. If value is too large to be a signed byte, it is truncated.
castore = 85	Store into character array	.., arrayref, .index, value ‡ ...	The integer value is stored at position index in the array. If value is too large to be a character, it is truncated.
sastore= 86	Store into short array	..., array, index, value ‡ ...	The integer value is stored at position index in the array. If value is too large to be an short, it is truncated.

Possible errors besides the ones already noted are as follows:

- In newarray, anewarray, and multianewarray, if it is not possible to allocate the memory for the array, the VM throws an OutofMemoryException. If size is negative, a NegativeArraySizeException is thrown.
- In the load, store, and length instructions, if arrayfref is null, the VM throws a NullPointer Exception, and if index is not within bounds, an ArrayIndexOutOfBoundsException is thrown.

Load/Store Instructions Remember that the value on the stack must be of the proper type for the instruction (see Table 10.9).

TABLE 10.9 Load/store Instructions

iload = 21 vindex	Load integer from local variable	... ‡ ..., value	Push the value of the local variables at vindex onto the operand stack.
iload_<n>: iload_0 = 26, iload_1 = 27, iload_2 = 28, iload_3 = 29	Load integer from local variable	... ‡ ..., value	Push the value of the local variables at <n> onto the stack.
lload = 22 vindex	Load long integer from local variable	... ‡ ..., value-word1, value-word2	Push the value of the local variables at vindex and vindex+1 onto the stack.
lload_<n>: lload_0 = 30, lload_1 = 31, lload_2 = 32, lload_3 = 33	Load long integer from local variable	... ‡ ..., value-word1, value-word2	Push the value of the local variables at <n> and <n>+1 onto the stack.
fload = 23 vindex	Load single float from local variable	... ‡ ..., value	Push the value of the local variable at vindex onto the stack.

Continued

TABLE 10.9 Continued

fload_<n>: fload_0 = 34, fload_1 = 35, fload_2 = 36, fload_3 = 37	Load single float from local variable	... ‡ ..., value	Push the value of the local variable at <n> onto the stack.
dload = 24 vindex	Load double float from local variable	... ‡ ..., value-word1, value-word2	Push the value of the local variables at vindex and vindex+1 onto the stack.
dload_<n>: dload_0 = 38, dload_1 = 39, dload_2 = 40, dload_3 = 41	Load double float from local variable	... ‡ ..., value-word1, value-word2	Push the value of the local variables at <n> and <n>+1 onto the stack.
aload = 25 vindex	Load object reference from local variable	... ‡ ..., value	The value of the local variable at vindex and vindex+1 is pushed onto the stack.
aload_<n>: aload_0 = 42, aload_1 = 43, aload_2 = 44, aload_3 = 45	Load object reference from local variable	... ‡ ..., value	Push the value of the local variable at <n> onto the stack.
istore = 54 vindex	Store integer into local variable	..., value ‡ ...	Set local variable vindex to value.
istore_<n>: istore_0 = 59, istore_1 = 60, istore_2 = 61, istore_3 = 62	Store integer into local variable	..., value ‡ ...	Set local variable <n> to value.
lstore = 55 vindex	Store long integer into local variable	..., value-word1, value-word2 ‡ ...	Set local variables vindex and vindex+1 to value.

lstore_<n>: lstore_0 = 63, lstore_1 = 64, lstore_2 = 65, lstore_3 = 66	Store long integer into local variable	..., value-word1, value-word2 ‡ ...	Set local variables <n> and <n>+1 to value.
fstore = 56 vindex	Store single float into local variable	..., value ‡ ...	Set local variable vindex to value.
fstore_<n>: fstore_0 = 67, fstore_1 = 68, fstore_2 = 69, fstore_3 = 70	Store single float into local variable	..., value ‡ ...	Set local variable <n> to value.
dstore = 57 vindex	Store double float into local variable	..., value-word1, value-word2 ‡ ...	Set local variables vindex and vindex+1 are value.
dstore_<n>: dstore_0 = 71, dstore_1 = 72, dstore_2 = 73, dstore_3 = 74	Store double float into local variable	..., value-word1, value-word2 ‡ ...	Set local variables <n> and <n>+1 to value.
astore = 58 vindex	Store object reference into local variable	..., value ‡ ...	Value must be a return address or a reference to an object. Local variable vindex is set to value.
astore_<n>: astore_0 = 75, astore_1 = 76, astore_2 = 77, astore_3 = 78	Store object reference into local variable	..., value ‡ ...	Value must be a return address or a reference to an object. Local variable <n> is set to value.
iinc = 132 vindex const	Increment local variable by constant	no change	Local variable vindex must contain an integer. Increment its value by const, which is treated as a signed 8-bit quantity.

Continued

| wide = 196 vindex2 | Wider index for accessing local variables in load, store and increment. | no change | This instruction must precede a load/store local variable instruction. Wide assembles the vindex of the following instruction and vindex2 from this instruction into an unsigned 16-bit index to a local variable. The following instruction uses this wider index in its operations. |

Object Field Instructions See Table 10.10 for object field instructions.

If objectref is null, Java throws a NullPointerException; if the field to be changed is static in a putfield instruction, or vice versa, an IncompatibleClassChangeException is thrown.

These instructions can handle both 32-byte and 64-byte fields.

Table 10.11 shows some other object commands.

TABLE 10.10 Object Field Instructions

putfield = 181 indexbyte1 indexbyte2	Set field in object	..., objectref, value ‡ ... or ..., objectref, value–word1, value–word2 ‡ ...	Set field indexed by indexbytes in object referenced by objectref to value.
getfield = 180 indexbyte1 indexbyte2	Fetch field from object	..., objectref ‡ ..., value or ..., objectref ‡ ..., value–word1, value–word2	Replace objectref on stack with value of field indexed by indexbytes in obect referenced by objectref on the stack.
putstatic = 179 indexbyte1 indexbyte2	Set static field in class	..., value ‡ ... or ..., value–word1, value–word2 ‡ ...	Set field indexed by indexbytes to value.

| getstatic = 178
indexbyte1
indexbyte2 | Get static field
from class | ..., ‡ ..., value
or
..., ‡ ..., value-word1,
value-word2 | Put value of field indexed
by indexbytes on the stack. |

TABLE 10.11 Other Object Instructions

new = 187 indexbyte1 indexbyte2	Create new object	... ‡ ..., objectref	Create a new object, of the class indexed in the constant pool by indexbytes, and push a reference to it onto the stack.
checkcast = 192 indexbyte1 indexbyte2	Make sure object is of given type	..., objectref ‡ ..., objectref	Check to see if objectref can be cast to be a reference to an object of the class indexed in the constant pool by indexbytes. If not, a Class CastException is thrown. (Null can be cast to any class.)
instanceof = 193 indexbyte1 indexbyte2	Determine if an object is of given type	..., objectref ‡ ..., result	Check to see if objectref can be cast to be a reference to an object of the class indexed in the constant pool by indexbytes. If so, objectref is replaced on the stack by 1. If not, or if objectref is null, it is replaced by 0.

Method Call and Return Instructions   See Table 10.12 for method call and return instructions.

TABLE 10.12 Method Call and Return Instructions

| invokevirtual = 182
indexbyte1
indexbyte2 | Invoke instance
method, dispatch
based on run-time
type | .., objectref,
[arg1, [arg2 ...]],
. ... ‡ ... | Call virtual method indexed
by indexbytes using args
from the stack. |

Continued

TABLE 10.12 Continued

invokenonvirtual = 183 indexbyte1 indexbyte2	Invoke instance method, dispatching based on compile-time type	..., objectref, [arg1, [arg2 ...]], ... ‡ ...	Call nonvirtual method indexed by indexbytes with args from the stack.
invokestatic = 184 indexbyte1 indexbyte2	Invoke a class (static) method	..., [arg1, [arg2 ...]], ... ‡ ...	Call static method indexed by indexbytes with args from the stack.
invokeinterface = 185 indexbyte1 indexbyte2 nargs reserved	Invoke interface method	..., objectref, [arg1, [arg2 ...]], ... ‡ ...	Call interface method indexed by indexbytes using args from the stack. Nargs is the number of arguments.
ireturn = 172	Return integer from function	..., value ‡ [empty]	Push value onto the stack of the previous execution environment. Discard all other values on the current stack and return control to the caller.
lreturn = 173	Return long integer from function	..., value-word1, value-word2 ‡ [empty]	
freturn = 174	Return float from function	..., value ‡ [empty]	
dreturn = 175	Return double from function	..., value-word1, value-word2 ‡ [empty]	
areturn = 176	Return object reference from function.	..., value ‡ [empty]	
return = 177	Return void from function.	..., ‡ [empty]	Discard all values on the current stack and return control to the caller.
breakpoint = 202		no change	Stop and pass control to breakpoint handler.

Special-Purpose Instructions to Load Constants

See Table 10.13 for those instructions that load constants.

TABLE 10.13 Constant Instructions

bipush = 16 byte1	Push one-byte signed integer	... ‡ ..., value	Push byte1, interpreted as a signed 8-bit value and expanded to an integer, onto the stack.
sipush = 17 byte1 byte2	Push two-byte signed integer	... ‡ ..., item	Assemble byte1 and byte2 into a signed 16-bit value, expand it to an integer, and push it onto the stack.
ldc1 = 18 indexbyte1	Push item from constant pool	... ‡ ..., item	Use indexbyte1 as an unsigned 8-bit index into the constant pool, resolve the item at that index, and push it onto the stack. Unsigned 8-bit index into the constant pool of the current class.
ldc2 = 19 indexbyte1 indexbyte2	Push item from constant pool	... ‡ ..., item	Use indexbyte1 and indexbyte2 to calculate an unsigned 16-bit index into the constant pool, resolve the item at that index, and push it onto the stack.
ldc2w = 20 indexbyte1 indexbyte2	Push long or double from constant pool	... ‡ ..., constant-word1, constant–word2	Use indexbyte1 and indexbyte2 to calculate an unsigned 16-bit index into the constant pool. Resolve the two-word constant at that index and push it onto the stack.
aconst_null = 1 reference	Push null object	... ‡ ..., null	Push the null object reference onto the stack.
iconst_m1 = 2	Push integer constant –1	... ‡ ..., –1	Push the integer –1 onto the stack.

Continued

TABLE 10.13 Continued

iconst_<n>: iconst_0 = 3 iconst_1 = 4 iconst_2 = 5 iconst_3 = 6 iconst_4 = 7 iconst_5 = 8	Push integer constant	... ‡ ..., <n>	Push the integer <n> onto the stack.
lconst_<l>: lconst_0 = 9 lconst_1 = 10	Push long integer constant	... ‡ ..., <l>-word1, <l>-word2	Push the long integer <l> onto the stack.
fconst_<f>: lconst_0 = 9, lconst_1 = 10	Push single float	... ‡ ..., <f>	Push the single-precision floating point number <f> onto the stack.
dconst_<d>: dconst_0 = 14, dconst_1 = 15	Push double float	... ‡ ..., <d>-word1, <d>-word2	Push the double-precision floating point number <d> onto the stack.

Miscellaneous Instructions See Table 10.14 for exception and monitor instructions.

TABLE 10.14 Miscellaneous Commands

athrow = 191	Throw exception or error	..., objectref => [undefined]	Throw the Throwable object referenced by objectref. If objectref is null, a NullPointerException is thrown.
monitorenter = 194	Enter monitored region of code	..., objectref => ...	Attempt to get a lock on objectref. If another thread already has a lock, the current thread waits until it is unlocked. If it is already locked, there is no effect.
monitorexit = 195	Exit monitored region of code	..., objectref => ...	Release the lock on objectref.

Programming: The Bare Plastic

If this discussion has piqued your interest and you want to try your hand at programming the Virtual Machine in assembly language, or even write your own compiler to compile to it, good for you! An ADA 95 to bytecode compiler has already been produced, and other compilers of this sort could breathe new life into some languages that are currently stagnating. Thus instead of being the fascist "one-world language" some have made it out to be, Java may actually revive some of the languages that never caught on. It's worth a shot!

One tool you may be interested in is K.B Sriram's jas, a Java assembler. This package is written in Java and can generate Java class files using either a script or another Java program to drive it. You'll find a pointer to this on our web page. To disassemble your classes, you can use the javap program that comes with the JDK. The usage is as follows:

```
javap [options] classname
```

Classname is the name of the class (with no extension), and options may be one or more of the following:

- -c Disassemble the code
- -classpath <directories separated by colons>
- h Create info that can be put into a C header file
- -p Include private fields and methods

Chapter 11

Internet Capitalism: Shopping Carts and Databases

Virtual Materialism

Most people who aren't in the business of selling something on the web look at the commercialization of the Internet with some dismay. As a rule, I refuse to even check out URLs which end in com unless I know exactly what file I'm looking for, because the odds of finding anything but blatant bandwidth-wasting advertisements are about 100 to 1. Still, programmers have to eat, and you may be creating commercial web sites. The two applications people are most likely to pay you to design are so-called "shopping carts" and database front ends. Shopping carts are fairly easy to pull off in Java, at least compared to using CGI. In the first half of this chapter, we'll hack together a skeleton shopping cart you can use as a framework for your own projects. On the database side, we'll look into the JDBC and ways to get your applets to access data.

Shopping Carts

The neighborhood I live in is pretty strange. I live just down the street from Valueland, arguably the worst supermarket in the state, and it isn't unusual to see people exit the store with their shopping carts, cross the parking lot, and calmly wheel the cart down the street to their home, where they ditch the cart in the street. In fact, the supermarket has to hire a truck to go around once a week and collect them. Fortunately, we won't have to deal with those sort of problems, because the carts we are talking about here are virtual.

The basic idea is that the virtual shopping cart travels around with users as they browse an on-line catalog and keeps track of the items they purchase. Virtual shopping carts are notoriously hard to write because of the stateless nature of HTTP. Each HTTP transaction is treated as an entity in itself with no past or future. Luckily, Java allows you to keep track of things on the client side, making shopping carts simple.

The approach taken in writing this sample shopping cart may seem a little unusual. Normally, a shopping cart serves as a repository for objects and knows all about the prices, styles, colors, and other attributes of the objects you put into it. The objects are simply data, and the cart must arrange to gather this data and base its actions upon it. Our example takes the opposite approach. The objects are smart applets. They know how much they cost, and they place themselves in the cart, which is just a dumb receptacle for information. The cart itself knows how to take objects out of itself upon request and how to find the checkout when it's time to leave!

Basic Strategy

The first requirement we have for our cart is that it be available to our items on every page. This is relatively simple to accomplish if we make all our items instances of a single class and make the cart a static member of that class. With this arrangement, all the items on the page share the same cart, which makes sense.

The cart itself is not even an applet, because it doesn't need to be embedded in an HTML page. Instead, we make our cart a subclass of Frame: that way we can pop it up at will, and it can have a menu if we wish. The most important part of the shopping cart is the constructor, which is called just once in a static initializer when the item applet class is loaded. The constructor first creates a Vector object to hold the prices of the objects put into it. The cart does not have to download a list of the items and prices; instead, it waits for an object to tell it something like, "I cost $19.95, and I'm jumping into the cart!" You could say that our cart is ignorant but not entirely stupid.

After the Vector to hold the prices is created, the next section of the constructor simply sets up a simple user interface in the frame:

```
public Cart(){
    prices=new Vector(100);

    setLayout(new BorderLayout());
    list=new List();
    this.add("Center",list);
    list.addItem("no items in cart");

    Panel panel=new Panel();

    removeItem=new Button("Remove Item");
    panel.add(removeItem);

    purchase=new Button("Purchase All");
    panel.add(purchase);

    hideCart=new Button("Hide Cart");
    panel.add(hideCart);

    this.add("South",panel);
    Panel topPanel=new Panel();

    topPanel.add(new Label("Total Price:"));

    TOTAL=new TextField(6);
    topPanel.add(TOTAL);

    this.add("North",topPanel);
}
```

In this case we use the simplistic BorderLayout to good effect. The North component is a panel containing a label and a text field to display the total cost of the items in the cart. The Center component is the list of items in the cart, and it starts out containing a message saying that there are currently no items in the cart. The South component contains a panel containing buttons to delete an item from the list, purchase all items in the cart, and hide the cart.

Now that we have constructed our cart, let's look at the items that place themselves into it. Each item is an applet of the Item class. The constructor for Item first reads two values from the APPLET tag: the name of the item and its price.

```
try{
    price=Float.valueOf(getParameter("price")).floatValue();
}catch (Exception e){
    price=(float)19.95;      // universal default price
}
id=getParameter("name");
if (id==null){
    id="YellowMatter Custard(s)"; // universal default name
}
```

You may question the wisdom of embedding an applet in your page for every item in your on-line catalog, but remember that the class file needs to be downloaded only once because all the applets are the same class. The only things that differentiate one applet from another are the parameters passed in the tag. Here's an example of the HTML to show how this works:

```
<applet code="Item.class" width=300 height=60>
<PARAM name="name" value="Plantain Tartlet(s)">
<PARAM name="price" value="11.50">
</applet>
```

Next, our constructor sets up the interface for our item. This has several parts. First, we set up three TextFields. One TextField is for the fixed price of the item, one is for the quantity desired, and one is used to display how much that number of items will cost. Underneath this we place a panel with buttons to add an item to the cart, empty the cart, and show the cart in order to review its contents.

```
this.add(new Label("QTY:"));

QTY=new TextField(6);
this.add(QTY);
QTY.setText("1");
QTY.selectAll();
```

```
this.add(new Label("PRICE"));

PRICE=new TextField(6);
PRICE.setEditable(false);
PRICE.setText("$"+Float.toString(price));

this.add(PRICE);
this.add(new Label("TOTAL:"));

TOTAL=new TextField(6);
TOTAL.setEditable(false);
TOTAL.setText("$"+Float.toString(price));

this.add(TOTAL);

Panel panel=new Panel();

addToCart=new Button("Add to cart");
panel.add(addToCart);

showCart=new Button("Show the Cart");
panel.add(showCart);

emptyCart=new Button("Empty the Cart");
panel.add(emptyCart);

this.add(panel);

/*
** force a layout
*/
validate();
```

Now that we have our user interface laid out, we can worry about how to handle events. Let's start with keystrokes. In our handleEvent(Event e) method we check to see if the event is a keypress. If it is, we snag it and pass it to the parent container's postEvent(Event) routine so that it shows up in our TextField. Next we try to parse the value of the field to get our quantity. If we can't, because the user entered a nonnumeric value, we set the

TextField's value to 1. Next we calculate the cost of the items, use a little dodgy code to make sure it has the proper format for a dollars and cents value, and put it in the result field. The code looks something like this:

```
if (evt.id==Event.KEY_PRESS && evt.target==QTY){

    /* send keystroke to the
    ** textfield so it shows up onscreen
    */
    Component parent = this.getParent();
    parent.postEvent(evt);

    /* try to parse the new info
    ** and set the value to 1 if invalid
    */
    StringBuffer sb=new StringBuffer(QTY.getText());
    try{
        quantity=Integer.parseInt(sb.toString());

    }catch (Exception e){
        quantity=1;
        QTY.setText("1");
    }

    /* calculate the string to put in the
    ** result field. This section makes sure
    ** we end up with a value of the form $xx.xx
    */
    sb=new StringBuffer().append(price*(float)quantity);
    int len=sb.length();
    int last=sb.toString().indexOf(".");
    if (last==-1){
        sb.append(".00");
    }else{
        if ((len-last)==2){
            sb.append("0");
        }
```

```
    }
    TOTAL.setText("$"+sb.toString());


    /* return true to fool caller into thinking
    ** we have handled the event!
    */
    return true;
}
```

Handling button events is straightforward enough. If the "show cart" button is pressed, we simply call cart.show(). If the "empty cart" button is pressed, we call the emptyCart() method. If the "add item" button is pressed, we call the addItem(String, int, float) method with the name of the item, the quantity, and the price. Since these are all method calls, our event handling is quite simple:

```
/* if one of our buttons was the target
** then call the approprate routine.
*/
if (evt.target==showCart){
    cart.show();
}


if (evt.target==emptyCart){
    cart.emptyCart();
}


if (evt.target==addItem){
    cart.addToCart(id,quantity,price);
}
```

Having completed our Item applet with a minimum of pain, we can now turn our attention to the cart itself. If the remove-item button is pressed, we first need to make sure that it's really an item that is selected and not the "no items in cart" message. If the item meets this criterion, we remove it from the list, retrieve its cost from the Vector we use to store it, and subtract the cost from the total. If the button to hide the cart is pressed, we simply call the frame's hide() method. If the purchase button is pressed, we do nothing, but here you would put the code to send the information back to your server. You have plenty of options. You could set up a Java server to listen for connections, take your orders, and store them in a file. If you have a server-side program that expects an HTTP POST method, you can open a connection to port 8080 (usually) and mimic the data your server expects. You could even use something like the NormanMailer applet to mail yourself the orders.

Let's take a look at the code used to add and remove items from the cart. Removing all the items is simplest:

```
public void emptyCart(){
    list.clear();
    numitems=0;
    list.addItem("no items in cart!");
    total=0;
    updatefield();
    prices.removeAllElements();
}
```

Here we just empty our list, add the default message, and call our updatefield() method to update our total field to reflect the fact that the cart is now empty. The code to add an item to the list is only a little more complicated. First we check to see if the cart is empty. If it is, we remove the default message. Next we add a string containing the quantity and the type of the item to the list, change our total to reflect the new addition, and call the updatefield() method to make the TextField reflect the change. Finally, we add the price of this item (or group of items) to our Vector of prices so that we can remove it later if necessary.

```
public void addItem(String s,int qty,float price){
    if (numitems==0){
        list.clear();
    }
    StringBuffer sb=new StringBuffer();
    sb.append(qty+"   ").append(s);
    list.addItem(sb.toString());
    numitems++;
    total=total+qty*price;
    updatefield();
    prices.addElement(new Float(qty*price));
}
```

That's it! When all the pieces are put together (Listing 11.1), the results look something like Figures 11.1 and 11.2.

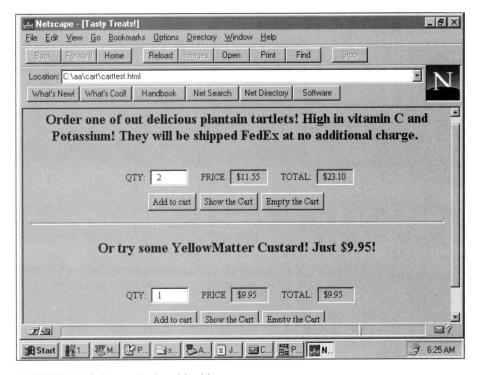

FIGURE 11.1 Items displayed by Netscape.

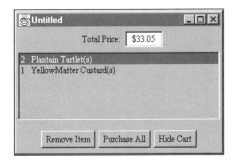

FIGURE 11.2 The Shopping Cart.

LISTING 11.1

```
import java.awt.*;
import java.util.*;
import java.applet.*;
```

Continued

```java
public class Item extends Applet implements Runnable{

    Thread T=null;

    /* initialize out static cart when
    ** the class is first loaded
    */

    static Cart cart=new Cart();
    static{cart.resize(300,200);}

    /* some global-ish variables
    ** for the price,id,quantity
    */

    String id="widget";
    float price;
    int quantity=1;

    /*
    ** our GUI components
    */

    TextField QTY,PRICE,TOTAL;
    Button addToCart,showCart,emptyCart;

    /*
    ** Just launch a thread
    */

    public void start(){
        T= new Thread(this);
        T.start();
    }

    public void run(){
```

```
/*
** get our parameters (name and price)
*/

try{
    price=Float.valueOf(getParameter("price")).floatValue();
}catch (Exception e){
    price=(float)19.95;    // universal default price
}
id=getParameter("name");
if (id==null){
    id="YellowMatter Custard(s)" ;
}



/*
** build our GUI
*/

this.add(new Label("QTY:"));

  QTY=new TextField(6);
this.add(QTY);
QTY.setText("1");
QTY.selectAll();

this.add(new Label("PRICE"));

PRICE=new TextField(6);
PRICE.setEditable(false);
PRICE.setText("$"+Float.toString(price));

this.add(PRICE);
this.add(new Label("TOTAL:"));

  TOTAL=new TextField(6);
```

Continued

```
TOTAL.setEditable(false);
TOTAL.setText("$"+Float.toString(price));

this.add(TOTAL);

Panel panel=new Panel();

addToCart=new Button("Add to cart");
panel.add(addToCart);


showCart=new Button("Show the Cart");
panel.add(showCart);

emptyCart=new Button("Empty the Cart");
panel.add(emptyCart);

this.add(panel);

/*
** force a layout
*/

validate();

}

public boolean handleEvent(Event evt){


    if (evt.id==Event.KEY_PRESS && evt.target==QTY){

        /* send  keystroke to the
        ** textfield so it shows up onscreen
        */
        Component parent = this.getParent();
        parent.postEvent(evt);
```

```
        /* try to parse the new info
        ** and set the value to 1 if invalid
        */
        StringBuffer sb=new StringBuffer(QTY.getText());
        try{
            quantity=Integer.parseInt(sb.toString());

        }catch (Exception e){
            quantity=1;
            QTY.setText("1");
        }

        /* calculate the string to put in the
        ** result field. This section makes sure
        ** we end up with a value of the form $xx.xx
        */
        sb=new StringBuffer().append(price*(float)quantity);
        int len=sb.length();
        int last=sb.toString().indexOf(".");
        if (last==-1){
            sb.append(".00");
        }else{
            if ((len-last)==2){sb.append("0");}
        }
        TOTAL.setText("$"+sb.toString());

        /* return true to fool caller into thinking we have
        ** handled the event!
        */
        return true;
    }
    /* if one of our buttons was the target
    ** then call the approprate routine.
    */
    if (evt.target==showCart){
        cart.show();
```

Continued

```
        }

        if (evt.target==emptyCart){
            cart.emptyCart();
        }

        if (evt.target==addToCart){
            cart.addItem(id,quantity,price);
        }

        return false;
    }

    public void stop(){

    }

}

class Cart extends Frame{
    Button removeItem, purchase,hideCart;
    Label label1,label2,label3;
    TextField TOTAL;
    List list;
    float total;
    int numitems;
    Vector prices;

    public Cart(){
        prices=new Vector(100);
        setLayout(new BorderLayout());

        list=new List();
        this.add("Center",list);
        list.addItem("no items in cart");

        Panel panel=new Panel();
```

```
    removeItem=new Button("Remove Item");
    panel.add(removeItem);

    purchase=new Button("Purchase All");
    panel.add(purchase);

    hideCart=new Button("Hide Cart");
    panel.add(hideCart);

    this.add("South",panel);
    Panel topPanel=new Panel();

    topPanel.add(new Label("Total Price:"));

    TOTAL=new TextField(6);
    topPanel.add(TOTAL);


    this.add("North",topPanel);

}

public void emptyCart(){
    list.clear();
    numitems=0;
    list.addItem("no items in cart!");
    total=0;
    updatefield();
    prices.removeAllElements();


}

public void addItem(String s,int qty,float price){

    if (numitems==0){
```

Continued

```java
            list.clear();
        }
        StringBuffer sb=new StringBuffer();
        sb.append(qty+"    ").append(s);
        list.addItem(sb.toString());
        numitems++;
        total=total+qty*price;
        updatefield();
        prices.addElement(new Float(qty*price));


    }


    public boolean handleEvent(Event e){
        if (e.target==removeItem){
            if (list.getSelectedIndex()!=-1 & numitems>0 ){
                int index= list.getSelectedIndex() ;
                Float f=(Float)prices.elementAt(index);
                total=total-f.floatValue();
                prices.removeElementAt(index) ;
                 list.delItem(index);
                numitems--;
                if (numitems==0){
                    list.addItem("No items in cart!");
                }
                updatefield();


            }
        }
        if (e.target==hideCart){
            this.hide();
        }
        return false;
    }
    public void show(){
        super.show();
        this.toFront();
```

```
        repaint();
    }


    public void updatefield(){
        StringBuffer sb=new StringBuffer().append(total);
        int last=sb.toString().indexOf(".");
        if (last==-1){
            sb.append(".00");
        }else{
            if ((sb.length()-last)==2){sb.append("0");}
        }
        TOTAL.setText("$"+sb.toString());


    }

}
```

Databases

Getting involved with databases these days is a good career choice because data is prolifer-ating at an alarming rate. It seems like the amount of information in the universe doubles every couple of months. I'm sure this violates some unwritten law of thermodynamics, but it's true. There's just one problem. Databases aren't fun. Very rarely will anyone exclaim "Yahoo, a table join!"

The offshoot is that the people currently learning to use database tools with Java proba-bly aren't doing it because they want to—they're doing it because the have to, or because someone drove a dumptruck full of money up to their front door.

For this reason, I'm going to make this section as quick and painless as possible. Remember those yellow Cliff's Notes from high school—or college for that matter—those wonderful little booklets which saved you from having to read long-winded Thomas Hardy novels by providing you with just enough information to get a C on the exams? Well, this section is pretty much the equivalent of those. The long-winded book in question is the *JDBC Specification*, and the information given here can save you from destroying your eyesight by viewing it with the Acrobat Viewer, or killing countless trees (and toner cartridges) by printing it out.

JDBC

We've seen how easy it is to make forms and user interfaces in Java, so creating a database front end is simple, but how do you actually interface to the database? Answer: JDBC. Let's start with the basics. JDBC stands for Java Database Connectivity, and it is a call-level SQL API. No fancy object-oriented database stuff here — just classes to encapsulate connections to a database, SQL statements, and result sets.

To use JDBC, you must download the basic JDBC driver manager package and at least one driver. The JDBC package is available from the following:

```
http://splash.javasoft.com/jdbc/
```

When you have extracted everything into a directory, add that directory to your CLASS-PATH so that Java can find it. In the examples below, we used the JDBC-ODBC Bridge driver that translates JDBC operations into the appropriate ODBC calls. This is also available from the same source. With this package, we put a couple of DLLs in places where Java could find them, so make sure to follow the instructions in the README file that comes with the particular driver you download. If you are using some other driver, what follows will be accurate on the whole, but some details will be different, such as the URL format (see below).

The decision was made to use a URL type syntax to access databases (but not a java.net.URL object). The URL starts with "jdbc:" followed by the sub protocol ("odbc" in this case) followed by any driver-specific information. Some of these URLs take a host name and port as part of the subprotocol, giving you easy access to remote databases. The JDBC-ODBC Bridge takes an additional string indicating the data source, so the URL would be as follows:

```
jdbc:odbc:mydatasource
```

The DriverManager

The DriverManager class is used to find drivers appropriate to given JDBC URLs. It does this by querying methods in the Driver class that you shouldn't really have to worry about unless you are writing a driver yourself. When the DriverManager class is loaded, it looks in the properties in the .hotjava directory for the "jdbc.drivers" property. It then attempts to load any drivers it finds there. The "jdbc.drivers" property is a string list of Driver class names separated by colons, so it might look something like this:

```
jdbc.drivers=foo.bah.Driver:vatican.pope.sql.Driver
```

Alternately, you may load a driver by name using the static Class.forName(String) method. In this case, we can use the following:

```
Class.forName("jdbc.odbc.JdbcOdbcDriver");
```

When it is loaded, the driver will automatically register itself with the DriverManager.

You may have noticed that all the methods in the DriverManager class are static, so you will not need to instantiate an object to use them. The most useful method in DriverManager is getConnection(String url), which returns a connection to the given JDBC URL. Once you have a Connection, you can use the createStatement() method to return a Statement object. The Statement object's executeQuery(String) method can be used to execute a raw SQL query. This method returns a ResultSet. The ResultSet's cursor is initially positioned before the first row, and the next() method will move to the next row (returning false if there is no next row).

You can find out how many columns are in the ResultSet using getColumnCount() and find out the name of a column with getColumnName(int index). You can use the methods in the ResultSet to get the values of different columns using either their index or the name of the column. It's easier to use the names to get data, but using the index of the columns is safer, of course, because the name might not be unique. (In this case, the first matching column is used.)

We can also get "meta-data" about the result set using its getMetaData() method. Using this method will return you a ResultSetMetaData object with lots of useful information about the result set such as the column count, the column heading, name, width, and much more.

To get the data for the current row, you may use either the get<datatype>(int) to get the data in the given column or the get<data>type(String name) to get the data in the column with the given name.

If you like details, you can use a Connection's getMetaData() method to return you an instance of a class that implements the DatabaseMetaData interface. A DatabaseMetaData object has about nine million methods to give you fascinating information such as the JDBC driver's minor version number and whether the database sorts NULL values. As Corbin Bernsen would say about the woman in Yorkshire who found a potato resembling Richard Nixon, it's truly extraordinary.

JDBC won't make database programming fun, but it does make it tolerable. These brief notes should be enough to get you started.

If you will be doing any heavy-duty database programming in Java, check out the book *Java Database Programming* by Brian Jepson. The author has a knack for bringing highly technical topics down to earth, and he manages to make one of the driest subjects almost entertaining.

Just What You Need

The classes and interfaces shown in Tables 11.1 through 11.7 are about the bare minimum you will need to get started with JDBC. As noted earlier, if you are interested in such things as DatabaseMetaData, you're on your own—my eyes glaze over at the very sight of the word.

TABLE 11.1 DriverManager

public static synchronized Connection getConnection(String url, String user, String password) throws SQLException	Returns a Connection to the given JDBC URL using the given user name and password. The first available driver capable of handling the URL is used.
public static synchronized Connection getConnection(String url) throws SQLException	Returns a Connection to the given JDBC URL. The first available driver capable of handling the URL is used.
public static synchronized Connection getConnection(String url, Properties info) throws SQLException	Returns a connection to the given JDBC URL passing along a Properties object with driver-specific parameters.
public static void deregisterDriver(Driver driver) throws SQLException	Removes the given Driver from the list of registered Drivers.
public static Driver getDriver(String url) throws SQLException	Returns a Driver that can handle the given JDBC URL from the set of registered drivers.
public static Enumeration getDrivers()	Returns an Enumeration of the currently registered Drivers.
public static int getLoginTimeout()	Returns the current maximum login time in seconds.
public static PrintStream getLogStream()	Returns a reference to the stream used for logging/tracing information.

public static synchronized void println(String message)	Prints a message to the current log stream.
public static synchronized void registerDriver(Driver driver) throws SQLException	Registers a Driver with the DriverManager.
public static void setLoginTimeout (int seconds)	Sets the maximum login time for all Drivers in seconds.
public static void setLogStream (PrintStream out)	Sets the stream used to print logging/tracing information.

TABLE 11.2 Connection

public final static int TRANSACTION_NONE	Transactions are not supported. Used in setTransactionIsolation(int level) and getTransactionIsolation( ).
public final static int TRANSACTION_READ_UNCOMMITTED	Dirty reads are done. Used in setTransactionIsolation(int level) and getTransactionIsolation( ).
public final static int TRANSACTION_READ_COMMITTED	Only reads on the current row are repeatable. Used in setTransaction Isolation(int level) and getTransaction Isolation( ).
public final static int TRANSACTION_REPEATABLE_READ	Reads on all rows of a result are repeat able. Used in setTransactionIsolation(int level) and getTransactionIsolation( ).
public final static int TRANSACTION_SERIALIZABLE	Reads on all rows of a transaction are repeatable. Used in setTransactionIsolation(int level) and getTransaction Isolation( ).
public final static int TRANSACTION_VERSIONING	Reads on all rows of a transaction are repeatable. Updates proceed and the old state is preserved for current readers. Used in setTransactionIsolation(int level) and getTransactionIsolation( ).
public abstract Statement createStatement() throws SQLException	Returns a new Statement object.

Continued

TABLE 11.2 Continued

public abstract CallableStatement prepareCall(String sql) throws SQLException	Creates a stored procedure statement.
public abstract void close() throws SQLException	Immediately releases any JDBC and database resources held by the connection.
public abstract void commit() throws SQLException	Commits the transaction and releases any database locks the connection holds.
public abstract void clearWarnings() throws SQLException	Causes a subsequent call to getWarnings to return a new SQLWarnings object.
public abstract void disableAutoClose() throws SQLException	Disable auto-closing on commit and rollback.
public abstract String getCatalog() throws SQLException	Returns the current catalog (null if none).
public abstract DatabaseMetaData getMetaData() throws SQLException	Returns a MetaData object for this connection.
public abstract int getTransactionIsolation() throws SQLException	Returns the transaction isolation mode. DisableAutoClose.
public abstract SQLWarning getWarnings() throws SQLException	Returns an SQLWarnings object containing the first warning (or null if none). Any subsequent warnings are chained to this SQLWarnings.
public abstract boolean isClosed() throws SQLException	Returns true if the connection has been closed.
public abstract boolean isReadOnly() throws SQLException	Returns true if the connection is in read-only mode.
public abstract String nativeSQL (String query) throws SQLException	Returns the native form of the given query string.
public abstract PreparedStatement prepareStatement(String sql) throws SQLException	Creates a compiled statement from the given SQL string.

public abstract void rollback() throws SQLException	Forgets all changes since the previous commit or rollback and releases and locks on the database held by the connection.
public abstract void setAutoCommit (boolean enableAutoCommit) throws SQLException	Causes SQL statements to be executed and committed as individual transactions (the default). If set to false, causes subsequent statements to all be part of one transaction (terminated by a commit or rollback call).
public abstract void setCatalog(String catalog) throws SQLException	Selects a catalog for this datadase. Silently ignored by databases that do not support catalogs.
public abstract void setReadOnly(boolean readOnly) throws SQLException	Makes this connection read only. (Cannot be called in the middle of a transaction.)
public abstract void setTransactionIsolation (int level) throws SQLException	Sets the transaction isolation level on a new connection. Cannot be used in the middle of a transaction.

TABLE 11.3 Statement

public abstract void cancel() throws SQLException	Can be used by another thread to cancel an executing query.
public abstract void clearWarnings() throws SQLException	Causes a subsequent call to getWarnings() to return a new SQLWarnings object.
public abstract void close() throws SQLException	Releases all JDBC and database resources.
public abstract boolean execute (String sql) throws SQLException	Executes the given statement.
public abstract ResultSet executeQuery(String sql) throws SQLException	Executes the given SQL statement and returns a single ResultSet.

Continued

TABLE 11.3 Continued

public abstract int executeUpdate (String sql) throws SQLException	Executes an SQL INSERT, UPDATE, or DELETE statement. Returns the row count.
public abstract int getMaxFieldSize() throws SQLException	Returns the maximum amount of data returned by any column in bytes, or 0 if unlimited.
public abstract int getMaxRows() throws SQLException	Returns the maximum number of rows to be returned in a ResultSet, or 0 if unlimited. Excess rows are silently dropped.
public abstract boolean getMoreResults() throws SQLException	Returns the next result. Returns true if it is a ResultSet and false if it is an integer.
public abstract int getQueryTimeout() throws SQLException	Returns the number of seconds a driver will wait for an SQL statement to execute before throwing an exception.
public abstract ResultSet getResultSet() throws SQLException	Returns the ResultSet for the last executed statement (that is, if it is a ResultSet, null if it is an update count).
public abstract int getUpdateCount() throws SQLException	Returns the update count.
public abstract SQLWarning getWarnings() throws SQLException	Returns an SQLWarnings object. Subsequent warnings will be chained to this one.
public abstract void setCursorName(String name) throws SQLException	Names the cursor in the ResultSet generated by this statement. Cursor names must be unique in a connection (may not be supported by all databases).
public abstract void setEscapeProcessing (boolean enable) throws SQLException	If true, the driver will do escape substitution before sending the SQL statement to the database.
public abstract void setMaxFieldSize(int max) throws SQLException	Sets the maximum amount of data (in bytes) to be returned by a column. Data beyond this limit is discarded.

public abstract void setMaxRows(int max) throws SQLException	Sets the maximum number of rows to be returned in a ResultSet (0 indicates unlimited).
public abstract void setQueryTimeout (int seconds) throws SQLException	Sets the number of seconds a driver will wait for an SQL statement to execute before throwing an exception.

TABLE 11.4 ResultSet

public abstract void clearWarnings() throws SQLException	Clear the warning chain.
public abstract void close() throws SQLException	Close this ResultSet's database and release its resources.
public abstract int findColumn(String columnName) throws SQLException	Return the index for the given column name.
public abstract InputStream getAsciiStream(int columnIndex) throws SQLException	Return the value of the given column as a stream of ASCII characters. When another call to a get method is made, the stream is automatically closed.
public abstract InputStream getAsciiStream(String columnName) throws SQLException	Return the value of the given column as a stream of ASCII characters. When another call to a get method is made, the stream is automatically closed.
public abstract InputStream getBinaryStream(int columnIndex) throws SQLException	Return the value of the given column as a stream of bytes. The stream is automatically closed when another get method is called.
public abstract InputStream getBinaryStream(String columnName) throws SQLException	Return the value of the given column as a stream of bytes. The stream is automatically closed when another get method is called.
public abstract boolean getBoolean(int columnIndex) throws SQLException	Get the value of the given column in the current row as a Boolean.
public abstract boolean getBoolean(String columnName) throws SQLException	Get the value of the given column in the current row as a Boolean.

Continued

TABLE 11.4 Continued

public abstract byte getByte(int columnIndex) throws SQLException	Get the value of the given column in the current row as a byte.
public abstract byte getByte(String columnName) throws SQLException	Get the value of the given column in the current row as a byte.
public abstract byte[] getBytes(int columnIndex) throws SQLException	Get the value of the given column in the current row as a byte array, the bytes being the raw values returned by the driver.
public abstract byte[] getBytes(String columnName) throws SQLException	Get the value of the given column in the current row as an array of bytes, which are the raw values returned by the driver.
public abstract String getCursorName() throws SQLException	Return the name of the SQL cursor used by this ResultSet.
public abstract Date getDate(int columnIndex) throws SQLException	Get the value of the given column in the current row as a java.sql.Date object.
public abstract Date getDate(String columnName) throws SQLException	Get the value of the given column in the current row as a java.sql.Date object.
public abstract double getDouble(int columnIndex) throws SQLException	Get the value of the given column in the current row as a double.
public abstract double getDouble(String columnName) throws SQLException	Get the value of the given column in the current row as a double.
public abstract float getFloat(int columnIndex) throws SQLException	Get the value of the given column in the current row as a float.
public abstract float getFloat(String columnName) throws SQLException	Get the value of the given column in the current row as a float.
public abstract int getInt(int columnIndex) throws SQLException	Get the value of the given column in the current row as an int.
public abstract int getInt(String columnName) throws SQLException	Get the value of the given column in the current row as an int.
public abstract long getLong(int columnIndex) throws SQLException	Get the value of the given column in the current row as a long.

public abstract long getLong(String columnName) throws SQLException	Get the value of the given column in the current row as a long.
public abstract ResultSetMetaData getMetaData() throws SQLException	Return the number, types, and proper ties of the columns in this ResultSet.
public abstract Numeric getNumeric(int columnIndex, int scale) throws SQLException	Get the value of the given column in the current row as a java.sql.Numeric object, with scale being the number of digits to the right of the decimal.
public abstract Numeric getNumeric(String columnName, int scale) throws SQLException	Get the value of the given column in the current row as a java.sql.Numeric object, where scale is the number of digits to the right of the decimal.
public abstract Object getObject(int columnIndex) throws SQLException	Get the value of the given column as an objcct.
public abstract Object getObject(String columnName) throws SQLException	Get the value of a parameter as an object.
public abstract short getShort(int columnIndex) throws SQLException	Get the value of the given column in the current row as a short.
public abstract short getShort(String columnName) throws SQLException	Get the value of the given column in the current row as a short.
public abstract String getString(int columnIndex) throws SQLException	Get the value of the given column in the current row as a String.
public abstract String getString(String columnName) throws SQLException	Get the value of the given column in the current row as a String.
public abstract Time getTime(int columnIndex) throws SQLException	Get the value of the given column in the current row as a java.sql.Time object.
public abstract Time getTime(String columnName) throws SQLException	Get the value of the given column in the current row as a java.sql.Time object.
public abstract Timestamp getTimestamp (int columnIndex) throws SQLException	Get the value of the given column in the current row as a java.sql.Timestamp object.

Continued

TABLE 11.4 Continued

public abstract Timestamp getTimestamp (String columnName) throws SQLException	Get the value of the given column in the current row as a java.sql.Timestamp object.
public abstract InputStream getUnicodeStream(int columnIndex) throws SQLException	Return the value of the given column as a stream of unicode characters. The stream is automatically closed when another get method is called.
public abstract InputStream getUnicodeStream(String columnName) throws SQLException	Return the value of the given column as a stream of unicode characters. The stream is automatically closed when another get method is called.
public abstract SQLWarning getWarnings() throws SQLException	Return the first warning reported by calls on this ResultSet. Warnings following this one will be chained to the end of this SQLWarning. Note: Reading a new row clears the warning chain.
public abstract boolean next() throws SQLException	Make the next row the current row. Clear the warning chain when the new row is read. Returns false if there are no more rows, true otherwise.
public abstract boolean wasNull() throws SQLException	Return whether the last column read was SQL NULL.

TABLE 11.5 ResultSetMetaData

public final static int columnNoNulls	Does not allow NULL values.
public final static int columnNullable	Allows NULL values.
public final static int columnNullableUnknown	Nullability unknown.
public abstract String getCatalogName(int column) throws SQLException	Return the catalog name of the column table.
public abstract int getColumnCount() throws SQLException	Return number of columns in ResultSet.

public abstract int getColumnDisplaySize(int column) throws SQLException	Return normal maximum width of the given column, in chars.
public abstract String getColumnLabel(int column) throws SQLException	Return suggested column title.
public abstract String getColumnName(int column) throws SQLException	Return the name of the given column.
public abstract int getColumnType(int column) throws SQLException	Return SQL type of the given column.
public abstract String getColumnTypeName(int column) throws SQLException	Return the type of the column's data source.
public abstract int getPrecision(int column) throws SQLException	Return number of decimal digits in given column. Return the name of column's schema.
public abstract int getScale(int column) throws SQLException	Return the name of column's schema.
public abstract String getSchemaName (int column) throws SQLException	Return the name of column's schema
public abstract String getTableName(int column) throws SQLException	Return name of column table.
public abstract boolean isAutoIncrement (int column) throws SQLException	Return whether column is automatically numbered.
public abstract boolean isCaseSensitive (int column) throws SQLException	Return whether column is case sensitive.
public abstract boolean isCurrency (int column) throws SQLException	Return whether the column is a cash value.
public abstract boolean isDefinitelyWritable(int column)	Return whether a write to the column is guaranteed to succeed.
public abstract int isNullable(int column) throws SQLException	Return whether you can write a NULL to this column.

TABLE 11.5 Continued

public abstract boolean isReadOnly(int column) throws SQLException	Return whether column is read only.
public abstract boolean isSearchable(int column) throws SQLException	Return whether column is searchable.
public abstract boolean isSigned(int column) throws SQLException	Return whether the column is a signed number.
public abstract boolean isWritable(int column) throws SQLException	Return whether the column is writable.

TABLE 11.6 SQLWarning

public SQLWarning(String reason,String SQLstate,int vendorCode)	Construct a fully specified SQLWarning. Reason is a description, SQLstate is an XOPEN code specifying the warning, and vendorCode is a database vendor-specific code.
public SQLWarning(String reason,String SQLstate)	Construct an SQLWarning without a vendorCode.
public SQLWarning(String reason)	Construct an SQLWarning with only a reason.
public SQLWarning()	Construct an unspecified SQLWarning.
public SQLWarning getNextWarning()	Get the warning chained to this one (i.e., the next SQLException in the chain).

TABLE 11.7: ResultSetMetaData

public final static int columnNoNulls	Does not allow NULL values.
public final static int columnNullable	Allows NULL values.
public final static int columnNullableUnknown	Nullability unknown.
public abstract String getCatalogName(int column) throws SQLException	Return the catalog name of the column table.

public abstract int getColumnCount() throws SQLException	Return number of columns in ResultSet.
public abstract int getColumnDisplaySize (int column) throws SQLException	Return normal maximum width of the given column, in chars.
public abstract String getColumnLabel (int column) throws SQLException	Return suggested column title.
public abstract String getColumnName(int column) throws SQLException	Return the name of the given column.
public abstract int getColumnType(int column) throws SQLException	Return SQL type of the given column.
public abstract String getColumnTypeName (int column) throws SQLException	Return the type of the column's data source.
public abstract int getPrecision(int column) throws SQLException	Return number of decimal digits in given column. Return the name of column's schema.
public abstract int getScale(int column) throws SQLException	Return the name of column's schema.
public abstract String getSchemaName (int column) throws SQLException	Return the name of column's schema.
public abstract String getTableName(int column) throws SQLException	Return name of column table.
public abstract boolean isAutoIncrement (int column) throws SQLException	Return whether column is automatically numbered.
public abstract boolean isCaseSensitive(int column) throws SQLException	Return whether column is case sensitive.
public abstract boolean isCurrency(int column) throws SQLException	Return whether the column is a cash value.
public abstract boolean isDefinitelyWritable(int column)	Return whether a write to the column is guaranteed to succeed.
public abstract int isNullable(int column) throws SQLException	Return whether you can write a NULL to this column.

Continued

TABLE 11.7 Continued

public abstract boolean isReadOnly(int column) throws SQLException	Return whether column is read only.
public abstract boolean isSearchable(int column) throws SQLException	Return whether column is searchable.
public abstract boolean isSigned(int column) throws SQLException	Return whether the column is a signed number.
public abstract boolean isWritable(int column) throws SQLException	Return whether the column is writable.

Chapter 12

The Future

I like to think

(it has to be!)

of a cybernetic ecology

where we are free of our labors

and joined back to nature,

returned to our mammal

brothers and sisters,

and all watched over

by machines of loving grace.

> "All Watched Over by Machines of Loving Grace"
>
> —Richard Brautigan

Visionaries

Speeches made by representatives from Sun are reminiscent of the phrase "machines of loving grace" from Richard Brautigan's poem. The combination of boundless child-like optimism with real technological know-how is quite interesting. Let's take a peek into the future to see what happens if all the predictions come true.

The Java World

Sensing Artie Choke's approach, the terminal turned itself on as he entered the room. Three hundred forty messages waiting. Artie stared at the auto-filter button and blinked twice. Two messages waiting. That was more like it. One message was the perky voice of his plumber's secretary confirming that the new software had been uploaded. Thank goodness! That new EuroStyle 3000 toilet had been throwing null-pointer exceptions for weeks, and Artie had had to reboot it twice the day before. He quickly confirmed payment of the bill.

The second message was business; he decided to save it for later and check out the news. As usual, his retrieval agent had sorted the articles into almost the order he wanted. He made a mental note to reprogram the preferences to give a lower weight to articles about that attractive Hollywood actress he had been obsessed with until her stand on animal cruelty (pro) had caused him to reevaluate her attractiveness. While he was skimming the paper on the VidScreen (tm), his stock monitoring applet popped up to warn him of some strange fluctuations in the commodities futures exchange. Along with millions of others, he reflexively blinked at the sell button and helped to start the long chain of events which would lead to the Great Crash of 2002, but this would not be apparent for another 30 minutes. He noted that the Internet Consciousness Suppression Team had had a close call overnight. No surprise there. The emergent consciousness had been rearing its head more and more frequently, and Artie was thankful there were professionals to handle things like this. At least no one was killed this time.

After reading the VidPaper, Artie reviewed the figures his associate in Hong Kong had sent him overnight. He reviewed the text summary, and then viewed the spreadsheet for the figures and the dynamically updated dataflow charts in the document. As he watched the graphs change and flicker, he noted that things were behind schedule. He decided to dock the monitoring component to the desktop using the familiar left-blink right-blink double-nose-twitch combination that had become second nature. Something on the readout troubled him. It looked like there was a data obstruction in sector seven. Oh, well—on with the VR helmet. In the three-dimensional view, the source of the blockage was immediately apparent from both its bright red color and the grating rusty-nail-on-a-chalkboard sound it was emitting. Of course, Artie had never seen a chalkboard, but that's how the documentation described it. Once he knew the source of the blockage, a barely perceptible head motion zoomed him to the affected server. He pulled out his cyber scalpel and . . .

The Reality

Now that we've taken a fanciful look at the future, let's look at some of the facts behind it. Just about everything mentioned above (with the exception of the emerging Internet Consciousness) would involve only technology we have today, but developing technology and getting it into people's lives are two different things.

Componentware

Here's the idea: You produce simple reusable components and then you or others hook them together later inside a container like a browser or a word processing program. Today there are several different standards that are standard in name only, but it's not that hard to come up with an API and get several "industry leaders" to sign on. The test comes when you look at the marketplace a year later. Is anybody using it? Is everybody using it? On what platforms?

The Microsoft Solution

Whenever somebody starts talking about componentware, there is bound to be talk of Microsoft and COM, OLE, ActiveX, and any other "standards" that have come up lately. These standards usually go through three stages. At birth they are overcomplicated proprietary APIs that are said to be the only standard anyone will ever need. Many "industry leaders" sign on. Next the standards languish for a while, with nobody rushing out to support them except for very large companies that can afford to wait and see if the standard flies or not. The final stage occurs when Microsoft turns them over to an "independent standards organization" and they become, essentially by fiat, "open standards." Still, Microsoft is no slouch on the technology front, and it supports the integration of Java and COM (component object model) on several levels:

- Controlling Java applets using VBScript—The VBScript can modify public Java variables and call Java methods.
- Controlling a COM object from Java—Microsoft provides Java "wrapper" classes to encapsulate a COM component, so the COM object acts just like a normal Java class.
- Exposing a Java class as a COM object—This allows a Java applet to appear to the rest of the system as if it were a COM object.

All of this sounds great, and it works, but there are a couple of problems. When creating a Java class to be used as a COM object, you must deal with many COM-specific details. The question is, why bother? Wouldn't it be nice to be able to put no platform-specific effort into a project and still get all the advantages of the reusable component approach?

Java Beans

If you're like most people, you have an unnatural fear of Microsoft which you can neither justify nor eliminate. In fact, many people who fear Microsoft have embraced Java because they believe it embodies the opposite of the Microsoft view of the universe. Therefore not too many Java programmers are likely to jump on the COM/OLE bandwagon (though one should never underestimate the appeal of the proverbial dumptruck full of money). Sun is working on a "pure Java" solution code-named "Java Beans," a platform-neutral set of APIs for reusable software components. Sun's plans for Java Beans are pretty ambitious, as the following quote from the API overview demonstrates:

> "The goal of the Java Beans initiative is to allow ISVs to develop reusable software components that end users can then hook together using application builder tools. The Java Bean APIs are portable and platform neutral and will be supported on all Java-enabled systems. The Java Bean APIs will also be connected by bridges into existing industry component models such as Microsoft's ActiveX, OpenDoc, and Netscape's LiveConnect. Software components that use the Java Beans APIs will thus be portable to a wide range of environments (including containers such as Internet Explorer, Netscape Navigator, HotJava, CyberDog, Visual Basic, Word, ClarisWorks, ...) and will work with a range of different application builder tools."

In other words, look out. There are two basic parts of the Sun model, components and containers. If this reminds you of the component model of the AWT, the idea is to scale up from the AWT so that the components may be as simple as an AWT button or as complex as a spreadsheet. AWT components will become Java Beans components with no additional effort. The Container may be a browser or even something like a Microsoft Word document. There are four major components to the API:

- GUI—Merging APIs will allow Java components to merge their user interface with that of their container, providing seamless integration of the components and making them indistinguishable from the container itself. These APIs also specify a protocol to be used to negotiate geometry layouts.

- Persistence—The Java Beans persistence APIs define a method whereby a component may save its state along with that of its container. This is important so that user preferences will not be lost between sessions.
- Event Handling—This component too might remind you of the AWT. The event handling APIs specify a mechanism by which components can deliver events to a specific component or broadcast them to a range of components.
- Application builder support—These APIs allow a component to expose its properties to other classes, which then customize their properties and behavior. This will allow an "editor" application to modify components and then hook them together without any low-level knowledge of the object's implementation.

Undoubtedly some of the interaction between components will take place across the network, but the mechanism for this is not specified. This was a conscious decision and not an oversight. Sun believes it is better not to saddle the Java Beans initiative with any particular distributed computing mechanism, but rather to allow developers to take their pick of those available (e.g., RMI, CORBA).

The bottom line is that Java Beans promises a pure Java cross-platform componentware solution.

A False Dichotomy

You can probably guess which of the competing component technologies we're betting on, but these technologies aren't as mutually exclusive as they may appear to be. If you already develop COM/ActiveX components and you don't care about other markets, keep doing what you're doing: it won't hurt Java, and Java won't hurt you. Your objects will be able to live in perfect harmony with Java Beans components.

Secure Commercial Transactions

The Java Electronic Commerce Framework (JECF) promises secure E-cash, credit card, and debit card transactions. Many different standards and protocols will be supported through cassettes. A cassette is a software module that plugs into the JECF. Cassettes may reside on the client or be dynamically loaded across the Internet. This solution requires no heavy-duty databases or processing on the server side; everything is done on the client, the Java way.

Java Server API

The server API is designed to make it easy to build high-powered network servers. Also promised is the ability to create something that resembles an applet's evil twin. These "servelets" will allow users to upload Java programs that can then be uploaded to the server and plug into it using a well-defined interface.

Multimedia

Sun has announced the Java Media APIs to address some of the early shortcomings of Java. At the top of the list is the lack of decent multimedia support. The basis of this is the Java Media Framework, which will allow different multimedia displays to "synchronize their clocks." To this framework the following features will be added:

- Advanced 2D and 3D graphics
- Audio and video
- Application sharing (i.e., "whiteboard" style sharing)
- MIDI (musical instrument digital interface)
- Telephony

Security

The Java Security API provides a framework for the coming flood of encryption technology. This API will provide tools for standard data encryption/decryption and the generation and verification of digital signatures. Digital signatures can be attached to documents and programs to prevent forgery and uniquely identify the source. This type of technology is in a legal gray area for several reasons. First, any encryption technology with a key size large enough to be effective may not be legally exported from the United States. Second, the courts have yet to decide if digital signatures are legally binding. This state of affairs may change as soon as we get a mathematician on the Supreme Court.

Embedded Systems

Sun has announced a subset of the core Java APIs to be used in embedded systems. This is not so much for use in "Internet Toasters" as it is for use in real toasters, CD players, televisions, bathtubs, and soda bottles. This API consists of the entire java.lang package, the java.util package, parts of java.io, and some extensions for network I/O. I don't even want to think about the kind of Orwellian nightmare this could all lead to when your boss gets the logs from your new smart liquor cabinet.

Just in Time

One of the most exciting recent developments has been the release of so-called "just in time" (JIT) compilers. In a JIT system, the Java bytecodes are translated into native code as the program runs. The first pass through a loop, for example, will be marginally slower than in a non-JIT system, but subsequent iterations will be much (about 10 times) faster. The early versions of this technology work but are nowhere near as stable as the normal Java interpreter. Remember, however, that the first generation of any technology is bound to be buggy.

Java Chips

After looking at the Virtual Machine instruction set, you may be impressed at how much simpler it is than the instruction sets of the CPU in your computer right now. It's natural to wonder how hard it would be to make a nonvirtual machine to implement it. People are already doing it, so it is possible to imagine a pure Java machine running Java bytecodes on a chip and using an operating system written in Java.

Virtual Reality

I must admit I've never been a big fan of VRML. I guess the main reason for this is that I've never owned a high-end workstation and one of those VR helmets. That fact aside, I think that the combination of Java and VRML is one of the most exciting "not quite there yet" technologies I've seen in a long time. The mapping between the objects in a VRML scene and the Java objects is one-to-one, making it easy to understand. Messages traveling to and from objects and things like time sensors and tactile sensors are simply Java method calls. For all this talk of objects, nobody ever gets to see them, but with VRML, it's not hard to imagine stepping into a three-dimensional model of your program and watching it execute. You could actually watch as messages fly back and forth between the objects and change shape and color (or taste and smell, for that matter) to represent their internal state. Imagine jumping into the network to watch data flow between a large distributed Java programs. When William Gibson started writing about "Cyberspace," he probably never expected that we would be seeing the first examples of this type of technology within our lifetimes. The obvious application for this technology, and undoubtedly the first to see the light of day, will be games and simulations, but it's not hard to imagine practical applications as well.

The Road Ahead

In the computer industry, the "road less traveled" leads to death. This often means that vendors are forced to support third-rate standards because "everybody else is doing it." They have no choice. For this reason, it's understandable that people are casting a critical eye toward Java. After all, anything that popular must have some serious flaws. Even under close scrutiny, though, the future looks good, at least so far. The only safe course is to keep a cool head and think positive thoughts.

Glossary

abstract Used when declaring classes whose methods have no implementation.

API Application Programming Interface.

applet A class derived from Panel that may be embedded in Web pages.

AWT Abstract Windowing Toolkit.

Boolean A variable type that may have one of two values: true or false.

break Statement to break out of a loop. Multiple loops may be exited by using labeled break.

byte An 8-bit signed variable.

catch Used to label a block of code to executed if an error occurs in a try block.

char A 16-bit unicode value.

class A blueprint for an object.

component The parent of all classes used in Java GUIs.

constructor The special method that is automatically executed when an object is instantiated.

Container The parent class of components that may contain other components.

continue Causes loop execution to skip the rest of the loop and start over.

default Used to label the default statement in a switch block.

do Creates a loop that executes at least once before the test is executed.

double A 64-bit IEEE 754 floating-point number.

else Introduces a block that is executed when and if a test evaluates to false.

encapsulation The act of protecting your data.

exception A subclass of Throwable that is used to signal an error.

extends Used to indicate the parent class in a class definition.

false One of the two Boolean values.

final Labels a class, method, or variable as unsubclassable, unoverridable, and unchangeable, respectively.

finalize A special method executed when an object is garbage collected. Must have the form "protected void finalize()throws Throwable."

finally Labels a block that is executed regardless of any exceptions encountered in a try block.

float A 32-bit IEEE 754 floating-point value.

Frame A subclass of Window that may have a title and a menubar.

garbage collector The background thread that deletes unreferenced objects from the heap.

GUI Graphical user interface.

if A statement used to conditionally execute a code block.

implements Used to indicate interfaces a class implements.

import Makes a class name or names from another package visible in the current file.

inheritance The ability to receive methods and variables of a parent class.

instance A manifestation of a class. The class is said to have been instantiated.

instanceof Used to determine if the given object is a member of a given class or implements a given interface.

int A 32-bit signed integer value.

interface A description of the methods a class must implement to be an instance of the interface.

JDK Java Developers Kit.

layout manager A class that implements the java.awt.LayoutManager interface. Responsible for arranging components in a container.

long A 64-bit signed integer value.

mark Method used to mark a position in a data stream.

method A function contained in a class or object.

NaN (not a number) Special value for floating-point variables. Always returns false if used in a comparison.

native Used to label code as being implemented in a language other than java.

native method A method written in another language that may be called from Java.

new Used to create a new instance of a class.

null Special value for reference variables that indicates the variable points to no object.

null Placeholder value for reference variables that do not point to an object.

object A combination of data and methods.

overloading Defining methods with the same name, but that take different arguments.

override To define a method with the same namer signature as a method in a superclass. Superclass method may still be called using super.

package Used to indicate that a class belongs to a group of classes. Used to avoid "namespace pollution."

peer The object that serves as an interface between a Java AWT component and a native widget.

private Used to mark methods and variables as being visible only inside a class.

protected Used to mark variables and methods as being visible only in the current package, in the current class, and in subclasses.

public Used to mark variables and methods as being visible everywhere.

return Used to return a value from a method.

Shempnum A very large integer. Defined in the java.shemp package.

short A 16-bit signed integer variable.

SMTP Simple mail transfer protocol.

Socket One end of a logical Internet connection.

SQL Structured Query Language.

static Used to mark variables and methods as belonging to a class and not an instance of a class.

stream A generic source of sequential data. Some streams support marking a point in the stream and returning to it later. The Java stream classes are defined in the java.io package.

String An immutable string of characters.

StringBuffer A mutable string of characters.

subclass A class that extends another class.

super Keyword used to access methods and variables in a superclass. May also be used in a constructor with a parenthesized argument list to execute a superclass constructor.

superclass A parent class of another class.

synchronized Used to mark methods and blocks of code that may not safely be executed by concurrent threads.

this Special variable that holds a reference to the object in which it is used.

thread An independent path of execution.

ThreadGroup A logical grouping of threads.

throw Used to toss exceptions.

throws Used to warn of exceptions thrown in a method. All exceptions that are not subclasses of RuntimeException must either be caught or declared using throws.

true One of the two values a Boolean variable may contain.

try Used to introduce a block of code where an exception might occur. Must be followed by one or more catch blocks (which may be empty).

unicode A 16-bit character coding scheme. The Java char data type is a unicode character.

virtual machine A software emulation of a CPU that has no physical counterpart (yet!).

void Used to indicate the absence of a return value in method declarations.

VRML Virtual Reality Modeling Language

while Used to introduce a loop that may be executed zero or more times.

Index

About The Web Site

You can download the source code for any of the applets/applications in this book through our World Wide Web site. The URL is www.wiley.com/compbooks. The Source listings are all contained in one zipped file. This site also contains examples of some of the applets at work, plus some links to various Java resources on the Web. Enjoy!